TRACING YOUR
POTTERIES
ANCESTORS

Best wishes

Mike Syme

FAMILY HISTORY FROM PEN & SWORD

TRACING YOUR POTTERIES ANCESTORS

A Guide for Family and Local Historians

Michael Sharpe

Pen & Sword
FAMILY HISTORY

First published in Great Britain in 2019
PEN & SWORD FAMILY HISTORY
an imprint of
Pen & Sword Books Ltd
47 Church Street, Barnsley, South Yorkshire, S70 2AS

Copyright © Michael Sharpe, 2019

ISBN 978 1 52670 127 5

Typeset in Palatino and Optima by CHIC GRAPHICS

Printed and bound in England by CPI Group (UK), Croydon, CR0 4YY

Pen & Sword Books Ltd incorporates the imprints of Pen & Sword
Airworld, Archaeology, Atlas, Aviation, Battleground, Discovery, Family
History, Fiction, History, Maritime, Military, Military Classics, Politics,
Select, Social History, True Crime, Frontline Books, Leo Cooper,
Remember When, Seaforth Publishing, The Praetorian Press,
Wharncliffe Local History, Wharncliffe Transport,
Wharncliffe True Crime and White Owl.

For a complete list of Pen & Sword titles please contact

PEN & SWORD BOOKS LTD
47 Church Street, Barnsley, South Yorkshire, S70 2AS, England
E-mail: enquiries@pen-and-sword.co.uk
Website: www.pen-and-sword.co.uk
or
PEN & SWORD BOOKS LTD
1950 Lawrence Rd., Havertown, PA 19083, USA
E-mail: Uspen-and-sword@casematepublishers.com
Website: www.penandswordbooks.com

CONTENTS

ABBREVIATIONS

BAA	Birmingham Archdiocesan Archives
BMDs	Births, marriages and deaths
BMSGH	Birmingham & Midland Society for Genealogy and Heraldry
FHS	Family history society
GRO	General Register Office
LCC	Lichfield Consistory Court
LRO	Lichfield Record Office
MI	Monumental Inscription
NSR	North Staffordshire Railway
PCC	Prerogative Court of Canterbury
PCY	Prerogative Court of York
PLU	Poor Law Union
PMAG	Potteries Museum & Art Gallery
SNI	Staffordshire Name Indexes (website)
SRO	Staffordshire Record Office
SRS	Staffordshire Record Society
SSA	Staffordshire and Stoke-on-Trent Archives (Service)
STCA	Stoke-on-Trent City Archives
TNA	The National Archives
WSL	William Salt Library

INTRODUCTION

The Proud Potteries

This book is about the Staffordshire Potteries: how it became one of the most distinctive industrial districts in the world and how you can find your ancestors there.

North Staffordshire is rightly proud of its industrial heritage. For almost 300 years from the mid-1700s, this isolated community on the western edge of the Peak District became a microcosm of the Industrial Revolution. Working with the simplest of tools and raw materials, often in wretched conditions, a skilled and industrious workforce produced objects of great beauty that were admired and desired around the world. Their efforts secured for Britain a pre-eminent place in a key industry that had previously been thought of as unprofitable, or reliant on royal patronage or Far Eastern expertise.

The processes and skills required were extraordinary. The factories, or potbanks, with their distinctive bottle ovens turned out ceramic wares of every shape and description from domestic utility items and fine bone china, to decorative tiles, sanitary ware and building materials, and later on specialized industrial products such as electrical insulators. But this innovation and creativity came at a cost. Working conditions in the potbanks were often grim, and the bottle ovens – along with the area's other staple industries, mining and steelmaking – heavily polluted the environment, with consequent impacts on health.

It was not a promising start. A visitor to the area in the Middle Ages would have found a few farmer potters eking out a living on the sides of the windswept hills. They would tend their farms during the summer and spend the winter months fashioning butterpots to use in their dairies and crude domestic items to sell in the local markets. But slowly and surely a body of expertise began to accumulate. Driven by the values of the Midlands Enlightenment – a conviction that science and technology should be applied to improve the human condition – pottery entrepreneurs such as Josiah Wedgwood began to apply inventions and discoveries to improve their wares. Some of these innovations were of their own making, others came from far and wide. In doing so, they turned what had been a craft into an industry with a worldwide reputation.

While names such as Wedgwood, Josiah Spode, Thomas Minton, John Astbury, John Doulton and Enoch Wood are credited with laying the foundations of the pottery industry in Staffordshire, many of the most talented people are known only to history. For hours on end, year in year out, these unknown craftspeople (both men and women) toiled in the potbanks producing some of the most exquisite creations ever made by human hand. It is these people we set out to find when we embark on the search for our Potteries ancestors, and we can be proud of them too.

That this distinctive heritage has tended to be overlooked is due, at least in part, to the Potteries being its own worst enemy at times. In the nineteenth century, civic rivalry between the six Pottery towns continually held the district back, denying it the momentum and influence it deserved. A municipal building boom within the rival towns led to a proliferation of town halls, market halls, theatres, libraries, schools of art, mechanics institutes and public parks far greater than the relatively modest population warranted. Often these public baubles were elaborately decorated with locally produced ceramic tiles and other adornments. Many of these buildings have been lost but a significant proportion still survives, making a visit to the city a feast for the amateur photographer and the architectural historian alike.

More than any other city in the country, Stoke-on-Trent came to be defined by what it made. The ceramic industry's grip on the area was immense – hence the name 'the Potteries' – giving it the greatest concentration on a single product of any industrial centre in Britain. At the industry's height before the Second World War, more than 2,000 bottle ovens punctuated Stoke-on-Trent's skyline. Emerging without any form of masterplan, there seemed to be at least one potbank on every street, interspersed with workers' housing (often of very low quality), like drones around the queen bee. It was a dramatic landscape, captured most evocatively in the novels of Arnold Bennett, the Potteries' most famous son. And the fall, when it came, was equally dramatic.

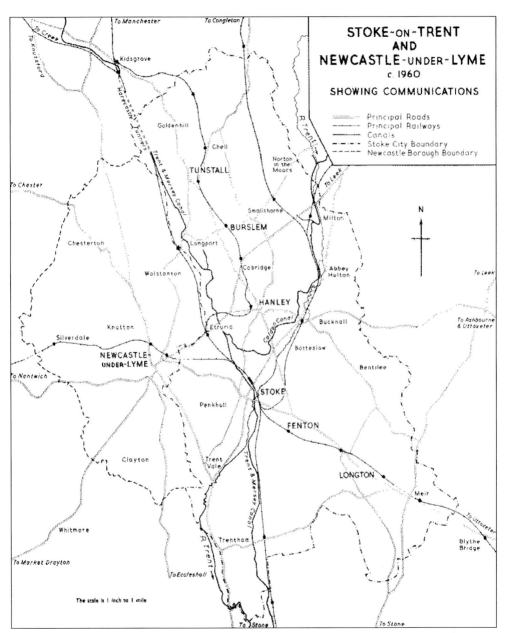

Environs of Stoke-on-Trent and Newcastle-under-Lyme, c. 1960. (Victoria County History)

When the economic tide turned, taking the pottery jobs abroad, the blow dealt to Stoke-on-Trent was severe and for a while appeared almost fatal. In other industrial cities redundant factories, warehouses and mills have been repurposed: after lying derelict for a while, regeneration efforts have seen them converted into offices and flats, breathing new life into the original fabric. But no one can live or work in a bottle kiln. The potbanks were levelled in their hundreds, ripping the heart out of the communities they served. Probably no urban landscape in Britain has changed more dramatically in the last 100 years than that of the Potteries. Today, the area is bouncing back, led by a new wave of pottery entrepreneurs such as Emma Bridgewater, as well as focusing on high-tech manufacturing industries and services.

The Potteries is an area with a resilient working class, industrious entrepreneurs, a strong reforming tradition and a rich cultural heritage. For family historians this means that we may find our ancestors in many settings and across all social and religious groups. While, in all likelihood, they will be living in a small terraced house in Burslem or Hanley, do not be surprised if your ancestor turns out to be a Methodist preacher, a performer in one of the many theatres, a school teacher, or a train driver on 'The Knotty' (North Staffordshire Railway (NSR)). Even working in the potbanks they are likely to have been highly skilled.

SCOPE: THE LAND IN BETWEEN

North Staffordshire was, and in many senses still is, a land in-between. Ever since the Romans first cut Ryknield Street linking Derby and Chester, people have been hurriedly traversing the area on their way to somewhere else. Although only 40 miles from major conurbations, historically the Potteries identified neither with the textile-based economy of the North-West, nor with the metal-bashing economy of the West Midlands. The harsh landscape of the Staffordshire Moorlands, to the east, and the lush arable land of the Cheshire plain, to the west, were equally alien.

Unusually among British cities, Stoke-on-Trent is what geographers call 'polymorphic'. Rather than a single historic settlement that grew out radially over time, the city of Stoke-on-Trent was formed through the amalgamation of a number of smaller towns that had gradually coalesced. There were six of these towns, running more or less in a line from north to south: Tunstall, Burslem, Hanley, Stoke, Fenton and Longton. The city itself is relatively young, federation having been achieved only in 1910. It was the need for a collective moniker for an area that had long been a single economic (though not administrative) unit that led to the name 'the Potteries' (the term was in use as early as 1802). Stokies, as the locals call themselves, have a strong sense of identity that even today often owes more to the constituent towns than the city as a whole.

For the family historian, then, research in 'the Potteries' has to take into account this multi-layered picture. While the primary focus in this book is the modern city of Stoke-on-Trent, on occasion the discussion necessarily moves down a level to consider the circumstances of the six constituent towns. At other times, the focus shifts up to address North Staffordshire as a whole. Two districts frequently mentioned are Newcastle-under-Lyme, the historic borough town on the city's western fringe, and the Staffordshire Moorlands, a rugged hinterland to the north and east. Stoke-on-Trent – and therefore our ancestors who lived there – had close links with both these neighbours and therefore it makes sense to include them in a family history guide such as this.

As a late arrival on the national scene, Stoke-on-Trent is a constituent part in some of the jurisdictions used by family historians and is the defining entity in others. Much of the modern city was originally accounted for by the ancient parish of Stoke-upon-Trent (now generally known simply as Stoke to distinguish it from the city of Stoke-on-Trent). The relevant jurisdictions in relation to aspects such as civil registration, the Poor Law, local government and legal matters are described at appropriate points in the text.

View of the Potteries, 1926. (Wellcome Collection, Creative Commons)

RESEARCHING IN THE POTTERIES

One of the pleasures of family history is that every story is unique. Every family will have followed its own winding road and left its own trail, and generalizations have limited value. Nevertheless it is useful to highlight some of the key issues and themes the family historian is likely to encounter in the search for their Potteries ancestors.

Firstly, researchers have the facilities of an excellent archives service at their disposal. Staffordshire and Stoke-on-Trent Archives Service (SSA) is recognized as one of the best performing and most professional in the country, and is the home to world-class collections. As the name suggests, it is a shared service funded jointly by Staffordshire County Council and Stoke-on-Trent City Council. The archives are split between sites at Stoke-on-Trent and Stafford, with search rooms at both locations, and as a researcher you may need to travel between one and the other to find the sources you are looking for. Fortunately, the SSA is investing heavily in digitization and many of the key sources, including parish registers and wills, are available online. The SSA's facilities and how to access them are described more fully below in the sections on Principal Archives and Sources and How To Use This Book.

Introduction

Sooner or later, you are almost certain to encounter Nonconformists in your family tree. North Staffordshire had a strong Nonconformist tradition. Baptists, Methodists, Presbyterians and Congregationalists (also known as Independents) all flourished. Methodism was particularly strong: John Wesley visited the area frequently and the region even spawned its own sub-branch of Methodism, called Primitive Methodism, in the early 1800s, and members were known for their huge open air meetings.

But the circumstances of the time mean there may be problems in tracing our Nonconformist ancestors. Firstly, the persecution experienced by many dissenters (a term that includes also Roman Catholics), particularly during the second half of the seventeenth century, gave rise to a reluctance to keep written records. Often a minister would retain the church registers for safe keeping and take them with him when he moved on. The independent nature and lack of a formalized and centralized structure in Nonconformist churches made systematic record keeping difficult to impose. There was considerable variation in the way records were kept, even within the same denomination. Thus, only a fraction of the records have survived and in certain cases not all surviving records have been deposited with the Archive Service.

Most likely there will be pottery industry workers in your tree as well. Given how quickly (in historical terms) businesses come and go, in general it can be difficult to find details of ancestors who worked for private firms. The size and longevity of the main pottery businesses mean that the surviving company records are better than in many other sectors. Documents such as apprenticeship papers, wages and salaries books, and employment contracts can throw light on our ancestors' working lives. On the other hand, there were so many pottery businesses – many of which were short-lived and never made a name for themselves – that it may not be possible to find occupational details. Similar variation applies in North Staffordshire's other principal industries – coal mining, iron and steel, and railways – and it is a matter of luck as to what survives.

Migration is another common theme. Like other towns during the Industrial Revolution, the Potteries grew by drawing in workers from elsewhere. So at some stage Stokies are likely to find that their heritage leads back to other areas. Most likely, these ancestors did not move very far, however. Unlike the industrial cities of the North and Midlands, migration in North Staffordshire was highly localized. In 1851, only around 19 per cent of the population of Burslem was born more than 30 miles from the town. This is low by national standards: in some industrial towns only a quarter of the population was native born. Rural Staffordshire, Shropshire, Cheshire and Derbyshire were the most likely locations, as well as movement within the Six Towns. Immigration was also relatively low. Around 10 per cent of the Burslem population was born outside England and Wales in 1851, the majority (8 per cent) being from Ireland.

PRINCIPAL ARCHIVES AND SOURCES

North Staffordshire is served by a diverse range of archives, several of national and international significance. In common with public archives elsewhere, these face two major, and in some senses inter-related, challenges. On the one hand, there is the shift towards digital access and delivery, while at the same time an increasing strain on archive services in the wake of public sector cutbacks. Several archives are reviewing their service provision, amending opening hours and/or closing certain facilities as a result. For these reasons, no information is given here on aspects such as opening hours or cost of services; you should check each organization's website for details before visiting. While information about online resources and collections is as up-to-date as possible, this too may be subject to change.

The main archives referred to in this book are listed below. The entries here merely summarize the services available and the main classes of archives held. Further details, including full postal addresses, are provided in Appendix 2 and specific references are made throughout the text.

Staffordshire and Stoke-on-Trent Archives
www.staffordshire.gov.uk/archives

The records and archive service covering the historic county of Staffordshire, which is funded jointly by Staffordshire County Council and the City of Stoke-on-Trent. Archive collections and series relating to North Staffordshire are split between the Stoke-on-Trent City Archives (STCA) at Hanley Library, Stoke-on-Trent, and Staffordshire Record Office (SRO) at Stafford. In addition, the SSA manages the William Salt Library (WSL) in Stafford, a specialist local history library (**www.staffordshire.gov.uk/salt**). The former Lichfield Record Office (LRO), which was operated by the SSA, has now closed and its collections have been transferred to the SRO. The move is the first stage of a centralization and modernization programme that will see the SRO, LRO and WSL collections brought together under one roof at a new site to be called the Staffordshire History Centre in Stafford.

Stoke-on-Trent City Archives grew out of the Horace Barks Reference Library at the City Central Library, which was named after a former Lord Mayor. Its records include parish registers, poll books and electoral registers, Poor Law records, newspapers and trade directories, and the records of local government, health and education. Its collections relating to the pottery industry are of national and international significance, and include the archives of industry pioneers and major businesses such as Wedgwood, Minton and Spode. The Search Room computers allow free access to commercial and other genealogy websites for library users, as well as a variety of additional resources.

The SSA has published guides to some of its record series, which may be downloaded from its website; these are referenced here individually at appropriate places in the text. As well as the SSA's own collections, its online catalogue Gateway to the Past, **www.archives.staffordshire.gov.uk**, covers the archival collections of the Potteries Museum & Art Gallery (PMAG), and is explained in greater detail below. Several specialist websites relating to the SSA's collections are also available:

- Staffordshire Name Indexes (SNI),
  www.staffsnameindexes.org.uk: A series of online indexes
  compiled from SSA records. Subjects include apprentices, canal
  boats, jurors, police officers, prisoners, workhouses and wills.
- Staffordshire Place Guide,
  www.staffordshire.gov.uk/leisure/archives/history/placeguide:
  A finding aid for information on Staffordshire parishes.
  Information is summarized under various headings, with direct
  links to the online catalogue.
- Staffordshire Past Track, **www.staffspasttrack.org.uk**: Allows
  users to explore Staffordshire's history through photographs,
  images, maps and documents, using a range of easy to use search
  tools.
- The Sutherland Collection, **www.sutherlandcollection.org.uk**:
  Contains records and papers relating to the estates of the Leveson-
  Gower family, Dukes of Sutherland.

Other notable collections and sources for North Staffordshire
research are:

Keele University, Specialist Collections
www.keele.ac.uk/library/specarc/collections/
The University holds a number of specialist collections relating to
individuals, families and organizations associated with North
Staffordshire. Among these, the Local Collection comprises around
5,000 books, plus pamphlets, newspapers, periodicals and
directories, and publications by the Staffordshire Record Society and
Staffordshire Parish Registers Society.

Midland Ancestors
http://midland-ancestors.uk and http://midland-ancestors.shop
Now known as Midland Ancestors, the organization was previously
the Birmingham & Midland Society for Genealogy and Heraldry
(BMSGH), and is the main family history society (FHS) for

researchers with interests in Staffordshire and other Midlands counties. North Staffordshire Family History Group, based in Stoke-on-Trent, is one of several branches affiliated to the Society. Through the indexing and transcription work undertaken by its volunteers, the Society is now a major data provider in its own right. It operates a series of indexes, several of which contain data not available elsewhere. Many datasets are available as downloads or on CD-ROM. There is also a specialist Midland Ancestors Reference Library in central Birmingham.

Newcastle Library
www.staffordshire.gov.uk/libraries
Now relocated within the new Castle House Civic Hub, the Library holds genealogical resources and a local history collection relating to the historic borough of Newcastle-under-Lyme.

Staffordshire BMD
www.staffordshirebmd.org.uk
A collaboration between Staffordshire's register offices and family history societies to transcribe the original, locally held indexes of births, marriages and deaths back to the start of civil registration in 1837. Has good coverage for North Staffordshire.

Staffordshire Collection on Findmypast
www.findmypast.co.uk
Under licence from the SSA, parish registers for Staffordshire are available online in the Staffordshire Collection at Findmypast. Approximately 200 parishes are covered, including all those within North Staffordshire. Coverage comprises entries for baptisms, marriages and burials from the beginning of the registers through to 1900, and includes digitized images of the original registers. In addition, the Staffordshire Collection covers probate records and marriage allegations and bonds (both with digitized images) issued through the Consistory Court of Lichfield, previously held at LRO.

Findmypast is available by personal subscription or free of charge at the SSA search rooms and in Staffordshire libraries.

Staffordshire Record Society
www.s-h-c.org.uk

The Staffordshire Record Society (SRS) originated in 1879 as the William Salt Archaeological Society. It publishes books and transcriptions of records on the history of the county under the title *Collections for a History of Staffordshire* (sometimes abbreviated here to *Collections*), some of which are of particular relevance to family history.

LOCAL HISTORY

As well as providing a guide to genealogical records, this book discusses the history of the Potteries and the surrounding area. It is only possible to sketch the region's rich history in a volume such as this. Thus, the presentations provide snapshots around particular themes rather than exhaustive accounts. The subjects have been chosen in order to better understand how our North Staffordshire ancestors lived and to enable us to interpret the records they left behind.

If you wish to delve further into the Potteries' fascinating past, a whole variety of sources is available. Staffordshire's first historian was Dr Robert Plot, keeper of the Ashmolean Museum at Oxford, who travelled throughout the county before publishing his *Natural History of Staffordshire* in 1686. It has been reprinted several times since. Antiquarian Walter Chetwyd, who lived at Ingestre Hall near Stafford, wrote a history of Pirehill hundred, which covered Newcastle-under-Lyme and what became the Potteries, in the 1680s. It remained unpublished until the early twentieth century, when it was published by the SRS.

An early publication, part directory and part history, is *The Staffordshire Potteries Directory: An Account of the Pottery Manufacture*, published in 1802 (available at **www.revolutionaryplayers.org.uk**). The first to attempt a comprehensive account of the area was Simeon Shaw in his book *History of the Staffordshire Potteries*, published in 1829 (reprinted in 1900). This was followed by John Ward's *The Borough of Stoke-upon-Trent*, which was first published in 1843 and republished in 1969. Robert Nicholls updated and expanded Ward's account in his book *The History of the City of Stoke-on-Trent & the Borough of Newcastle-under-Lyme*, published in 1931.

A mid-twentieth-century perspective is provided in Ernest Warrillow's *A Sociological History of the City of Stoke-on-Trent* (1960, republished by Ironmarket, 1977). A more personal history, quoted several times in the text here, is Charles Shaw's *When I Was A Child*, an evocative account of growing up in the Potteries in the mid-nineteenth century which is said to have inspired Arnold Bennett's writings. Digitized versions of many of these early publications can be found online, for example, through the Internet Archive (**www.archive.org**), Hathi Trust (**www.hathitrust.org**) and Project Gutenburg (**www. gutenberg.org**).

In the modern era, John Gilbert Jenkins's *Stoke-on-Trent: Federation and After* (Staffordshire County Library, 1985), *The Making of the Six Towns* by Cameron Hawke-Smith et al. (1985) and Alan Taylor's *Stoke-on-Trent: A History* (Phillimore, 2003) are key reading. Also of note is the thought-provoking and beautifully illustrated *The Lost City of Stoke-on-Trent* by Matthew Rice (Frances Lincoln Ltd, 2010), which surveys the city's rapidly disappearing industrial heritage. Gateway sources for the specific themes covered are indicated in each chapter.

Each of the Six Towns, as well as some outlying localities, has its own historical account: GENUKI Staffordshire pages provide lists by parish (**www.genuki.org.uk/big/eng/STS/parishes**). Newcastle-under-Lyme is especially well documented. Although it has now ceased trading, Churnet Valley Books for many years published a huge array of local history titles for North Staffordshire, some of which are still available through bookshops.

The Staffordshire History website has links to various

organizations and resources for local history across the county, including indexes to the former *Staffordshire History Journal* which ceased publication in 2013 (**www.staffshistory.org.uk**). Keele University's Centre for Local History publishes the specialist journal *Staffordshire Studies* (**www.keele.ac.uk/history/centreforlocalhistory**). The Centre is home to the Victoria County History (VCH) of Staffordshire, a long-running project to compile the definitive history of the county: Volume 8 covers the Potteries and Newcastle-under-Lyme and can be read for free online (**www.british-history. ac.uk/vch/staffs/vol8**). *Midland History* is an academic journal, available on subscription, but certain articles are free to download (search at **www.maneyonline.com**). The *History West Midlands* website publishes popular history articles by the region's leading historians (**www.historywm.com**).

Steve Birks's Potteries.org website is an essential resource for the Potteries historian (**www.thepotteries.org**). The design is old-school and a logical structure conspicuously lacking but delve in and you will find a cornucopia of interesting material on the history of the area. Local historian Fred Hughes has a regular column in the *Sentinel* newspaper and blogs about Stoke-on-Trent history (**https://fredhughesblog.wordpress.com**). Most districts have their own local history society (sometimes more than one); website addresses are given in Appendix 2 or contact the nearest Staffordshire community library.

The Six Towns Collection, the local studies collection at the STCA in the City Central Library, Hanley contains books, reports, pamphlets and other items relating to the city. Key items from this collection are on the open shelves in the STCA Search Room, with early books and many pamphlets held in store.

HOW TO USE THIS BOOK

This book aims to provide a comprehensive guide to genealogy resources for tracing your family history within the Potteries and the surrounding area. It is not intended as a general 'how-to' guide. The

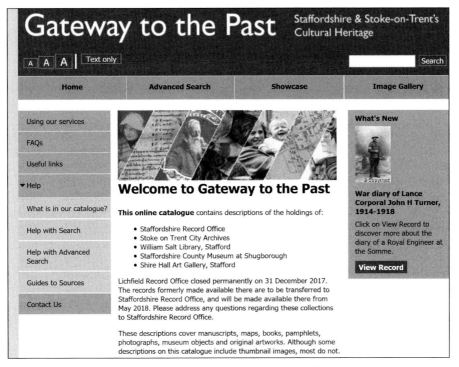

The Gateway to the Past website is the online catalogue of Staffordshire & Stoke-on-Trent Archives.

reader is assumed to be familiar with the basic approaches and processes for genealogical research: the main focus here is how to further and apply this knowledge within the specific context of North Staffordshire. For the beginner, there are numerous excellent guides and tutorials that will help you to get started. *Who Do You Think You Are?: Encyclopedia of Genealogy* by Nick Barratt (HarperCollins, 2008), *Tracing Your Ancestors* by Simon Fowler (Pen & Sword, 2011) and *Tracing Your Ancestors from 1066 to 1837* by Jonathan Oates (Pen & Sword, 2012) all provide useful introductions. Periodicals such as *Family Tree* and *Who Do You Think You Are?* magazine have 'getting started' guides (**www.family-tree.co.uk/ how-to-guides** and **www.whodoyouthinkyouare magazine.com**).

Many general sources, such as censuses, parish registers, and civil registration indexes are now readily available online. While these are addressed, the book also encourages you to go further and deeper, seeking out sources that you may not have considered previously. Only by digging down into the lives of our ancestors will we be able to understand how they lived and worked within the extraordinary place that is the Potteries. Hence, there is, hopefully, something for the beginner and the experienced researcher alike.

Where relevant, references are given to original sources within the catalogues of the archives concerned. **Not all of the individual catalogues are online**, so if you are unable to locate a reference given in the text it may be necessary to check with the repository directly.

The catalogue referred to most frequently is that of the Staffordshire and Stoke-on-Trent Archives Service, known as Gateway to the Past, which can be found at the following web address: **www.archives.staffordshire.gov.uk**. This contains descriptions of the holdings of five organizations managed by the Archives & Museums Service: Staffordshire Record Office (SRO); Stoke-on-Trent City Archives (STCA); William Salt Library, Stafford (WSL); Staffordshire County Museum at Shugborough; and Shire Hall Art Gallery, Stafford. The Gateway to the Past catalogue allows searches to be made in a number of ways, for example, by title, free text, document reference, and for the results to be filtered by various criteria. The references given in this book relate to the DocRefNo (Document reference number) field.

Within the text, **original archive references according to this system are given in square brackets [ ]**. For example, document reference number [Q/RLv] within the SSA catalogue is 'Victuallers and Alehousekeepers Recognizances'. In cases where the repository is not mentioned explicitly, the reference will include the archive's abbreviation. Thus, the above example may also appear as [SRO: Q/RLv] clarifying that this record series is held at Staffordshire

Record Office rather than at any of the SSA's other sites. The referencing is highly sensitive and spaces are required within the reference codes where given in the text.

Computers are meant to make our lives easier but as we know this is not always the case. The Gateway to the Past catalogue is a fine example. It can be difficult to use, crashes frequently and searches often fail to retrieve the relevant information even though the entries are in the catalogue. An alternative means of searching, which is often more successful, is to access via The National Archives (TNA) Discovery catalogue which links to archive databases across the country (**http://discovery.nationalarchives.gov.uk/**). In compiling this book, Discovery was regularly able to identify records held by the SSA that its own catalogue was unable to retrieve. To use this method, select Discovery's 'Advanced Search' option, then click 'Search other archives' and type 'Staffordshire and Stoke-on-Trent Archives' or one of its sub-divisions (SRO, STCA, WSL, etc.). Then enter document references or other search terms in the main search fields. If you wish, the results can be downloaded as a spreadsheet for easier viewing.

Website addresses generally appear in the text in conventional brackets ( ) and in bold, e.g. (**www.staffspasttrack.org.uk**). For the sake of brevity, only addresses that are referenced once (or on a few occasions) are written in full. General sources, such as main repositories and commercial websites, are given in the lists above and in the Directory in Appendix 2.

Chapter 1

THE POTTERIES AND
ITS PEOPLE

STOKE-ON-TRENT AND ENVIRONS
The area we now know as Stoke-on-Trent lies in a shallow depression on the south-western edge of the Peak District. The landscape is characterized by high plateaus punctuated by a series of steep ridges and river valleys. To the west, the industrialized and densely settled conurbation forms a boundary with the sweep of the Cheshire, Shropshire and Staffordshire plain. To the south, the incized landscape gives way to rolling Midlands countryside in the Trent and Dove valleys. At the eastern flank, the Churnet Valley runs through smoothly undulating upland pasture linked by short, steep, wooded valleys known locally as 'cloughs'. The river that gives its name to the city, the Trent, traverses from north to south. From its source on the southern edge of Biddulph Moor, a few miles north of the city, the Trent flows through Stoke merging with the Lyme, Fowlea and other streams that drain this area of North Staffordshire.

Archaeological finds show that this part of the north Midlands has been populated for thousands of years. Caves in the Manifold Valley were occupied during the Palaeolithic era, probably on a seasonal basis. Barrows on prominent hilltop sites, such as the Bridestones on the Cheshire border, suggest that the area was being farmed by the Neolithic or Bronze Age (*c.* 3000 BC). Names such as Trent, Lyme (as in Burs*lem*) and Penkhull are Celtic in origin and suggest that this was an important place of settlement in pre-Roman and Roman times. The Romans built several roads across North Staffordshire and established a fort at Chesterton. Near this road at Trent Vale, on the banks of the

Trent, a Roman pottery kiln has been found: possibly the first instance of pottery-making in the area.

The discovery of the Staffordshire Hoard in a field near Lichfield is a reminder that the Kingdom of Mercia was home to a vibrant culture during the period known as the Dark Ages. Saxon crosses at Stoke and Leek testify to the strong Christian heritage in the period before the Norman Conquest. The name 'Stoke' is Old English for 'place' and is especially used of a 'holy place', again suggesting very early Christian connections. Although there is evidence of pottery being made during medieval times, the wares were crude and utilitarian, showing little promise of the glory that was to come.

For family history purposes, we can think of North Staffordshire in terms of three distinct localities: the Six Towns that eventually joined together to form the city of Stoke-on-Trent; the ancient borough of Newcastle-under-Lyme; and the hinterland towns and villages of the Staffordshire Moorlands from which many people migrated to find work in the rapidly growing industrial centre on their doorstep.

The Six Towns

The city of Stoke-on-Trent came into being in March 1910 through the federation of six neighbouring towns. These were the boroughs of Burslem, Hanley, Longton and Stoke, plus the districts of Fenton and Tunstall. Stoke was chosen as the administrative centre, despite Burslem and Hanley being better established. The constituent towns still retain a strong sense of identity and many locals identify more with their hometown while referring to 'the Potteries' for the wider administrative unit.

Broadly speaking, the city has developed along a linear axis, from Tunstall in the north, through Burslem, Hanley and Stoke clustered in the centre, to Fenton and Longton on the southern fringes. During the nineteenth century each of these towns displayed great civic pride, as attested by the array of town halls, parks and other civic amenities that sprang forth.

BURSLEM

Although not the first of the six to be incorporated, Burslem was the largest town in the Potteries and the first to develop with the onset of the Industrial Revolution. As early as the seventeenth century Burslem

Burslem Old Town Hall and the bottle kiln of the Central Pottery, 1967. (Courtesy of thepotteries.org)

was noted for the quality of its pottery production. Thus, it became known as 'The Mother Town of the Potteries'. It was no coincidence, perhaps, that the greatest exponent of the potters' art, Josiah Wedgwood, was born here.

In the Domesday Survey Burslem appears as 'Bacardeslim' and frequent references (under various spellings) are found in records and charters throughout the medieval period. The Church of St John the Baptist served as a chapelry to Stoke for many years, until Burslem became a separate parish in 1807. During the eighteenth century Burslem became closely associated with Nonconformism and John Wesley visited the area frequently.

Following the opening of the Trent & Mersey Canal the manufacturing district of Longport became an important trading centre with many wharfs from where boats dispatched finished wares the length and breadth of the canal network. Other nearby villages, which eventually became populous suburbs, included Brownhills, Sneyd, Hulton Abbey and Cobridge. Burslem was incorporated as a borough in June 1878.

FENTON

Historically, Fenton consisted of the two townships of Great Fenton (also known as Fenton Culvert) and Little Fenton (or Fenton Vivian). In 1832 the boundaries were formed to the west by the River Trent, by the Cockster Brook to the south and the east (the common boundary with Longton), while the northern boundary adjoining the township of Botteslow followed an irregular line. Little Fenton was the site of a medieval manor house and the manor is listed in Domesday as thane land amounting to about 30 acres held by the Saxon Alward. The Hearth Tax returns of 1666 list seventeen people in Fenton Vivian and sixteen in Fenton Culvert liable to pay the tax. By 1775 the population was strung out along the main Newcastle to Uttoxeter road, with separate settlements at Lower Lane, Lane Delph and Lane End. Fenton developed more slowly than the other towns: as well as pottery manufacture, mining and iron working were important industries.

HANLEY

Hanley grew up as two separate hamlets about half a mile apart, known as Hanley Upper Green (centred on the junction of Keelings Lane and Town Road) and Lower Green (now the Market Square). By the mid-sixteenth century the area was known as Hanley Green. By 1775 the built-up area had spread westwards into Shelton township and there was continuous building along what are now Town Road, Old Hall Street, Albion Street and Marsh Street.

The growth of the town is reflected in the building of the church in 1738, its extension in 1764 and its rebuilding in 1787–90. By the 1790s Hanley, though still smaller than Burslem, was described as 'an improving and spirited place'; it was, however, 'built so irregularly that, to a person in the midst of it, it has scarcely the appearance of anything beyond a moderate village'. In the 1830s Hanley was considered 'a large modern town', the largest in the Potteries and the second in Staffordshire. Its streets were 'generally spacious and well paved', its houses were of 'neat appearance, and some of them, as well as the public edifices . . . spacious and elegant'. On the other hand, much of the town was overcrowded and insanitary. In 1850 it was noted that 'the principal streets have some good shops; and there has been lately finished a range of shops far above the standard of everything else in the Pottery district'. A planning official in the 1960s described the centre of Hanley as 'an archipelago of island sites' and the town's village roots are preserved in the irregular layout of the present-day town centre.

LONGTON
Longton (meaning 'long village') is the newest of the Six Towns and was originally laid out as an agricultural village in the thirteenth century. It was at the end of a lane which ran from Tunstall and hence was known originally as Lane End, and colloquially as 'Neck End'. Coal mines and iron works were the main industries but the building of the Newcastle to Uttoxeter turnpike in 1759 and shortly after the Trent & Mersey Canal brought the pottery industry to the town. Later its position on the Stoke and Derby branch of the North Staffordshire Railway (NSR) also served it well. Numerous small pot works gave the new town a distinctive irregular appearance with pot banks lining the main streets jumbled in and around the workers' houses. During the nineteenth century it became established as one of the most important centres of the pottery industry, in particular for the production of bone china. But its huge concentration of ovens and position in a slight hollow earned Longton the reputation of being highly polluted.

STOKE
The town of Stoke-upon-Trent (generally known simply as Stoke to distinguish it from the city of Stoke-on-Trent) is the oldest of the six communities. The ancient parish of Stoke spanned a huge area, from Whitmore in the west to Bagnall in the east, and from Burslem in the north to Longton in the south. These outlying districts had their own chapelries and maintained their own parish registers. A series of Acts of Parliament in 1807, 1832 and 1889 saw the various chapelries split off into separate parishes.

Curiously, Stoke itself was for centuries little more than a church and a few houses. It is recorded as such in the Domesday Survey of 1087 and remained virtually unchanged until the arrival of the turnpike roads and the Trent & Mersey Canal in the eighteenth century. The church served the neighbouring village of Penkhull, a hilltop settlement which remained an important township into the nineteenth century. *Pigot's Directory of Staffordshire 1841* notes that Stoke:

owes its increase in population and opulence to the establishment of numerous potteries, for which its situation, on a navigable river and a great canal, renders it favourable, and for which it has for many years been distinguished. The town contains many handsome houses, commodious wharfs and warehouses, and extensive china and earthenware manufactories, and is deemed the parish town of the Potteries.

The towns of Stoke, Penkhull and Boothen were incorporated as the Borough of Stoke-upon-Trent in January 1874.

TUNSTALL

Tunstall is the most northern town of the city. It stands on a ridge surrounded by old tilemaking and brickmaking sites, some of which probably date back to the late Middle Ages. Historians have found that iron was being produced here as early as 1280. By the sixteenth century Tunstall comprised about 100 acres of land contained within six open fields, which were later enclosed. In 1795 it was described as the 'pleasantest village in the pottery'. The neighbouring village of Goldenhill existed by 1670 and by 1775 was almost as large as Tunstall, becoming a major centre for the iron industry as well as pottery manufacture. By the time of the cutting of the Trent & Mersey Canal mining had also become established at Goldenhill. The canal passes within ½ mile of Tunstall village and the Harecastle Tunnel, which runs nearly 2 miles underground, is nearby.

Newcastle-under-Lyme

Strictly speaking, Newcastle-under-Lyme is not and never has been within the Potteries. Its origins are much older, having grown up around the twelfth-century castle which stood in an extensive tract of

The marketplace Newcastle-under-Lyme, c. 1890 showing the Guildhall. (Public domain)

water fed by the Lyme Brook and other streams from the surrounding hills. The presence of a permanent garrison attracted traders and craftsmen, and there was a market by at least the early 1200s. A Guildhall was built and the town is thought to have been granted borough status around 1172–3.

The town blossomed further during the Georgian period, due mostly to its strategic position on both north–south and east–west coaching routes. The High Street contained several important coaching inns by the middle of the eighteenth century. Surrounded by a large agricultural district, Newcastle became a key centre for trading in cattle. Mining also sprang up in the districts of Silverdale and Apedale to the west. Although there was a church here from the thirteenth century, it was for many years a chapel dependent upon the parish church at Stoke-upon-Trent. The current Church of St Giles dates from the 1870s and was designed by Sir Gilbert Scott.

Newcastle largely escaped the industrialization that beset its neighbours during the nineteenth and twentieth centuries and today may be regarded as a suburb of Stoke-on-Trent.

The Staffordshire Moorlands

Although never administratively part of Stoke-on-Trent, the people of the Potteries have always felt intimately connected with the Staffordshire Moorlands. This rugged upland on the district's eastern flank was where many of their ancestors originated before moving to the rapidly expanding pottery towns in search of work. The agricultural economy, centred on the market towns of Leek, Cheadle and Biddulph, helped to feed the burgeoning population down the valley. Once working conditions began to improve and people were granted more time off, rural locations such as the Churnet Valley and Rudyard Lake provided much-needed recreation for the Potteries' hard-pressed workers.

Historically, the present-day Staffordshire Moorlands area was mostly contained in the hundred of Totmonslow, one of Staffordshire's ancient divisions. During the eighteenth century the area underwent its own mini industrial revolution, with textile mills being established at Leek, Cheadle and other locations: silk working in particular came to dominate. Coal mining was also an important industry.

Most of the district is over 180m (600ft) above sea level and Flash, at 463m (1,518ft), is reputedly the highest village in Britain. Much of the area now falls within the Peak District National Park.

GROWTH OF THE POTTERIES

The growth of the Potteries is intimately bound up with the growth of the ceramics industry. As industry adopted the factory system, ever larger numbers of people were required living closer to hand. Higher wages enticed people from the rural areas into the new industrial and urban areas that were clustered initially around the canals and coalfields, and later the railways.

By the nineteenth century the villages of the Potteries had grown into sizeable towns, of which Burslem was the largest. Calls for them to be amalgamated into one administrative unit began as early as 1817. Administrative rationalization began in 1857, when the towns of Hanley and Shelton were combined into the Borough of Hanley. In 1865 Longton and Long End became the Borough of Longton; and in 1874 the towns of Stoke, Penkhull and Boothen were brought together as the Borough of Stoke-upon-Trent (generally known as Stoke). The remaining towns, Fenton and Tunstall, gained urban district status in the 1890s. In 1910 the rationalization process was completed when all six towns were brought together to form the County Borough of Stoke-on-Trent. The borough gained city status in 1925.

Stoke-on-Trent's borders have expanded on a number of occasions since then. The main change came in 1922 with the addition of areas to the south and east of the city. This comprised all or part of the civil parishes of Smallthorne, Caverswell, Stone, Trentham, Hanford, Bucknall, Norton, Chell, Newchapel and Milton.

Reliable population statistics are hard to come by. According to one estimate, in 1738 there were as few as 4,000 people living across the 6 districts (John Ward, *The Borough of Stoke-upon-Trent*, 1843). The first census in 1801 recorded a population of more than 26,000 and by the time of the 1841 census this had more than doubled, to around 63,000. Official statistics for the Stoke-on-Trent local authority area cite slightly different figures for the historical population, partly due to boundary changes over the years. It is these that are quoted in Table 1.1 overleaf.

Table 1.1: Population of Stoke-on-Trent Urban Area

Year	Population, 000s
1801	17.5
1811	23.7
1821	29.8
1831	42.7
1841	55.5
1851	59.5
1861	74.2
1881	121.0
1891	139.5
1911	257.5
1931	272.1
1971	260.0
2011	249.0

Source: GB Historical GIS/University of Portsmouth, A Vision of Britain through Time. **www.visionofbritain.org.uk/unit/10217647/cube/TOT_POP.**

FINDING PEOPLE: KEY SOURCES
Censuses
When it comes to using the censuses, the situation for North Staffordshire is very much 'business as usual'; which nowadays, of course, means searching online. All of the publicly available censuses, 1841–1911, are available through commercial websites as well as being free to access at FamilySearch. The FreeCEN project is aiming to provide free online access to UK nineteenth-century census returns (**https://freecen2.freecen.org.uk**). At the time of writing, coverage for North Staffordshire is limited to 1861 and part of 1891; check the 'Database Coverage' page for updates. Stoke-on-Trent City Archives has various legacy products and indexes on microfiche, CD-ROM and hard copy but these are much inferior to online alternatives.

The four censuses taken prior to 1841 (i.e. 1801–31) generally listed only the head of the household rather than the entire population. Coverage for these pre-1841 listings is extremely patchy: the only ones known to survive for North Staffordshire are for Biddulph, 1801 [SRO: D3539/1/48] and Newcastle-under-Lyme, 1811 [SRO: D3251/9/1]. In addition, Staffordshire Record Office has earlier ad hoc population listings for Stoke-on-Trent, 1701 (gives all names and ages); and Biddulph, 1779. *A List of Families in the Archdeaconry of Staffordshire* is a survey of 1532–3 listing over 51,000 names for mid- and North Staffordshire; it has been published by the Staffordshire Record Society (*Collections*, 1976). Chapter 8 has further details of these early listings.

Civil Registration
At the introduction of civil registration on 1 July 1837, England and Wales were divided into a series of registration districts based on the Poor Law Unions (PLUs) introduced a few years before. North Staffordshire comprised six registration districts, each with several sub-districts:

1. Stoke-upon-Trent: covered the heart of the urban area, encompassing the parishes of Bagnall, Fenton, Hanley, Longton, Stoke Rural and Stoke-upon-Trent.
2. Wolstanton: covered ten parishes to the north and west of Stoke-upon-Trent, including Burslem, Chell, Chesterton, Tunstall and Wolstanton.
3. Newcastle-under-Lyme: covered around twenty parishes in north-west Staffordshire. There were sub-districts at Audley, Kidsgrove, Newcastle-under-Lyme, Whitmore and Wolstanton.
4. Stone: was a large district to the south of Stoke-upon-Trent that included the parishes of Barlaston, Blurton, Hanford and Trentham. It was abolished in 1937 to become part of Stafford registration district.
5. Cheadle: covered parishes to the east of Stoke-upon-Trent, including Caverswall and Cheddleton. It was abolished in 1974 to become part of Staffordshire Moorlands and East Staffordshire registration districts.

6. Leek: was a very large registration district to the north-east of Stoke-upon-Trent covering more than thirty parishes, the closest to the Potteries being Norton-in-the-Moors and Endon. It, too, was abolished in 1974 to become part of Staffordshire Moorlands registration district.

Jurisdictions within the main urban area have shifted several times over the years due to administrative and boundary changes. The original Stoke-upon-Trent and Wolstanton registration districts were abolished in 1922 to become part of a single Stoke & Wolstanton registration district. This, in turn, was abolished in 1935 with the creation of the Stoke-on-Trent and Newcastle-under-Lyme registration districts. The latter subsequently became part of the Staffordshire registration district. UKBMD (**www. ukbmd.org.uk/genuki/reg**) has further details of the evolution of registration districts within the Potteries and surrounding areas.

Civil birth, marriage and death registers for the historical registration districts referred to above are now held either by Stoke-on-Trent Register Office at Hanley Town Hall (for areas now within the city boundary, see **www.stoke.gov.uk/info/20011/births_marriages_and_ deaths**), or Staffordshire County Council Registration Service (other areas including Newcastle-under-Lyme and Staffordshire Moorlands, see **www.staffordshire.gov.uk/community/lifeevents/certificates/ certificates.aspx**). Both services offer an online ordering facility for purchasing certified copy certificates. Staff at Stoke-on-Trent will also undertake searches in the indexes for a period of three years but only where accurate details are provided. See council websites for opening hours and fees.

Copies and transcriptions of the General Register Office (GRO) indexes are widely available online, including on non-commercial sites such as FamilySearch and FreeBMD. The STCA has a copy of the GRO indexes for the whole of England and Wales on microfiche for 1837–1960.

The indexes held by the local civil registration service are often more accurate and more complete than the central indexes compiled by the GRO. Family history societies within Staffordshire are collaborating with the local registration services to transcribe their indexes and make them freely available online. The project is ongoing and there is already good coverage for all areas within the former registration districts of Stoke-on-Trent and Newcastle-under-Lyme (**www.staffordshirebmd.org. uk**). The site has the addresses of all register offices in Staffordshire and details of how to order certificates.

Wills and Probate

Probate is the general term for the management of a deceased person's estate. It is a legal process during which a will has to be proved

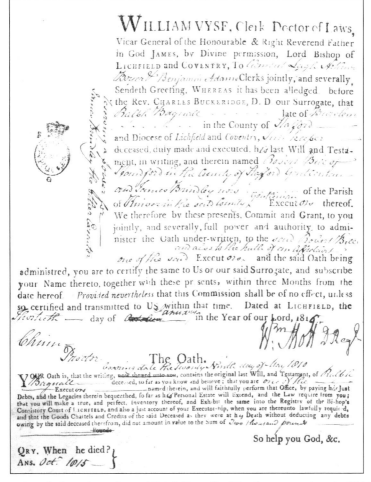

Executor's oath from the probate of Ralph Bagnall of Burslem, granted at the Lichfield Consistory Court, 9 April 1816. (Staffordshire Collection, FindMyPast)

(meaning 'approved') by persuading a court that it is valid and has not been superseded. Once the court is satisfied of these conditions then probate is 'granted'. Responsibility for carrying out the terms of the will falls to the executor (or executrix if female) appointed by the deceased as detailed in the will. Letters of Administration, or 'Admons', are issued when a person dies intestate (i.e. without leaving a will). Historically, other documents that may occur in the context of probate are inventories of the deceased's personal possessions (a statutory requirement between 1529 and 1782); and papers relating to death duties and other taxes. Raymond (2012) has further background on the history and purpose of probate records.

Since 1858, probate for England and Wales has been administered centrally through the Principal Registry of the Family Division. The index to these cases, known as the National Probate Calendar, is available to search free of charge at the Government's Probate Search Service website (**https://probatesearch.service.gov.uk/#calendar**). There are separate databases for 1858–1996, 1996 to present, and soldiers' wills. Copies of these wills can be ordered at the same site and currently cost £10 each. The National Probate Calendar is also available via Ancestry (1858–1966) and Findmypast (1858–1959).

Before 1858 probate was proved in ecclesiastical (church) courts. The whole of Staffordshire was within the Diocese of Lichfield & Coventry. The Bishop of Lichfield & Coventry had general jurisdiction over probate within this area, which was exercised through the Lichfield Consistory Court (LCC). Unlike many dioceses, there were no archdeaconry courts and the LCC covered the whole diocese. Some areas, known as peculiar jurisdictions or peculiars, were exempt from the bishop's jurisdiction. Here, probate was usually handled by other church officials or, in a handful of cases, lords of manors. There were no peculiars in this part of North Staffordshire, nor were there any significant changes in the jurisdiction of the Consistory Court over an extended period. Both of these factors significantly simplify the search for pre-1858 wills. Humphery-Smith (2003) maps parishes to probate jurisdictions for all pre-1974 counties (see Maps section below, p. 19).

Lichfield Record Office, which held most LCC records, has now closed and the records have been transferred to the SSA's main facility at Stafford. Survival of original consistory wills is good after 1600, although few inventories survive after around 1750. The LCC holdings are summarized in the *Handlist to the Diocesan Probate and Church Commissioners' Records* (2nd edn, 1978). There is a good nineteenth-century calendar to LCC Wills and Administrations, 1516–1857, and a separate index to records of peculiars. Printed versions of these indexes to 1652 (published by the British Record Society) are less accurate.

In a major boon for Staffordshire researchers, these indexes as well as digitized images of the original wills and administrations proved in the LCC are available as part of the Staffordshire Collection on Findmypast. Elsewhere online, partial indexes to LCC probates are available through Staffordshire Name Indexes for the period 1630–1780 (**www.staffsnameindexes.org.uk**) and Ancestry for the period 1516–1652.

In general, where someone held property or goods within one diocese only, the will was proved, or administration granted, in that court. If held in two dioceses, then the grant was made in higher courts at either Canterbury or York. Indexes to Prerogative Court of Canterbury (PCC) wills can be searched free of charge on the TNA website (with copy wills available to purchase), while Findmypast has indexes to wills proved in the Prerogative Court of York (PCY), 1688–1858.

LOCAL PHOTOGRAPHS
Photographic Collections
The SSA is the custodian of a wide range of photographic collections. Highlights from these collections are showcased at the Staffordshire Past Track website, which provides access to photographs, images, maps and film and audio clips through easy-to-use search tools (**www. staffspasttrack.org.uk**). The site covers more than 30,000 resources in total, some of which are available to purchase and download. The SSA's full photographic collection can be searched using the Gateway to the Past search engine (**www.archives.staffordshire. gov.uk**, specify 'photographs' under DocType).

Some of the images on Staffordshire Past Track are derived from the collections of private photographers. One such was J.A. Lovatt, who

Wharf Street, Longton, c. 1905 photographed by William Blake. (Staffordshire Past Track)

lived in Normacot and was a member of the North Staffordshire Field Club in the 1920s. His collection of photographs of Longton and area is held at the STCA [SD 1752]. Another Longton-based photographer with images on Past Track is William Blake. Born in the United States in 1874, Blake emigrated with his family to Britain and settled in Longton, where he set up a stationer's shop on Stafford Street (now the Strand). He was a key member of the North Staffordshire Field Club, acting as librarian for the society's photograph collection (which is now housed at the Staffordshire County Museum). He died in 1957.

Other notable image collections held at the STCA are:

- The Beard Collection: Photographs of Burslem, Hanley and Tunstall taken by Derek Beard, 1959–c. 1962 [STCA: SD 1635, currently uncatalogued].
- The J.R. Hollick Collection: Approximately fifty albums and loose photographs, mainly relating to railways in North Staffordshire during the 1920s and 1930s (not catalogued).

- The Bentley Slide Collection: A series of over 6,000 colour slides taken by Bert Bentley in the early 1960s under commission from Stoke-on-Trent Libraries [SD 1480].
- The Watson Collection: Photograph albums, photographs, film recordings and ephemera recording the city's industrial and social heritage compiled and donated by Stoke-on-Trent resident Mark Watson [SD 1537].
- The Morgan Photographic Collection: A large collection of late twentieth-century photographs donated by Jim Morgan [SD 1655].

The Warrillow Collection at Keele University comprises over 1,800 photographs of the Potteries area dating from the 1870s to the 1970s (**www.keele.ac.uk/library/specarc/collections/**). The majority were taken by Ernest James Warrillow, a press photographer with the *Sentinel* newspaper from 1927–74. He graphically recorded the changing landscape and people of the Potteries and collected old photographs and engravings. The STCA has a printed catalogue. Keele is also home to the William Jack Collection, comprising around 2,000 photographs of North Staffordshire's industrial heritage taken by Chatterley Whitfield Colliery employee William Jack during the 1920s and 1930s.

Other Imagery
Pastscape (**www.pastscape.org.uk**) is a portal to information on archaeological and architectural heritage across England, run by Historic England (formerly English Heritage). It has descriptions, and in some cases pictures, of sites and buildings referenced within historical sources, including over 5,000 in Staffordshire. A related service, ViewFinder, has historic photographs from the Historic England Archive (**http://viewfinder.english-heritage.org.uk**), while the full catalogue has over 1 million entries describing photographs, plans and drawings of buildings and historic sites (**http://archive.historicengland.org.uk**). Information on all buildings that have received listed status is available at **www.britishlistedbuildings.co.uk**.

Staffordshire Views is a unique series of illustrations of churches, public buildings, country houses and landscapes from all over Staffordshire, dating mainly from the 1830s and 1840s (**www. views.staffspasttrack.org.uk**). Staffordshire Prints offers artwork from local museums to purchase in various forms, including fine-art posters and prints (**www.magnoliabox.com/collections/staffordshire-prints**).

The photo-sharing site Flickr has many members and groups devoted to photography around and relating to the Potteries, both contemporary and historic. One of the largest is **www.flickr.com/groups/stoke-on-trent**. The Potteries Museum & Art Gallery and the Gladstone Museum each have social media channels where they share images from their collections (**www.stokemuseums.org.uk**). Facebook, Twitter and Instagram all have photo-sharing communities.

There are many Stoke-on-Trent galleries within the Geograph database, which aims to collect geographically representative photographs and information for every square kilometre of Great Britain and Ireland (**www.geograph.org.uk**).

Potteries.org has numerous photographs, both old and new, relating to the area and its heritage culled from various sources (**www.thepotteries.org/photos.htm**). The work of recent and contemporary photo historians is presented, alongside aerial photos of the city, watercolours, paintings and old postcards. The site has more than 100 drawings of buildings in the Potteries by artist Neville Malkin which originally appeared in the *Evening Sentinel* during the 1970s (**http://thepotteries.org/tour/index.htm**).

Several books have been published presenting the Potteries and surrounding area through old photographs and postcards (see Publishers section in Appendix 2).

The Moving Image

The Media Archive for Central England preserves the 'moving image heritage' for both the East and West Midlands (**www.macearchive. org**). Its online catalogue contains 50,000 titles for Staffordshire and Stoke-on-Trent. Many of these are part of the Staffordshire Film Archive, a specialist archive of original films for the county which was founded and developed by Ray Johnson MBE (**www.filmarchive.org. uk**). The

Media Archive for Central England offers a range of high-quality DVDs and films for sale and/or download.

The West Midlands History portal regularly produces short films, which are free to view online, uncovering the stories of the people and events that shaped the region (**www.historywm.com**). A collection of archive films on Staffordshire is available on the British Film Institute website (**http://player.bfi.org.uk**). *Stoke-on-Trent Past in Pictures* is a DVD from commercial publisher UK History Store (**www.ukhistory store.com**) containing recordings made between the 1930s and the 1970s, many of which have not been published before.

MAPS, GAZETTEERS AND PLANS

Maps are an essential resource for family historians, helping to provide a more detailed understanding of where and how our ancestors lived.

Before the advent of the Ordnance Survey in the nineteenth century, mapping relied on a series of county maps produced privately by individuals or small groups of surveyors with wealthy patrons. In some cases these would be bound into volumes of county atlases. The earliest map of Staffordshire dates from 1577 and was produced by the mapmaker Christopher Saxton. It is surprisingly accurate and detailed for its time, showing settlements and geographical features. In common with other early county maps, however, it shows no roads. Other early maps of the county include Smith's map of 1599 and Kip's map of 1607.

The famous John Speed mapped Staffordshire in 1610, again including main features but omitting the roads. Some of these early maps were reproduced at a small scale for inclusion in 'pocket atlases', while others started to feature town plans with key buildings and street names. John Bill's miniature version of 1626 was the first to show degrees of latitude and longitude. Robert Plot's map of 1682 was highly detailed and became a benchmark for others to follow.

During the eighteenth century county maps improved in accuracy, with the addition of roads and ways of differentiating between main routes and minor lanes. William Yates undertook a scientific survey to produce the first large-scale map of the county in 1775; a second smaller

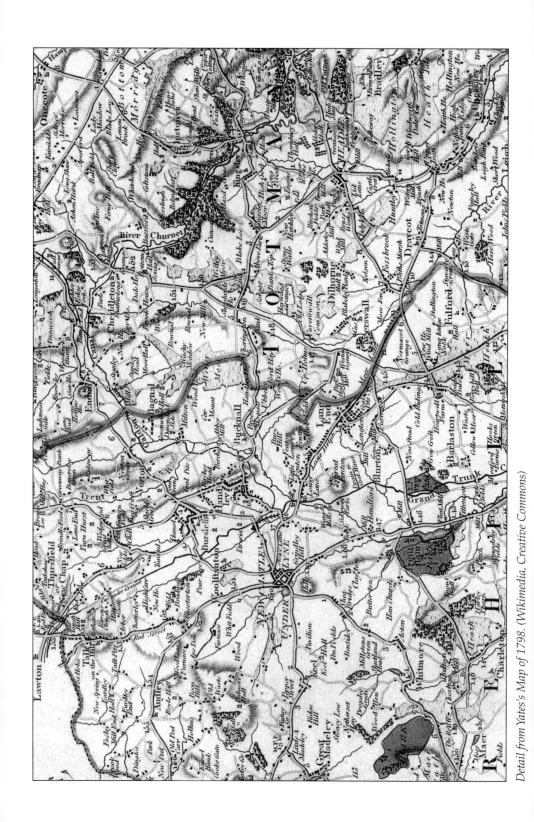

Detail from Yates's Map of 1798. (Wikimedia, Creative Commons)

edition followed in 1798. The first half of the nineteenth century saw further refinements and in 1820 Christopher Greenwood produced a large-scale, 1in-to-the-mile map based on a detailed survey. By this time, however, the Ordnance Survey had begun its work and the age of privately surveyed county maps was drawing to a close. The first edition 1in Ordnance Survey sheet of the Potteries was published in 1837, from survey work undertaken between 1831 and 1837. Second and third editions were released in stages around 1881 and 1908, respectively.

The SSA's map collection covers many types and periods. The majority of original printed county maps are held at the William Salt Library, while the SRO holds copies of Greenwood's map of 1820, reprints of earlier county maps and various printed and administrative county maps dating from the twentieth century. The collection can be searched using the Gateway to the Past search engine (**www.archives. staffordshire.gov.uk**, specify 'maps and plans' under DocType). The Staffordshire Past Track portal allows map-based searches across a variety of themes relating to the county's history (**www.search.staffs pasttrack.org.uk/mapexplorer.aspx?**).

Enclosure – the process by which land farmed in common was divided into enclosed fields – required the areas affected to be mapped in great detail (see Chapter 8). From the mid-eighteenth century, enclosure by Act of Parliament became standard practice and it is from this period that much of the documentation survives. The SRO holds documents relating to enclosure, mostly for the seventeenth and eighteenth centuries, which may include surveys, maps and plans. *SSA Guide to Sources No. 5: Staffordshire Enclosure Acts, Awards & Maps* has a detailed list of holdings.

Further change to agricultural communities came with the Tithe Commutation Act of 1836, which abolished the in-kind payment of tithes and substituted rent charges. This required accurate maps of the country measuring acreage and recording the state of cultivation. For some places the tithe maps were the first detailed maps, although the results were of variable quality. Together with the accompanying apportionment schedule, the tithe maps show who owned and who rented land. Most of the maps for North Staffordshire were produced between 1839 and 1852. Copies are likely to be found at TNA, the SRO and the WSL (explained further in Chapter 8). *SSA Guide to Sources No. 3: Tithe Maps and Awards* provides a detailed listing.

Potteries.org has a large collection of maps from across the area, including local detail from Yates's map of 1775 (**www.thepotteries.org/maps/index.htm**). Early Ordnance Survey maps and factory and estate plans are also well represented.

The City Surveyor's Map Collection [SA/CS] at the STCA contains numerous types of maps made by the Stoke-on-Trent City Surveyor's Department, mainly from the period 1920–50. Aspects covered include: bus and tramway routes, new housing schemes, utilities and maps of bomb damage and air raid precautions from the Second World War. There is a catalogue in the STCA Search Room.

Because the Six Towns had grown up independently many street names had been duplicated, which led to confusion as people started to move more freely around the city. For example, there were seven Albert Streets, eleven Church Streets and twelve High Streets. In the early 1950s a large number of streets were renamed. The STCA has a list of changed street names that was originally compiled by the City Council in 1955 and reprinted in 2001 by the North Staffordshire Branch of the BMSGH (now out of print). The listing is also available on Potteries.org, cross-referenced by old name, new name and district, together with more recent street listings (**www.thepotteries.org/streets/index.htm**).

When researching in a new area it is essential to know what parish registers are available and which are the neighbouring parishes. The definitive source for this is *The Phillimore Atlas and Index of Parish Registers* (Humphery-Smith, 2003). It lists the availability of registers for a given parish, and shows the neighbouring parishes as well as the relevant probate jurisdiction for wills and administrations. The parish maps from the *Phillimore Atlas*, produced by the Institute of Heraldic and Genealogical Studies, are available on Ancestry as *Great Britain, Atlas and Index of Parish Registers* (**https://search.ancestry.co.uk/search/db.aspx?dbid=8830**).

FamilySearch has a facility to compile maps made up of various layers, such as parishes and PLUs, to see how they relate to each other; this is very useful in an urban area such as Stoke-on-Trent (**http://maps.familysearch.org**).

The excellent National Library of Scotland website has a huge selection of Ordnance Survey and other maps covering the whole of the British Isles (**https://maps.nls.uk**). Other rich sites for historical maps are: Genmaps (**http://freepages.genealogy.rootsweb.ancestry.com/~genmaps/**); MAPCO (**http://mapco.net**); Old Maps Online (**www.oldmapsonline.org**); and Vision of Britain (**www.visionofbritain.org.uk**).

An Historical Atlas of Staffordshire (Phillips and Phillips, 2011) provides an academic perspective on Staffordshire's historical geography.

NEWSPAPERS

Provincial newspapers began to become established in England in the early eighteenth century. Before this news reached the English countryside through manuscript newsletters, printed newsbooks and newspapers produced in London. Politicians saw the growth of cheap newspapers as dangerous, fearing they would radicalize the lower classes, leading to social unrest and even revolution. Taxes were levied on paper and advertisements as well as a stamp duty on newspapers in an effort to restrict their growth. As the tax was per sheet of paper, the pages grew larger and larger and the print became smaller and smaller to accommodate more news. Many newspapers continued as so-called 'broadsheets' until recent times.

Newspapers are a valuable but often underused resource for the family historian. They can be a gateway to a wealth of information, some of which is not available elsewhere; or they may lead on to other sources. The types of information to be found include: obituaries, birth,

Masthead of the Staffordshire Sentinel, *19 May 1873.*

marriage and death announcements, bankruptcies and dissolution of partnerships, name changes, court cases, school and university examination results, military appointments and promotions, and gallantry citations and awards.

Court cases and inquests are a staple of all local papers. Usually a reporter would be sent along and took down, verbatim, what was said. Witnesses, such as family members, would be questioned, perhaps revealing key information, such as marital infidelity or a separation. Obituaries also give a lot of information: as well as a summary of the deceased's life, they may mention family relationships and provide a list of people who attended the funeral. As the areas covered by newspapers often overlapped, and some of the content was syndicated between titles, an event may not necessarily be reported (or have survived) in the nearest local newspaper.

The main newspaper for the Potteries was, and remains, the *Staffordshire Sentinel*, later the *Evening Sentinel* and now the *Sentinel* (**www.stokesentinel.co.uk**). Although not the first to be published in the area (see p. 26), it has outlived all others and has come to be regarded as a Potteries institution.

The STCA has a substantial collection of newspapers from the Potteries and the wider county available on microfilm (see Table 1.2 below). There are long runs of the *Staffordshire Sentinel* from 1854 through to 1985, and the *Staffordshire Advertiser*, a county wide newspaper, from 1795–1973, as well as two bound volumes of indexes to birth, marriage and death announcements published in that newspaper between 1795 and 1840 (produced by the Staffordshire Record Society). A separate typescript index covers items from the *Staffordshire Advertiser*, 1870–84 for the parish of Audley and surrounding villages. The WSL also holds a complete run of the *Staffordshire Advertiser* from 1795–1973.

Newcastle-under-Lyme Library has an almost complete run of the *Sentinel*, in all its manifestations, from 1854 on microfilm, plus various others including two local titles: *Newcastle Guardian* (1900–9) and *Newcastle Times* (1938–73).

Table 1.2: Newspaper Series at Stoke-on-Trent City Archives

Newspaper	Years Held
Miner & Workman's Examiner	1874–8
North Staffordshire Advertiser	2000–3
Potteries Examiner	1871–81
Potteries Examiner & Workman's Advocate	1843–7
Pottery Gazette	1879–1914
Staffordshire Advertiser	1795–1973
Staffordshire County Herald	Occasional from 1831/2
Staffordshire Knot	1882–91
Staffordshire Mercury	1830–45
Staffordshire Sentinel	1854–2009
Stoke-on-Trent City Times	1935–69

Staffordshire is well represented in the British Newspaper Archive, an ambitious project to digitize British nineteenth-century newspapers being undertaken as a joint venture between the British Library and DC Thomson Family History (**www.britishnewspaperarchive.co.uk**). Titles relating wholly or partially to North Staffordshire include: *Leek Post & Times/Cheadle News & Times/Moorland Advertiser, Staffordshire Advertiser, Staffordshire Gazette and County Standard*, and *Staffordshire Sentinel* (including some under the original name of *Staffordshire Sentinel and Commercial & General Advertiser*). Ancestry has a very limited run (just four years) of the *Staffordshire Sentinel*. Print, microfilm and digitized newspapers can also be viewed at the Newsroom, the British Library's specialized reading room at St Pancras, London (**www.bl.uk /subjects/news-media**).

National newspapers can be an important source for legal and family announcements (especially for the upper classes). The *London Gazette*, published since the mid-1600s, is freely available online (**www.the gazette.co.uk**). National and some local titles are accessible through subscription services, such as the Gale Newspaper Database and The Times Digital Archive (1785–1985); many libraries offer free access either within library buildings or from home for library members.

SPREADING THE NEWS: NEWSPAPERS IN NORTH STAFFORDSHIRE

The first newspaper known to have been printed in North Staffordshire was the *Pottery Gazette and Newcastle-under-Lyme Advertiser*, which made its appearance in January 1809. Financed by pottery owners looking to advertise their wares, it was thought by some to be 'decidedly Tory and aristocratical' in tone and lasted a little over a year. Another *Pottery Gazette* was established in 1822 and lasted for six years. Meanwhile, Thomas Allbut had started the *Pottery Mercury* – later known as the *Staffordshire Mercury* – as a moderate Liberal newspaper in 1824 and this continued for around twenty years. Other titles that appeared around this time were the *Potteries Examiner* (published from 1823–46); the *North Staffordshire Independent* (early 1850s); and the *Staffordshire Potteries Telegraph* (dates unknown). Increasingly, such papers began to promote the interests of pottery workers, in some cases from a strong religious standpoint.

In 1853 a group of Liberal reformers decided to launch a new weekly paper. One of their objects was to campaign for the incorporation of Hanley to free it from the outmoded, and allegedly corrupt, Improvement Commissioners and other bodies who were running the town's affairs at that time. Among the newspaper's early supporters were: Edward Challinor, a local solicitor; Edmund Oswald, a potters' commission agent; and a commercial traveller named Samuel Taylor who was a pioneer of the 'penny readings', a primitive form of adult education in the area. All of these appear to have put money into the venture and secured the support of John Keates, a local printer.

The *Staffordshire Sentinel and Commercial and General Advertiser* was first published on 7 January 1854 from offices in Cheapside, Hanley. The publisher was Hugh Roberts, a former printer, and the editor was Thomas Phillips, a radical campaigner and former bookseller. By 1872 circulation of the *Sentinel* had increased to 5,000 copies weekly with 90 agents covering the whole of North Staffordshire and part of Cheshire. The following year, 1873, the paper became a daily, published from Monday to Friday, with a separate weekly edition on Saturdays.

Under its then editor, Thomas Andrews Potter, and his successors the *Sentinel* became a strong campaigning force that did not shy away from political controversy. It was a deep influence on Arnold Bennett, who made a newspaper called 'The Signal' a centrepiece of several of his novels. During the twentieth century the *Sentinel* shed its partisanship and extended its reporting horizons, both thematically and geographically. In March 2014, the *Sentinel* was awarded the Freedom of Stoke-on-Trent. It is now part of the Trinity Mirror Group.

TRADE AND COMMERCIAL DIRECTORIES

As a centre dependent on the production and sale of manufactured goods, trade directories were an essential means for North Staffordshire firms to publicize their wares. In the early years Stoke-on-Trent tended to be covered as part of county directories for Staffordshire (and sometimes neighbouring counties as well); later on, as the district's importance grew, dedicated directories were produced. Most directories provide a history of the locality and descriptions of amenities such as schools, workhouses and churches. As well as businesses, some directories list every resident or building and/or the members of local councils and other administrative bodies.

The STCA has a collection of trade and commercial directories covering Stoke-on-Trent and Staffordshire, 1783–1940. These are produced by well-known publishers such as Kelly, Pigot, the Post Office, Slater and White and are available in various formats. *City of Stoke-on-Trent Directory with Newcastle-under-Lyme*, published in 1963 (Barrett's Publications), gives a more recent picture of industry in the city, just at the point at which it was starting to decline. Also of note is *Leek Trade Bills* c. *1830–1930* – a source collection on trade and business in Leek compiled from letterheads, advertisements and directories (Poole, 2003–7).

The SRO and the WSL have their own collections. The excellent *Potteries, Newcastle and District Directory*, published by the Staffordshire Sentinel Ltd in 1907 and 1912, lists, with a few exceptions, every householder in the district including the rural areas [WSL: PN4246]. Keele University Library (which is open to the general public) and Newcastle-under-Lyme Library each have selections. Potteries.org has scans and transcriptions of various trade directories, including a 1955 publication by the North Staffordshire Chamber of Commerce.

Historical Directories of England and Wales, part of the University of Leicester's Special Collections Online, has many digitized trade directories for Staffordshire and other Midlands counties from the 1760s to the 1910s, which are free to download (accessible via **http://special collections.le.ac.uk**). Midlands Historical Data is a commercial publisher offering digitized copies of trade and commercial directories to purchase on CD-ROM; subscription and pay-as-you-go options are also available (**www.midlandshistoricaldata.org**). The Midland Ancestors Reference Library, the Society of Genealogists and TNA all have good runs of Midlands directories.

The introduction of the telephone brought the need for a new type of listing. Ancestry has a good collection of historical telephone directories from across the UK under 'British Phone Books, 1880–1984'. Forebears who worked in the Post Office are likely to be found in the British Postal Service Appointment Books, 1737–1969, and also on Ancestry.

NORTH STAFFORDSHIRE NAMES AND BIOGRAPHIES
Like other areas, North Staffordshire has its own collection of distinctive surnames, many of them unique to the district. Local historian Edgar Tooth has made an exhaustive study of the origins and distribution of such names. This scholarly work documents in extensive detail the origins of a multitude of surnames native to North Staffordshire and is required reading for any researcher tracing a distinctive name. The results were published in a four-volume series issued between 2000 and 2010 by Churnet Valley Books. Potential origins considered are local placenames and landscape features (Tooth, 2000); occupations, trade, rank and office (Tooth, 2002); nicknames (Tooth, 2004); and personal and pet names (Tooth, 2010).

Obituaries in newspapers and periodicals can provide important biographical details on our ancestors that might not be found elsewhere.

As well as mainstream publications, church and parish magazines can be useful in this respect (see Chapter 4).

Potteries.org has mini-biographies of leading figures in business, civic life and other fields, as well as an index to people mentioned elsewhere in this huge website (**www.thepotteries.org/biographies**). *Contemporary Biographies* by Cameron Pike, published in 1907, is a series of pen portraits of leading figures in 'Staffordshire and Shropshire at the opening of the twentieth century' (all men, of course!). *People of the Potteries: A Dictionary of Local Biography* by Denis Stuart (University of Keele, 1985) is a similar but much later listing.

FURTHER INFORMATION

Anonymous, *The Sentinel Story: 1873–1973* (James Heap Ltd, 1973)

Humphery-Smith, Cecil R., *The Phillimore Atlas & Index of Parish Registers* (3rd edn, Phillimore, 2003)

Phillips, A.D.M. and C.B. Phillips, *An Historical Atlas of Staffordshire* (Manchester University Press, 2011)

Poole, Ray, *Leek Trade Bills c.1830–1930*, 3 vols (Churnet Valley Books, 2003–7)

Raymond, Stuart A., *The Wills of Our Ancestors: A Guide for Family & Local Historians* (Pen & Sword Family History, 2012)

Tooth, Edgar, *Distinctive Surnames of North Staffordshire: Vol. One: Surnames Derived from Local Placenames and Landscape Features* (Churnet Valley Books, 2000); *Vol. Two: Surnames Derived from Occupations, Trade, Rank and Office* (Churnet Valley Books, 2002); *Vol. Three: Surnames Derived from Nicknames* (Churnet Valley Books, 2004); *Vol. Four: Surnames Derived from Personal and Pet Names* (Churnet Valley Books, 2010)

Chapter 2

THE POTTERY INDUSTRY

THE ORIGINS OF THE POTTERY INDUSTRY

The industry that would come to symbolize this part of North Staffordshire had an ignominious start. The subsistence farmers who worked the land in the Middle Ages sought to supplement their income in any way they could. Some took to quarrying, ironworking, charcoal burning and to making coarse earthenware products from the plentiful supplies of red clay. Simple cylindrical butter pots and other domestic wares were sold in markets as far afield as Birmingham and Nottingham. In 1603 a dish maker called Gervase Griffye is listed in Tunstall. Pottery was being made at Penkhull by about 1600 and by the end of the century there are records of butterpots being produced in Stoke and Hanley. Clay pipes were made at Newcastle using Shelton clay.

The first proper history of the area, Robert Plot's *History of Staffordshire* published in 1686, describes in detail the clays and techniques used in pottery making in the late seventeenth century. During this period yeoman farmers used common land or their own holdings to dig for clay and coal and adapted their sheds and outbuildings for pottery production, building kilns and digging clay pits. Pottery making, like farming, remained a seasonal activity but the surrounding landscape began to feature an increasingly familiar sight: the bottle kiln. By 1720 Burslem was a prominent pottery centre, probably the largest in the country, and most farms had bottle-shaped kilns attached. An illustration of Burslem from this period shows a cluster of houses and a large number of potbanks set beside the parish church.

The early eighteenth century saw increasing investment in

specialized buildings, such as drying and packing houses. Some potters expanded their trade sufficiently to employ small teams of skilled workers. Expertise was passed on from father to son, and some Staffordshire potters became aware of the opportunities for developing their trade to supply the increasingly sophisticated markets that were emerging for fashionable white tableware and ornamental ware. The time was right for enterprise and North Staffordshire had no shortage of innovative young men willing to try their hand.

FOUNDING FATHERS: POTTERY PIONEERS

Among the pioneers of English potting technology was the Astbury family. John Astbury established a factory at Shelton in the early eighteenth century, where he succeeded in producing yellowish-glazed red earthenware decorated with bits of white pipe clay. These are some of the earliest Staffordshire figures in brown and white clay covered with a lead glaze. He is said to have learned the technique from the secretive

Elers brothers who had emigrated to the area from Holland in 1688. Astbury's son, Thomas, experimented with this lead-glazed earthenware to create a form that became known as creamware, so called because of its cream colour. The cream colouring was considered a fault at the time and Staffordshire potters sought out a purer white alternative that would substitute for Chinese porcelain. It was Josiah Wedgwood who was able to capitalize on these innovations.

Born in 1730, Wedgwood had been apprenticed to his brother Thomas at the family's Churchyard Works in Burslem. From 1754 to 1758 he was in partnership with Thomas Whieldon, a distinguished potter from Fenton who had been a keen experimenter with creamware. By the time Wedgwood set up his own pottery works in

Statue of Josiah Wedgwood, Winton Square, Stoke. (Wikimedia, Creative Commons)

1759 there were already around 150 potters in the Burslem area, employing about 7,000 people. Wedgwood, too, was a keen experimenter and he set about refining and developing what other potters were doing. The introduction of Cornish clay and stone to provide a whiter body, coupled with more sophisticated shapes and glazes set his products apart. Wedgwood's highly durable cream-coloured tableware so pleased Queen Charlotte that in 1762 she appointed him royal supplier of dinnerware. His skill was as much as a businessman as a potter and he immediately named the range 'Queen's Ware'.

Wedgwood instinctively knew that royal patronage would boost his business and so it transpired. Demand for the ware that graced the Queen's table went through the roof and Wedgwood's already successful factory soon dominated the market. Writing to his friend, the merchant Thomas Bentley, in 1767, Wedgwood observed: 'The demand for this Creamcolour, Alias, Queen Ware, Alias, Ivory, still increases – It is amazing how rapidly the use of it has spread all most over the whole Globe.' In 1768 he built a second factory at Etruria, near Stoke, and in the same year went into partnership with Thomas Bentley. At first only ornamental pottery was made in Etruria, but by 1773 Wedgwood had concentrated all his production facilities there. Through the Lunar Society, a group of industrialists and thinkers in the English Midlands, Wedgwood got to know James Watt and this led, in 1782, to Etruria being one of the first factories to install a steam-powered engine.

Other notable successes were to follow. In 1774 Empress Catherine the Great of Russia ordered a massive creamware service of 952 pieces, further boosting its popularity. Other wares were produced with names such as rosso antico (red porcelain), cane, drab, chocolate and olive wares.

The most iconic development, however, was the introduction in 1775 of jasper ware. This fine-grained, unglazed stoneware was the result of a long series of experiments aimed at discovering the techniques of porcelain manufacture. The name derives from the fact that it resembles the natural stone jasper in its hardness. Jasper is white in its natural state and is stained with metallic oxide colouring agents. The most common shade is pale blue, but dark blue, lilac, sage green, black and yellow were also used. The familiar, densely uniform stoneware in solid colours ornamented in a contrasting hue was Josiah Wedgwood's most important contribution to ceramic art. One of the firm's most outstanding creations was the 1790 reproduction in jasper of the Portland Vase, which had been excavated from a tomb outside Rome in the early seventeenth century. One of these is now in the British Museum.

Wedgwood's achievements extended far beyond pottery. He was one of the wealthiest entrepreneurs of the eighteenth century and is credited as the inventor of modern marketing. As a leading thinker of his day he mixed with the likes of Matthew Boulton, James Watt, Joseph Priestley, Samuel Galton and Erasmus Darwin. Josiah's eldest daughter Susannah married Erasmus's son and was the mother of the naturalist Charles Darwin. Josiah was also an ardent Nonconformist and a prominent abolitionist and is remembered for his 'Am I Not a Man And a Brother?' anti-slavery medallion.

Josiah Wedgwood died on 3 January 1795. His contribution to the development of the pottery industry and the nation is well summarized in his epitaph in Stoke church, that he: 'converted a rude and inconsiderable manufactory into an elegant art and an important part of national commerce'. His descendants carried on the business at the Etruria site until 1940, when the Wedgwood factory was relocated to Barlaston. Years later the site was used as part of the National Garden Festival.

Spode, another famous pottery dynasty, was started by Josiah Spode in around 1760. He was born in 1733 in Lane Delph and was 6 when his father died and was buried in a pauper's grave. After serving an apprenticeship under Thomas Whieldon, Spode worked for and in partnership with other potters in the area before establishing his own business in Stoke. His son, Josiah Spode II, also trained as a potter and ran the firm's warehouse in London, eventually taking over the pottery factory from his father in 1797. Josiah Spode II led the

Josiah Spode (1733–97) by N. Freese. (Wikimedia, Creative Commons)

33

development of bone china, which became the standard English porcelain body from about 1800 onwards.

The Spode factory became renowned for its blue and white Willow pattern, developed by the original Josiah Spode in about 1790 from a pattern called Mandarin. After visiting the factory in 1806 the then Prince of Wales asked Spode to produce the banqueting service for his coronation as George IV. This was the first of many Royal Warrants to be received. In 1867 the company's official trade name was changed to W.T. Copeland & Sons, only reverting back to Spode in 1970. After passing into receivership in 2008 the business was bought by the Stoke-based Portmeirion pottery company.

The perfection of the formula for fine bone china has been described as the single most significant development in the history of the pottery industry. It set Spode on course to become one of the most well-known names in British pottery and brought the family great wealth. They built The Mount, an elegant mansion in Penkhull which was subsequently inherited by Josiah's son, Josiah Spode III.

Other early influences on the development of the Staffordshire pottery industry came from the Adams and Wood families. After being apprentice to John Astbury, Ralph Wood worked with Thomas Whieldon learning the manufacture of coloured glazes. Ralph's brother Aaron opened his own pottery and the family became closely associated with Josiah Wedgwood through both business and marriage. By 1833 Enoch Wood & Sons was the largest employer in Burslem with a workforce of 1,100: only Davenport's in Longport was of comparable size. The Adams family had potteries in Staffordshire as early as 1650, when two brothers, William and Thomas, had separate ventures in Burslem. The business continued in various incarnations at Burslem, Stoke and Tunstall into the twentieth century, being managed by members who were the eleventh and twelfth generations in direct descent from the seventeenth-century founders.

Other famous names include:

• The Davenport company: Founded by John Davenport, who began as a potter working with Thomas Wolfe of Stoke. In 1794, he acquired his own pottery at Longport and began producing cream-coloured blue-printed earthenware. The quality of his wares led to him becoming a supplier to the Prince of Wales, later to become George IV. John retired in 1830 and his sons, William and Henry, carried on the business. In 1887, the firm, by then known as William Davenport & Co., was acquired by Burleigh Pottery.

- The Doulton company: Founded by John Doulton in Lambeth, south London in 1815. Under his son, Henry Doulton, it became Britain's leading manufacturer of sanitary wares and other industrial ceramics, as well as a major producer of art pottery and of ornamental and commemorative pieces, and tableware. Doulton took over the Nile Street, Burslem factory of Pinder Bourne in 1877, where it began making bone china. Production has been concentrated at Burslem since 1956. Having taken over many of its rivals in both industrial and decorative wares, the Royal Doulton Group is now the largest manufacturer of ceramics in Britain.
- The Minton company: A rival to Spode, was founded by Thomas Minton in 1793. The factory's staple products consisted of useful and unpretentious tablewares in painted or printed earthenware or bone china, following the typical shapes and decorative patterns of the period. It also popularized the famous so-called Willow pattern. Figures and ornamental porcelains were made increasingly from the 1820s. After Thomas Minton's death in 1836, under his son, Herbert, the company diversified into producing printed and painted tiles. The factory, including office accommodation and the Minton Museum, was demolished in 2002 as part of rationalization within the Royal Doulton Group. The Minton Archive has been kept together and was transferred to the city of Stoke-on-Trent in 2015.
- The Moorcroft company: Origins in the work of William Moorcroft who worked as a designer for the Macintyre factory in Burslem in the 1890s. Working in the art nouveau style, Moorcroft developed designs that have become famous worldwide. In 1912 he purchased land at Cobridge where he opened his own factory. The company remained under his control until his death in 1945. The firm still operates from the original Sandbach Road site.

THE GROWTH OF POTWORKS

These, of course, are just the most well-known names. Over the years many hundreds of ceramics-based businesses came and went, some becoming established names, others leaving little impression or legacy. One study identified 391 pottery manufacturers in Stoke-on-Trent in 1907, working across a variety of sectors (see Table 2.1 below). Altogether, over 1,500 manufactories have been identified as being active within the North Staffordshire potteries at one time or another. Potteries.org lists all known potters in the Stoke-on-Trent area indexed by name, date of first operation and location of factory. Many entries also have details of the pottery marks, the factories they worked and examples of the ware produced.

Table 2.1: Potworks in Stoke-on-Trent in 1907

	Stoke	Hanley	Longton	Fenton	Burslem	Tunstall
Earthenware	16	47	31	18	46	11
China	11	11	50	12	11	3
Jet and Rockingham	1	4	2	3	12	3
Sanitary Ware	2	8	1	–	8	–
Tiles	14	14	–	1	13	10
Other	2	15	1	3	6	1
Total	**46**	**99**	**85**	**37**	**96**	**28**

Source: R.Whipp, *Patterns of Labour: Work and Social Change in the Pottery Industry* (Routledge, 1990), p. 25.

Pottery factories (often referred to as 'potworks', 'potbanks' or 'manufactories') ranged from vast and purpose-built facilities with thousands of workers, such as those of Enoch Wood in Burslem and Josiah Wedgwood in Etruria, to back-street hovels with one or two workers. Some potters built and owned their own works. Many were tenants in factories built by others and a succession of potters occupied

Bottle oven, Gladstone Pottery Museum. (Wikimedia, Creative Commons)

the same premises. It was also common practice for a works to be split between two different pottery companies or for a larger manufacturer to let out part of its works to a potter making a different type of product.

The core facility of the pottery industry, and one that came to define the landscape, was the bottle oven or kiln. From the eighteenth century until the 1960s bottle ovens were the dominating feature of the area. Nothing set the Potteries skyline apart more than these weird bottle-shaped brick buildings. At the peak of the industry in around 1913, there are estimated to have been up to 4,000 bottle kilns with as many as 2,000 still standing in the 1950s.

Some small factories had only one bottle oven, other large potbanks had as many as twenty-five. Ovens were not situated within a factory according to any set plan. They might be grouped around a cobbled yard or placed in a row. Sometimes they were built into the workshops with the upper part of the chimney protruding through the roof. No two bottle ovens were exactly alike. They were all built according to the whim of the builder or of the potbank owner. According to one recent study, only twenty-seven sites in Stoke-on-Trent still have bottle ovens or calcinating kilns (**https://staffordshirepotteries.wordpress.com/ bottle-ovens/**).

CERAMIC MATERIALS

The industry encompasses a bewildering array of products, processes and materials.

Firstly, there are various types of base materials, known as the ceramic body. Earthenware was the fabric first produced by the North Staffordshire potters. The local red clay was sorted and purified, and then fired at a fairly low temperature (950–1,050 °C) so that it remained porous. To make it waterproof, the fired object is covered with a glaze, a mixture of glass-forming minerals and melting agents, and then fired a second time. During the firing, the fine particles covering the surface fuse into an amorphous, glass-like layer, sealing the pores of the clay body. The main glazes used were lead, tin and salt.

By the 1720s ball clay from Devon and flint from the east coast were being imported into the Potteries to provide a better base for earthenware. Ball clays are plastic and so suitable for throwing and

The Glory of the Staffordshire Potteries

Clarice Cliff tableware in the 'Original Bizarre' pattern.

Minton floor tiles, c. 1845.

The Wedgwood Portland Vase, c. 1790.

Minton Willow pattern miniature dinner service.

Ironstone rectangular dish, c. 1820 by G.M. and C.J. Mason of Lane Delph.

Fine porcelain pieces by Spode.

machine use. The fine white earthenware evolved by Thomas Whieldon and then by Josiah Wedgwood (known as creamware) were based on these ingredients. From 1747 manufacturers turned instead to china clay from Cornwall in an effort to emulate the truly fine white body of imported china wares.

Stoneware is fired at a higher temperature than earthenware, so that the material partially vitrifies and the ware becomes impervious to liquids even when unglazed. Where a glaze is used, it serves a purely decorative function. Traditional stonewares, common in the Midlands and Continental Europe, were grey or buff coloured. A bright white stoneware body, suitable for salt glazing, had been perfected in North Staffordshire by 1730.

Porcelain is a vitrified pottery with a white, fine-grained body that is usually translucent, as distinguished from earthenware, which is porous, opaque, and coarser. There are three main types: soft-paste porcelain, hard-paste porcelain and bone china. Soft-paste porcelain is produced by mixing white clay with 'frit', a glassy substance. It was technically difficult to work with and significant losses in firing were common. In Europe, notable manufacturers such as Sèvres and Meissen were supported by royal patrons, an option not open to English competitors such as Worcester and Derby. In Staffordshire, the Longton Hall Company was one of the few firms to experiment with it. Hard-paste porcelain is made from a mixture of china clay (kaolin) and china stone (petuntse). Again, few British firms produced it successfully.

It was in bone china that the Staffordshire potters made their mark. Stronger than other types and easier to manufacture, bone china is created by adding bone ash to the ingredients for hard-paste porcelain. The resulting wares had an ivory white appearance that resembled fine translucent oriental wares. Bone china was easily modelled, withstood thermal shock and was equally well suited for practical as well as decorative wares. Importantly for the manufacturers, it was also not too costly or difficult to fire.

Starting with Josiah Spode II in around 1800, other manufacturers began to adopt the process including Minton, Davenport and, to a much more limited extent, Wedgwood. The quality, as much as form and decoration, varied from factory to factory. Some tended, after about

1820, towards brilliant colour, lavish gilding and overcrowded design; others produced tasteful, simply ornamented tableware. Since much early bone china was issued unmarked, it is often difficult to attribute the pieces.

MANUFACTURING PROCESSES AND INNOVATIONS

Traditionally raw clay was mixed with water in an open-air tank using a paddle and left to dry out through natural evaporation. As industrialization took hold during the eighteenth century, clay preparation moved indoors. The drying process was accelerated by placing hot flues under the slip tank. From the last third of the nineteenth century the job of stirring the clay manually was replaced by mechanically powered blungers. The slip was then strained through sieves to remove grit and other impurities. Later, this dewatering process was transformed by the use of the filter press. One design of press, by Needham and Kite, was originally used to separate yeast from beer but was readily adapted for use in pottery manufacture.

The clay is next prepared for shaping. It must be kneaded to remove air bubbles and ensure uniform plasticity, a laborious and even harmful process that was often carried out by women and children. From the early 1800s pug mills, a form of mechanical kneading, began to be used in brickworks but was only slowly and intermittently applied in potbanks. It is not thought to have been widespread before 1900.

When it comes to shaping, potters have used kick wheels for throwing pots since time immemorial. As matters were systematized during the eighteenth century, it was recognized that productivity could be improved by having the wheel turned by an assistant (generally a child) by means of a rope-driven flywheel, and by a 'baller up' to weigh and prepare the balls of clay.

Mechanical shaping techniques were slow to be introduced in the Potteries, partly because the potters opposed them and partly because of the imperfections left in plastic clay products. From the 1830s machines for making hollowware and flatware, known as jollies and jiggers respectively, were introduced. Both worked on the principle of shaping the plastic clay with a profile tool pivoted on the arm, simulating the hand of the thrower as the clay revolves.

Placing saggars in the oven at Parrott & Company, Albert Street, Burslem, c. 1936. (Courtesy of thepotteries.org)

From the mid-eighteenth century moulds made of plaster of Paris were also used in some cases. Sheets of plastic clay were flattened into a bat which was then draped and pressed on to the absorbent moulds for flatware. Holloware, such as figures, teapots, spouts and cup handles, was also made by this method. The seams and joints were tidied up by teams of fettlers while the ware was still in the fragile, unfired or 'green' state.

Some hollowares were made by slip casting which involved pouring slip, the liquid form of clay in suspension, into plaster of Paris moulds. From the early twentieth century this became the main means of producing holloware as a result of innovations in the preparation of slip. It was discovered that adding deflocculants to slip significantly increased the proportion of clay it could hold, thus reducing the amount of water needing to be absorbed by the moulds and speeding up drying times. Potbanks maintained mould shops and mould stores to prepare, produce and store the patterns for pressed wares. The more innovative also employed their own designers.

For certain applications, such as tile making, the use of clay in powder form was found to be advantageous. Fly-presses were used to make decorative tiles from powdered clay, resulting in fewer problems of uneven drying and warping than by using plastic clay.

Wares were then subjected to successive firings. The first, known as biscuit firing, set the ware, making it brittle. After any underglaze decoration and glazing were applied, a glost firing was then made to fix the glaze, enhancing both the ware's appearance and technical performance. Additional firings were made as necessary, especially where enamel decoration or gilding was added.

Although they grew in size and sophistication, the kilns used in the Potteries followed the same basic construction as those in the late medieval period: essentially an inner brick hovel surrounded by a bottle-shaped brick chimney. Wares ready for firing were placed in refractory containers called saggars, capable of withstanding high temperatures. Flatware was carefully bedded in flint to prevent warping and china figures were propped up with stilts to prevent sagging. Placing wares within the saggars and the saggars within the kiln both had to be done with great care and precision. The correct distribution of draught and heat within the kiln was essential. The sides and bottom of the oven would contain more densely packed saggars to absorb the most intense heat. The tops of the stacks, or bungs, were usually filled with empty ('green') saggars. During firing the fireman controlled the oven by regulating the dampers built into its crown and by adjusting the regulating holes set in the sides of the oven above the firemouths. Although measurement devices were used, an experienced fireman would be able to bring an oven up to temperature by eye alone, using the colour of the flames as a guide.

From the mid-twentieth century tunnel kilns gradually replaced bottle kilns. Wares were placed on trucks that were pulled through a long tunnel lined with refractory bricks until they emerged, fired, at the far end. This continuous process dispensed with saggars and allowed wares to be placed much more quickly. However, the new technology required a larger ground area that few traditional sites could accommodate. Wedgwood & Sons' move to a new purpose-built factory on a green-field site at Barlaston was motivated by the need for tunnel kilns. But other firms were slow to follow this lead and invest on the necessary scale.

After firing, biscuit ware was decorated and glazed. In the Potteries, as elsewhere, much use was made of cobalt for underglaze decoration from the mid-eighteenth century. It had to be fired on at a high temperature in order for the colour to develop and so was applied before the glost firing, often in the form of a transfer print. Biscuit wares were traditionally dipped by hand to coat them in the liquid glaze solution, which was then fired in the glost firing.

A distinguishing feature of the Staffordshire Potteries was the extent to which the final wares were decorated by hand. From chimney ornaments to the finest tableware, pieces were often finished by hand gilding and hand painting. Other techniques were bat printing, a method of applying a very delicate on-glaze stipple engraving effect, and ground-laying, a method of colour dusting to apply a richly coloured ground to glost tableware. On-glaze decoration required at least one further firing, which was traditionally carried out in a small enamel or muffle kiln.

The checking, sorting, wrapping and packing of finished wares was women's work and was done in the potbank's warehouse.

POTTERY INDUSTRY OCCUPATIONS

While we may think of the potter sitting at his wheel, the reality in the industrialized pottery factory was very different. There was no such job as an actual 'potter'. Rather the industry comprised a bewildering array of jobs, some skilled, many unskilled, often expressed in obscure terms.

The index at the Potteries.org website identifies over 150 job titles. Much of this rich occupational lexicon is now lost to us. Family historians are likely to encounter these terms in certificates, censuses and other documents.

One of the most skilled jobs related to the saggar, a fireclay box for holding ware during firing. As noted above, the saggar was used to protect pottery from marking by flames and smoke while in a bottle oven and was usually oval or round. Producing saggars to the correct specifications was a skilled job carried out by a craftsman, known as the saggar maker. He had several assistants. The bottom knocker (usually a young boy) made the base of the saggar from a lump of fireclay which he knocked into a metal ring using a wooden mallet or mawl (pronounced 'mow'). The frame filler (a male apprentice) flattened a mass of clay and produced a rectangle which was wrapped round a drum to make the side of the saggar. Placing wares in saggars required special knowledge and was the job of a dottler. Plates were carefully separated from each other by thimbles (known as 'rearing' or 'dottling') to prevent the glaze from making them fuse together in the glost firing. Ovenmen, or placers, placed the saggars in the ovens for firing and also emptied the ovens after firing. If not broken, a saggar could last for thirty to forty firings.

Other curiously entitled occupations within the industry included:

- A biscuit rubber brushed (scoured) pottery after the biscuit firing to remove loose particles. A similar role related to the second firing was known as a glost rubber or glost cleaner.
- A clay blunger operated a slip stirring machine, which slowly mixed clay with water in a huge tub or vat to produce a slip.
- A dipper dipped biscuit ware in glaze before the glost firing.
- A fritter poured mixed ingredients for glaze into a frit mill for mixing.
- A jigger used a profile tool to shape the outside of flatware, such as plates and saucers, on a revolving mould. The tool, also known as a jigger, was turned by hand and was often a young person's first job in a pottery factory. A good plate maker could produce around 400 to 500 plates a day.

- A pugger (also known as a pug miller or pugman) operated a pug mill, a machine that mixed and kneaded the clay to improve its texture and consistency.

WORKING CONDITIONS IN THE POTBANKS

Conditions for our ancestors in the potbanks were harsh. Workers toiled long hours for low wages in environments that were often extremely hazardous and sometimes downright deadly.

One of the dangers was heat. Obviously the fireman and his assistants in charge of a kiln worked in very hot conditions. But the need for repeated firings, including in smaller kilns and stoves, and the cramped layout of factories meant that other workers too were exposed to heat. The impact of so many coal-fired ovens and kilns was felt across the wider area in the form of air pollution that choked the population and besmudged the environment.

At least heat exhaustion had an easy remedy. This was not the case for those working with lead glazes which were ubiquitous throughout the industry. Lead poisoning was long known to be a problem and dippers were particularly prone. Although experiments with leadless glazes were conducted throughout the nineteenth century, lead was then essential. Only in the early twentieth century was a safe solution found: a glaze of low solubility produced by making the glaze suspension out of fritted lead. Other poisonous metals, such as cobalt, used in glazes and enamels also had to be controlled.

Another health risk endured by potters was silicosis. It was caused by the inhalation of flint-dust particles and resulted in gradual and often fatal damage to the lungs. Known locally as 'potters rot', it was a lingering disease which took many decades to diagnose and control. Those most at risk were flint millers, dottlers who had to pack biscuit ware in flint inside the saggars, sliphouse workers and fettlers of biscuit earthenware.

While we may think of working life for our Potteries ancestors as unhealthy and unsafe, this was not always the case. The partly seasonal, rural craft-based production that existed in the early stages of the Industrial Revolution created relatively benign working conditions. Only as industrialization progressed, bringing poor workers from the

Workers at the Middleport Pottery, c. 1930. (Public domain)

countryside into the overcrowded town centres, did the industry take on its unsavoury connotations.

One of the first to address this was Josiah Wedgwood, who built a separate village for his workers alongside his new factory at Etruria. The idea was prompted at least in part by necessity: the factory was some distance from the existing settled area and needed a large number of workers. But it was also motivated by Wedgwood's Nonconformism and concern for the common good. He provided his workers with simple dwellings lining both sides of the newly turnpiked road between Leek and Newcastle. Pre-dating other better known examples by many years, Etruria was the first industrial village of its kind anywhere in the world. A school and chapel were added later. Larger firms, such as Minton's, followed Wedgwood's example in building housing for their workers, but this remained the exception rather than the norm.

The pottery industry was unusual for the period in that men and women worked alongside each other. Women generally had the lighter but less agreeable work, such as dipping and scouring the wares. They were also involved in painting, decorating and other finishing processes, and could be highly skilled. At Ridgway, Morley, Wear & Co., an iron-stone china and earthenware factory in the early 1840s, government inspector Samuel Scriven found women and girls accounted for around 45 per cent of the workforce. Of 348 employees, 69 were women, 71 were females under 21 and 18 were girls under 13. Ann Baker, aged 19, told the inspector that she had worked at the Ridgway's factory for three years: 'first in the biscuit warehouse, then in the dipping house; my duty is to scrape the uneven dipping off the ware when dry. The occupation is a very unhealthy one. I cannot eat my food as I used to do; it affects my chest very much, makes me cough.'

CLARICE CLIFF: WOMEN'S PIONEER

By the early twentieth century women's roles in the pottery industry were not limited to the shopfloor: those with the talent and drive were beginning to make their way into the boardroom as well. Blazing the trail was Clarice Cliff, who established herself as one of the Potteries' most iconic designers.

Cliff was born into a working class family in Tunstall in 1899. Having shown artistic promise at school, she started work as an apprentice enameller at a local factory at the age of 13. Three years later she moved to another firm as an apprentice lithographer, at the same time attending evening classes at Tunstall School of Art.

In 1916, aged 17, she joined A.J. Wilkinson's pottery where her drawing brought her to the attention of the owner, Colley Shorter, and he allowed her to experiment on some old stock. In 1927 he arranged for her to study sculpture at the Royal College of Art in London, and later in Paris. After a few months she returned to Stoke-on-Trent where Shorter set her up in a decorating studio. By 1929 her designs went into full production as 'Hand Painted Bizarre by Clarice Cliff'.

By 1931 she was an Art Director of the factory with a decorating team of around 150. Clarice Cliff and Shorter eventually married. She died in 1972.

Sarah Bowers, aged 13, was a paper-cutter in the printing-room and had already been employed four years; her working day started at 7.00 a.m. and could go on until 9.00 p.m. Hannah Jay was even younger, just 11, and was two years into a seven-year apprenticeship as a painter.

As these reports show, the industry employed not only women but also children on a large scale. In 1861 there were 4,500 children under 13 at work. They were often expected to work long hours as mould runners or as assistants to dippers. Scriven observed how boys worked on flatware in conditions approaching 40 °C:

A little boy, without shoes or stockings, is kept constantly running between the plate-maker, from whom he receives the plate or dish newly formed on a mould, and the stove, into which he carries this mould with the moist plate upon it. These moulds, thus charged, are ranged upon shelves to dry, and as soon as they are sufficiently dried the boy liberates the mould and carries it back to receive a new layer of clay.

A fascinating insight into life in the Potteries in the mid-nineteenth century was provided by Charles Shaw in his autobiography, *When I Was a Child* (Shaw, 1903). Born in Tunstall in 1832, Shaw started work at the age of 7 as a mould-runner in Enoch Wood & Sons' factory in Burslem. In 1842, as a result of unemployment his family was forced into the workhouse at Chell for a period until his father found another job. This and other episodes recorded by Shaw helped inspire parts of Arnold Bennett's *Clayhanger* trilogy.

By the early nineteenth century workers were beginning to campaign for better conditions. The first proper trades union to emerge in the Six Towns was the Journeyman Potter's Union in 1824. By the following year it had embarked upon a series of confrontations with employers relating to the truck system and piece rates. These issues would dominate union affairs for years to come. In August 1825 a strike began. The manufacturers, who had closed ranks and promised to subsidize each other until the union's defeat, retaliated with a lockout. The strike failed, the union disintegrated and selected leaders were victimized. The main problem with this first union had been its lack of unity. Ovenmen, potters, cratemakers, printers and others all argued against each other and worked for the advantage of their own group. This tendency was repeated many times over the years.

Dr Samuel Scriven's factory visits, described above, were part of an investigation into the employment of children and young persons in the North Staffordshire Potteries. Through site visits, interviews and correspondence, Scriven and his team probed into working conditions including those in coal mines, cotton and woollen mills, as well as pottery factories. He visited 173 potteries and his report, published in 1842, paints a rich picture of life in the potbanks during that time, much of it told through workers' own testimony.

A second report published in 1862 found the situation little changed. Although the 1833 and 1844 Factory Acts started to improve conditions for women and children, they focused on coal mines and textile mills. The Staffordshire potteries were not mentioned because by the standards of the time working conditions in the average pottery factory were considered better than the minimum required by the new law. An Act of 1853 restricted children's hours of employment to between 6.00 a.m. and 6.00 p.m. on weekdays and no later than 2.00 p.m. on Saturdays. Not until the Factory & Workshop Act of 1878, which consolidated all previous Acts across all trades, was the employment of children in the pottery industry fully regulated. From 1 August 1898 pottery manufacturers could no longer employ anyone under the age of 14, and a year later they were prohibited from hiring anyone less than 15 years of age to work in the most hazardous occupations.

By this time a wider movement to improve working conditions for all pottery employees was afoot. In the 1860s Dr Robert Baker, the first Factory Inspector for the Potteries, attempted to introduce precautions against silicosis, such as proper ventilation, improved cleanliness in workshops and protective clothing. The proposals were met with considerable opposition from the potbanks' owners and managers. Small manufactories, especially, saw improved buildings, sanitary arrangements, welfare, ventilation and supervision of their workers as unnecessary and unaffordable. It was believed at the time that frequent oscillations between excessive heat and cold represented the greatest risk to health. Baker, with his colleague Dr John Thomas Arlidge, campaigned vociferously against industrial disease in the pottery industry and they are now seen as among the founders of occupational medicine.

ANCILLARY INDUSTRIES

The scale and diversity of the pottery industry in North Staffordshire supported an equally diverse network of suppliers. A range of ancillary industries grew up to service the specialist materials and equipment required by pottery manufacturers.

A trade directory of 1963 provides an indication of the importance of these ancillary industries. *Barretts City of Stoke-on-Trent Directory* lists more than thirty categories of supplier allied to ceramics in some way. There were suppliers of ceramic colours, ceramic materials, ceramic transfers, china-clay merchants, china decorators, china factors, kiln builders, kiln furniture manufacturers, potters' colours and glazes, potters' grinders, potters' millers and potters' workboards. The list indicates how, in the twentieth century, many functions had been outsourced by the pottery manufacturers. Colour-making, the mixing of colours and glazes for example, would previously have been done within the potbank.

POTTERY INDUSTRY RECORDS AND ARCHIVES

Staffordshire and Stoke-on-Trent Archives Service holds the business records of many pottery manufacturers as well as those working in processes allied to the pottery industry. Search in the catalogue for the company concerned or see under 'ceramics' in the *SSA Guide to Sources No. 4: Business Records*. Many of these are held within the Potteries Museum & Art Galleries collections [SD 4842]. As well as corporate and financial records, series may include pattern books, trade catalogues and general business correspondence. Wage and salary books are likely to be the best source for individual workers. These holdings are limited, however, considering the huge number of pottery businesses that are known to have existed, and most go back no further than the mid-twentieth century.

Stoke-on-Trent City Archives holds important collections relating to the industry. The Adams Collection is believed to have been assembled by P.W.L. Adams in around 1914 when writing his *History of the Adams Family of North Staffordshire*. Many of the items relate to the Adams family of potters during the eighteenth and nineteenth centuries [SD 1256]. A further series, known as the Hand Collection, comprises the papers of Frederick H. Hand who was secretary of the National Council of the Pottery Industry from 1919 to 1945. He was also a founder and secretary of the Association of Joint Industrial Councils. Again, the STCA has a handlist [PA/HAND].

The Spode Papers at Keele University comprise more than 1,000 documents relating to the company, mostly dating from the nineteenth century. They include the original articles of partnership signed by Josiah Spode and William Copeland in 1813, as well as important series of account books, price lists, volumes of technical data and pictorial material. Following its closure in 2008, material formerly held by the Spode Museum was deposited with the STCA .

The STCA is now home to the Minton Archive, which was gifted to the city in March 2015. It comprises the Minton company records as well as those of more than twenty companies that had been acquired by Royal Doulton plc, including such famous names as Adderley, Booth, Davenport, Paragon, Ridgway, Royal Albert and Shelley [SD 1705]. The Minton section alone contains more than 5,000 entries. Importantly for family historians, these include many employee records, from apprenticeships and wage books to artists' contracts and Minton Social Club records. The archive is gradually being catalogued and digitized and made available via a dedicated website, **www.themintonarchive. org.uk**.

Two notable ancillary companies among the records held at the STCA are Blythe Colour Ltd, a well-known colour-maker (1910–90) [SD 1682/2], and Allied Insulators Ltd, which pioneered the use of ceramics in the electricity industry (*c.* 1860–1989) [SD 1237].

Many of the surviving pottery manufacturers maintain their own archives, sometimes incorporating also the archives of businesses they have acquired.

Various business associations have represented the industry over the years. The STCA has records relating to: British Pottery Manufacturers Association, *c.* 1906–2006 [SD 1712]; British Stoneware Potters

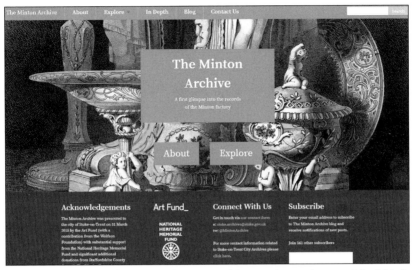

The Minton Archive website, www.themintonarchive.org.uk, contains a wealth of detail on the company and its employees.

Association, 1917–88 [SD 1316]; British Ceramics Confederation [SD 1558 & 1671]; and National Council of the Pottery Industry [PA/HAND, as above]. The records of the North Staffordshire Chamber of Commerce from 1874–1978 may also be relevant [SA/CC]. Although relatively sparse in relation to individuals, items such as newsletters, photographs and minutes can be useful in building up a picture of the industry from contemporary sources.

The Staffordshire Apprentice Index contains nearly 12,500 entries relating mainly to apprenticeship indentures and entries in apprenticeship registers held by the SSA (**www.staffsnameindexes. org.uk**). Most are derived from parish Poor Law records in the period prior to 1838 but some privately arranged apprenticeships are also referenced. Articles of apprenticeship are held by the Potteries Museum & Art Gallery and the Wedgwood Museum, in particular three series supported by the Leveson Charity between 1738 and 1799 [SD 4842/28/1-3]. Newcastle-under-Lyme Guild apprentice records, held at Newcastle Museum, are indexed 1767–1910 and on microfilm at Staffordshire Record Office (MF134/11-14).

Potters used a variety of marks to identify their wares. These ranged from letters and initials to more elaborate crests or symbols used as a trademark, all of which were embossed, printed or painted on the bottom of the ware. From 1842 there was also an official system of Diamond Marks to signify when a design was registered to prevent copying. Potteries.org has an extensive list of known marks associated with Staffordshire pottery, as well as a useful guide to understanding what they all mean. There are many published works, two of the most authoritative being Godden (1999) and Henrywood (2002).

Old habits die hard and despite the industry's decline it is not unusual to see locals turning pottery upside down to inspect the black mark. Familiarity with such marks is essential for the pottery collector. All of the main houses and brands have collectors clubs which provide insights into the company's work and there are many specialized books. Again, the Potteries.org site has introductions and links, and also lists of trade names.

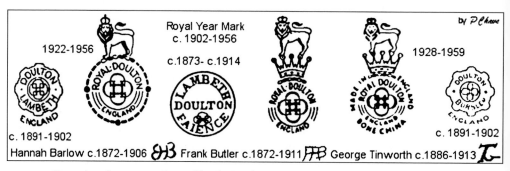

Examples of pottery marks used by the Doulton company. (Public domain)

POTTERIES HERITAGE

The Potteries has one of the highest concentrations of museums in the country, many dedicated to the area's predominance in ceramics. The PMAG provides an overview of the area's industrial heritage, including what is undoubtedly the world's best collection of Staffordshire ceramics (**www.stokemuseums.org.uk**). Over 5,000 pieces are on display and many more are held in storage, including items from the Minton Museum sale. Also operated by Stoke-on-Trent Museums are its sister institutions: the Gladstone Pottery Museum at Longton; and the Etruria Industrial Museum in Stoke-on-Trent, which has the last steam-powered potters' mill in Britain (**www.etruriamuseum.org.uk**).

The Wedgwood Museum at Barlaston houses a world-class collection of Wedgwood ceramics, alongside an archive of international acclaim. The UN cultural body UNESCO has described the Wedgwood Archive as 'one of the most complete ceramic manufacturing archives in existence' (**www.wedgwoodmuseum. org.uk/archives**). The lives of the Wedgwood family, the company's workers and the classical inspiration that drove Wedgwood design are just a few of the stories told through the archive material, some of which is accessible online.

The refurbished Middleport Pottery in Burslem offers tours of the working Burleigh factory as well as a visitor centre (**www.middleport pottery.co.uk**). Saved from closure by The Prince's Regeneration Trust, the building reopened in 2014. Visitors have the opportunity to see pottery being made using the same handcraft methods as in the 1880s and to see the mould store housing Europe's largest collection of ceramic moulds.

Other venues offering insights into pottery heritage are the Dudson Museum, Emma Bridgewater Factory, Moorcroft Heritage Visitor Centre and Spode Works Visitor Centre. Many of the potters who made Stoke-on-Trent world famous are buried at Stoke Minster (the Church of St Peter ad Vincula, **http://stokeminster.org**). These and other sites are part of The Ceramics Trail which covers museums, galleries, visitor attractions and shopping outlets across the Potteries (**www.visitstoke. co.uk/ceramics-trail**).

FURTHER INFORMATION

Burchill, Frank and Richard Ross, *A History of the Potters' Union* (Ceramic and Allied Trades Union, 1977)

Godden, Geoffrey A., *New Handbook of British Pottery & Porcelain Marks* (Barrie & Jenkins, 1999)

Henrywood, R.K., *Staffordshire Potters, 1781–1900: A Comprehensive List Assembled From Contemporary Directories With Selected Marks* (Antique Collectors Club, 2002)

Scriven, Samuel, *Employment of Children and Young Persons in the District of the North Staffordshire Potteries* (HM Government, 1840), transcribed at www.thepotteries.org/history/scriven_index.htm

Sekers, David, *The Potteries* (Shire Publications, 2013)

Shaw, Charles, *When I Was a Child* (Methuen, 1903), transcribed at www.thepotteries.org/focus/011.htm

Taylor, Alan, *Stoke-on-Trent: A History* (Phillimore, 2003)

Chapter 3

INDUSTRIAL DIVERSITY

COAL AND IRON MINING

Excavations indicate that coal and ironstone have been mined in North Staffordshire since Roman times. Medieval documents point to mining at Tunstall in 1282, Shelton in 1297 and Keele in 1333, and by 1467 surface coal was being mined and used for firing pottery. Visiting the area in 1686, Robert Plot wrote of coal being gained by 'footrails', meaning a sloping tunnel driven into the hillside to follow the coal seam. Some coal was mined in 'bell pits', a series of adjacent pits which in section looked like a bell. These early mines supplied diverse industries such as small metal-based trades, breweries, the Cheshire salt industry, glass making and tile making.

Large-scale mining began to take off from about 1750, driven primarily by the growth in the pottery industry, the switch from charcoal to coal in the iron industry and the improved road and canal systems. Innovations such as the steam engine allowed mines to be pumped clear of flood water and coal to be extracted from deeper underground. Previously drainage had depended on gutters being cut and this technique was still being relied upon as late as the 1820s. By 1830 mechanization allowed a depth of 2,000ft to be reached at Apedale Colliery, accessed by an inclined plan and a shaft of some 720ft. The North Staffordshire coal industry began to flourish, with areas such as Silverdale and Tunstall becoming hotbeds of mining activity. At the peak of the industry around 1900 there were about ninety collieries within the North Staffordshire coalfield.

In the late eighteenth century pottery manufacturers had begun to join together to form companies to mine coal for their mutual benefit. One at Fenton Park Colliery was typical, in which the principal partners

The Chatterley Whitfield Colliery, c. 1930. (Public domain)

included Josiah Spode II, Thomas Wolfe and Thomas Minton. The local aristocracy and gentry also played a crucial role. Earl Gower risked his fortune by investing in the canal networks and in mineral extraction. He was one of the main investors in the Trent & Mersey Canal and brother-in-law to the Duke of Bridgewater (who most likely introduced him to James Brindley). In 1833 his son, then 2nd Marquis of Stafford, became the 1st Duke of Sutherland, a family name that would be synonymous with the success of Stoke-on-Trent during the nineteenth century.

Ironstone was being mined at Meir Heath by 1679 and later a furnace was established there. Longton, too, had several ironworks during this period. William Sparrow mined ironstone at Lane End having acquired mineral rights from the Duke of Sutherland. By 1829 his forge was producing more than 1,300 tons of iron a year, mainly for the South Staffordshire nail-making industry. Many such forges were located beside canals since this was the only convenient way of transporting such a heavy product.

The long recession that ensued in the iron industry following the end of the Napoleonic Wars was eventually reversed in the 1830s with the introduction of the blast furnace. In 1850 Lord Granville (the 5th Earl) established a new works alongside the canal at Etruria, the Shelton Bar Iron Company. Its voracious furnaces were served by a large ring of local pits which included Slippery Lane, Racecourse and Hanley Deep. The Shelton Bar Company went from strength to strength, winning awards at several international exhibitions. By 1888 over 3,000 people were employed at the site and the company continued to expand into the early twentieth century. Apedale and Silverdale also saw the development of large-scale iron and steel works.

This prosperity came at a price, however. Apart from the squalid working conditions (a characteristic of many industries at the time) there was the environmental cost. Mining created huge spoil heaps, known as rucks, which only added to those produced by the pottery industry ('shard rucks'). In some collieries the waste slack accounted for as much as 75 per cent of the extracted material. Despite the risks, the heaps became favourite playgrounds for generations of Potteries children.

With few controls and constant pressures to maintain productivity, mines offered an extremely dangerous working environment. Flooding, roof collapses and explosions were all commonplace and those working in the mines were constantly aware of the dangers. In July 1860 an accident with a cage led to the deaths of five men at Adderley Green Colliery near Longton, and at Mossfield Colliery in 1889 a massive gas explosion claimed the lives of sixty-four miners. Even worse was to follow at Diglake Colliery, Audley, in January 1895 when a vast underground reservoir of water broke into the workings and threatened the lives of 240 men and boys. In the ensuing horror there were some miraculous escapes, but 77 lives were lost.

The situation improved only gradually. Despite early efforts, including the appointment of inspectors in coal mines, in 1870 over 1,000 lives were still being lost across the country each year in mining accidents. In 1872 the Coal Mines Regulation Act introduced the requirement for pit managers to have state certification of their training. Miners were also given the right to appoint inspectors from among themselves. The Mines Regulation Act, passed in 1881, empowered the Home Secretary to hold inquiries into the causes of mine accidents. It remained clear, however, that there were many aspects of mining that required further intervention and regulation. Casewell (2015) is an index of mining deaths in North Staffordshire 1756–1995: it lists around 4,450 deaths based on newspapers, official reports and burial records. Leigh (1993) describes the history of the North Staffordshire Mines Rescue Service and operations with which it was involved.

Matters were not much safer for those above ground either. With miles of underground workings criss-crossing the Six Towns subsidence was widespread. For example, by comparing historic maps and later photographs it has been shown that Wedgwood's Etruria factory sunk by about 2.5m. As early as 1844 a Mr Hilton of Union Street, Shelton brought an action for compensation against Lord Granville. By then more than 60 houses in Hanley and Shelton had been damaged by subsidence and over 160 rendered uninhabitable. Hilton's was a test case brought to scrutinize the accountability of Granville and his agents and the right of local copyholders to be compensated. While admitting that his works had caused the damage, Granville claimed that custom gave him a right to work the mines, without control, as near to the surface as he needed and without giving compensation. The case went on for several years and no compensation was paid.

The pivotal point for coal and steel in the Potteries came in the post-war period. In the steel industry, constant swapping between private and public ownership, combined with chronic under-investment, led to prolonged decline. In the 1960s competition from abroad forced the then British Steel Company to focus on sites with deep-water wharves able to handle huge quantities of imported raw materials. Land-locked Shelton was retained as an experimental facility for a while but finally closed in 1978. The rolling mill was kept on, producing 400,000 tonnes per year, until it too ceased production in 2000.

With many small collieries, deep mining too began to feel the pressure of international competition. Mine closures began in the 1960s with the closure of collieries such as Hanley Deep and Apedale. In the following decades there were many more, although the most productive, including Silverdale, continued to receive new investment. Despite producing over 1 million tonnes annually at its peak, eventually Silverdale too was considered uncompetitive: it closed in 1998, the last deep mine in North Staffordshire. Edwards (1998) and Stone (2007) present historical accounts of Staffordshire's collieries and coalminers, while Deakin (2004) provides a photographic record of most of the pits that were operating at the time of nationalization in 1947.

The area's coal mining heritage can be seen at Chatterley Whitfield Colliery, which is acknowledged to be the most comprehensive surviving deep mine site in Britain. Once operated as a commercial museum, it is now run as a charity and accessible on selected open days only (**http://chatterleywhitfieldfriends.org.uk**). The Northern Mine Research Society is dedicated to the preservation and recording of the mining history of the north of England and has various publications and resources (**www.nmrs.org.uk**). A useful resource for mines research, the Coal Mining History Resource Centre is no longer maintained but is still available via online archives (**https://archive.is/www.cmhrc. co.uk**).

Advertisement for the Shelton Iron & Steel Company, 1889. 'Granville' was one of its brands. (Public domain)

Mining Records

SSA Guide No. 6 Colliery Records summarizes holdings on collieries within the county. The records of the industry include the pre-1947 colliery company records, sporadic records of individual collieries and the divisional and area records of the nationalized industry after 1947. All of the series may need to be searched for material on individual pits. More general sources such as Ordnance Survey maps, local newspapers, tithe and estate maps, and trade directories may also be useful. Family members may be mentioned in materials relating to mining accidents, such as the Audley (Diglake) Colliery Disaster Fund [STCA: D021 and SD 1023].

The Peak District Mines Historical Society has reproduced lists of mines in Staffordshire from a 1896 publication; it lists both coal (**http://projects.exeter.ac.uk/mhn/1896-C1.htm**) and metalliferous mines (**http://projects.exeter.ac.uk/mhn/1896-C4.htm**). The records of the MacGowan Company contain many photographs, maps, plans and manuscripts relating to mining in the area, including the *Transactions of the North Staffordshire Institute of Mining & Mechanical Engineers, 1875–1891*: see the handlist in the STCA Search Room [SD 1090].

Staffordshire and Stoke-on-Trent Archives has a limited collection of trades-union records from the Midland Miners Federation [SRO: D4554] and the National Union of Mineworkers (NUM) [SRO: D4701], including photograph albums of NUM Area Galas from the 1950s [D4554/A/4]. Further records from the NUM Midlands Area: Staffordshire District, 1891–1971 are held at the Modern Records Centre, University of Warwick. Staffordshire University Special Collections has original records from Hem Heath and Silverdale collieries and some National Coal Board records.

A one-time employee of the Chatterley Whitfield Collieries Ltd, William Jack photographed and also collected photographs of North Staffordshire collieries, railways and mineral workings. This collection, now housed at Keele University, comprises typescripts of Jack's own contributions to North Staffordshire railway and mining history, as well as scrapbooks and minute books of the Chatterley Whitfield Colliery dating from the 1870s to 1926.

If your ancestor was a mine owner or manager, they may turn up in the records of the North Staffordshire Coal Owners Defence Association, North Staffordshire Colliery Owners Association or the North Staffordshire Iron Masters Association, all of which are held at Staffordshire Record Office.

CANALS
The Fluid Highway

The blossoming of the pottery industry in North Staffordshire is intimately bound up with the growth of canals. Pottery manufacture is a resource-intensive process requiring huge quantities of bulky raw materials, principally clay and coal. The finished products are extremely fragile and so not amenable to long distance transport by horse and cart on unpaved roads. As they expanded their operations, early manufacturers such as Josiah Wedgwood complained that even the short packhorse journey between the potbanks and the nearest navigable rivers resulted in too many breakages, was too costly and took too long.

Although sitting on the Trent, at Stoke the river was too shallow to navigate. The nearest points of access to natural waterways were Winsford in Cheshire, on the River Mersey (leading to Liverpool), and Willington in Derbyshire, on the River Trent (leading to the North Sea). In fact, the Potteries lie on high ground close to the east–west watershed between these two basins. Breaching this watershed by a canal was seen as bringing opportunities to exploit trade routes in either direction.

Schemes to link the Trent and Mersey had been discussed as early as 1717 but surveying work did not begin in earnest until 1758. A pamphlet of 1765 explained the vital importance of such a scheme to the future of the industry. Noting that finished wares had to be transported up to 30 miles to a navigable watercourse, it continued:

The burden of so expensive a land carriage to Winsford and Willington, and the uncertainty of the navigations from those places to Frodsham in Cheshire and Wilden in Derbyshire, occasioned by the floods in winter and the numerous shallows in summer, are more than these low priced manufactures can

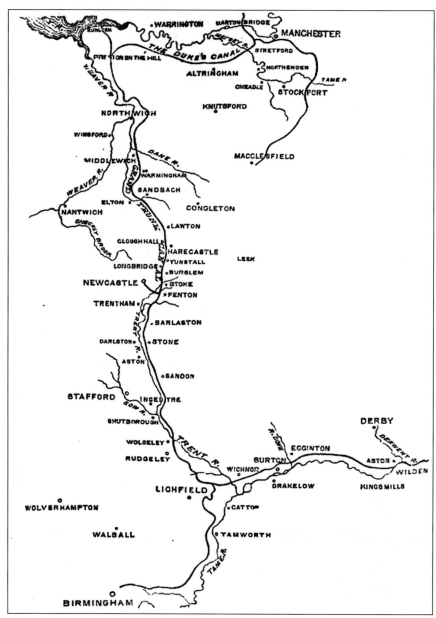

Plan of the Trent & Mersey 'Grand Trunk' Canal showing connections to the north and south. (Victoria County History)

bear; and without some such relief as this under construction, must concur, with their new established competitors in France, and our American colonies, to bring these potteries to a speedy decay and ruin.

The grand idea was to link the Trent, Mersey, Severn and Thames rivers with a system of canals, and the Potteries would be one of the first to benefit. The success of the enterprise was down to two men: Josiah Wedgwood, who secured the patronage and goodwill of the large landowners and politicians; and James Brindley, who masterminded the engineering.

Brindley was born near Chapel-en-le-Frith and set up his own mill in Leek before moving north to tackle an engineering problem at a colliery in Lancashire. His ingenious work brought him to the attention of the Duke of Bridgewater who employed him to build a canal to transport coal from his collieries to Manchester. Wedgwood and his fellow entrepreneurs, who included Earl Gower and John Sneyd, commissioned Brindley to build the Trent & Mersey Canal. An Act of Parliament authorizing its construction was passed in 1766 and Wedgwood himself cut the first sod.

It was clear from the outset that the main obstacle to success would be the Harecastle Tunnel between Kidsgrove and Tunstall. The technical feat of cutting a tunnel of 2,880yd through sandstones and coal deposits was unprecedented at the time. During construction of the tunnel many fossils were discovered which were a great source of puzzlement to Wedgwood. 'These wonderful works of nature' were, he said, 'too vast for my narrow microscopic comprehension.'

The canal was completed in eleven years, opening in 1777, though parts were in use long before. At the time the Harecastle Tunnel was described as the eighth wonder of the world. Brindley did not live to see the fulfilment of his project: he contracted pneumonia while out surveying and died in 1772.

Navigable waterways brought huge benefits to the area. Transport costs dropped dramatically, from 10*d*. to 1½*d*. per ton per mile. Yet between 1774 (before the whole stretch was opened) and the arrival of the railway in 1848, the total canal tolls collected increased four-fold.

Wedgwood's Etruria Works was the first of many new factories to be built along the line of the waterway. Gateways to the canal at Longport, Middleport and Newport all became important manufacturing districts. The original subscribers to the Canal Company received an impressive return for their investment. The benefits were felt in the wider community too. A visitor in 1788 noted that: 'the value of manufactures arises in the most unthought of places; new buildings and new streets spring up in many parts of Staffordshire where it passes; the poor no longer starving on the bread of poverty; and the rich grow greatly richer'.

Further canals and tunnels were soon needed. The Caldon Canal linked the Churnet Valley to the Potteries and included a feeder reservoir known as Rudyard Lake. The Harecastle Tunnel became a bottleneck and in 1827 a second tunnel was built by another master engineer, Thomas Telford. At 2,926yd, Telford's tunnel was longer than Brindley's. It also had a towpath so that horses could be used, rather than having to rely on bargees to walk their heavily laden boats through by lying on their backs (known as 'legging').

Although the main purpose of the canals was to link the manufactories with their markets at home and abroad, they also allowed the inflow of raw materials. A canal connection to Newcastle in 1795 provided a direct link to the main source of coal, while other links facilitated the flow of ground flint and stone from corn mills that had been converted to serve the pottery industry.

Dean (1997) maps all of the waterways of the Potteries, showing opening dates and key features, while Davies (2006) records the memories of the last of the boat people who worked the Midlands canals from the 1930s to the 1960s.

Canal Records

The canal age has left a huge legacy of records and archives. The National Archives holds the bulk of the surviving canal company records: minute books, wage books, correspondence, deeds of partnership, bankruptcy orders, canal share certificates and shareholders' registers, prospectuses, pamphlets, accounts, maps, deposited plans, photographs and surveys, etc. Canal records are

Barges and bottle ovens: pottery manufacturers were heavily reliant on the canals. (Public domain)

archived with docks, road and railway records in addition to many other categories. Relevant authorities include the Board of Trade, Ministry of Transport and the British Waterways Board and its predecessors. TNA Research Guide *Domestic Records Information 83 (Canals)* gives an overview of the many types of record available. See also Wilkes (2011) and the checklist compiled by the London Canal Museum (**www.canalmuseum.org.uk/collection/family-history.htm**).

The SSA has important collections relating to canals within Staffordshire. *SSA Guide to Sources No. 8: Transport Records* summarizes the holdings, which are of three main types:

1. **Records of the Canal Companies**: These cover the initial planning and construction of the canals and their subsequent operation, and may include employee records. They comprise plans, maps, letter books, correspondence (for example, negotiations between canal and railway companies) and other records.

2. **Canal Boat Registers and Inspection Reports**: An Act of 1795 required vessels using navigable rivers and canals to register with the local Clerk of the Peace; the legislation seems only to have lasted a few years. Where they survive, registers of vessels and applications to register vessels under the Act are found in the Quarter Sessions records. Registers may be consulted at the SRO [Q/Rub/1] with an online index at **www.staffsnameindexes.org.uk**.

3. **Miscellaneous Documents and Correspondence:** Documents from non-official sources relating to the canal era, such as letters, diaries, newspaper cuttings, etc.

Cheshire Archives and Local Studies has certificates issued by the Stoke-upon-Trent Registration Authority for canal boats owned by the North Staffordshire Railway Co., 1879–90 [LNW/36]. The Basil Jeuda Collection contains more general material on the NSR's involvement in canals (see below) [SD 1653].

Prosecutions under the Canal Acts will appear in the Quarter Sessions records. The Staffordshire Quarter Sessions, for example, has a number of convictions of boatmen for wasting water from locks, allowing a boat to hit lock gates and so on. Depositions (witness statements) may have names of canal workers or boatmen if they were accused of theft or other crimes.

Canal people lived an itinerant life: they could have been born, married and buried in three different counties and their children born in yet another. Therefore you may need to search for them across a wide area. Often the boat families made connections to Nonconformist churches such as Primitive Methodists and Salvation Army.

The Waterways Archive at the National Waterways Museum in Ellesmere Port is the national archive for the canal network. Its collections include boat registers, toll and tonnage records, and photographic collections covering canal life. Coverage for the Trent & Mersey Canal is patchy, however. More useful are its indexed transcripts of boat registers (from late nineteenth century) for the Cheshire canals (Chester, Nantwich, Northwich and Runcorn) and those in the West Midlands as far as Gloucester, all of which would have been used by Staffordshire boatmen (**http://collections.canalrivertrust.org.uk**).

Longport railway station in the early 1960s. (Trevor Ford, courtesy of thepotteries.org)

NORTH STAFFORDSHIRE RAILWAYS

The Railway Mania of the early 1840s left the Potteries without a railway, although the surrounding towns of Stafford, Crewe, Derby and Macclesfield were all connected to the railway system. The nearest access to the growing national network was at Whitmore, on the Grand Junction Railway (GJR) from Birmingham to Manchester via Stafford and Crewe, which opened on 4 July 1837.

Various schemes were put forward that were eventually amalgamated into a combined proposal with two main lines. The Pottery Line would run from Congleton to Colwich, providing connections with the Manchester & Birmingham Railway and GJR respectively. It was promoted as 'giving the most ample accommodation to the towns of Tunstall, Burslem, Newcastle-under-Lyme, Hanley, Stoke, Fenton, Longton and Stone'. A second route, the Churnet Line, was to run from Macclesfield through Leek, Cheadle and Uttoxeter to join the Midland Railway between Burton-upon-Trent and Derby, thus forming a direct link between Manchester and Derby. A third route from Harecastle to Liverpool had to be abandoned in the face of fierce opposition from the Grand Junction Railway. The only section to be built was the short branch from Harecastle to Sandbach, where it connected into the London & North Western Railway.

The North Staffordshire Railway Company was formed to push forward the proposals, which received parliamentary approval in June 1846. Construction work began three months later with John Lewis Ricardo, Member of Parliament for Stoke-on-Trent and chairman of the NSR Company cutting the first sod.

Known locally as 'The Knotty', the North Staffordshire Railway officially opened to passengers on 17 April 1848, with trains running from a temporary station at Whieldon Grove, Stoke, to Norton Bridge. By 1849 more than 113 miles of track had been laid in North Staffordshire, along with stations, warehouses and sidings. At the heart of the NSR's little empire was Stoke station, in Winton Square, widely acknowledged as one of the finest examples of Victorian architecture in Staffordshire. Serving also as the headquarters of the NSR Company, the building was designed by H.A. Hunt of London and opened in 1848.

At the turn of the century, the still-independent NSR was enjoying a boom, both in passengers and tons of freight carried. An example was the first-rate service on the Loop Line which ran from Tunstall via Burslem, Cobridge, Hanley, and Etruria to Stoke, continuing along the Derby line to Fenton, Longton and finally to Normacot. It boasted an each-way daily service of fifty trains, running at 15-minute intervals during peak periods.

Serving a relatively small population and being surrounded by larger railways, the NSR was always on a precarious financial footing. Having resisted takeover bids since the 1850s, the decline in railways after the First World War meant 'The Knotty' could hold out no longer. In 1923 the NSR was absorbed by the powerful London, Midland and Scottish Railway Company and the name disappeared from the network. Later, like communities across Britain, the area suffered heavily from the Beeching cuts of the 1960s.

Jeuda (1986) is an illustrated guide to the NSR from its creation through to 1923 using photographs from the company's official archive. The Churnet Valley Railway is a heritage railway that operates steam trains along a part of the NSR's former Churnet Valley Line.

Railway Records

TNA holds the records of many of the railway companies that existed prior to nationalization in 1947; these are catalogued in the TNA Class RAIL. Many are employment related, including staff registers (the commonest type), station transfers, pension and accident records (which may include date of death), apprentice records (which may include father's name), caution books and memos. The main series, more than 2 million records in total, is available on Ancestry (search for 'UK Railway Employment Records, 1833–1963']. Stoke-on-Trent City Archives has NSR employee records, *c.* 1898–1950 but it is not clear how these relate to the Ancestry series [SD 1184]. For further information on railway staff records see specialist guides: Hawkings (2008), Hardy (2009) and Drummond (2010).

The SSA has an extensive collection relating to the NSR, much of which is uncatalogued. It includes property deeds, legal papers, maps, timetables and prospectuses and is filed under numerous catalogue references. The Basil Jeuda Collection contains material relating to the NSR throughout the nineteenth and twentieth centuries, including the company's master photographic archive [SD 1288, SD 1416, SD 1688, SD 1698 and D1415, uncatalogued]. The Jack Hollick Collection [Hollick] and Lancefield-Walker Collection [SD 1319, SD 1419] also relate to the NSR. Little of this archive relates to employees, however. The holdings are summarized in *SSA Guide to Sources No. 8: Transport Records*. Midland Ancestors has the Wages Ledger, 1850–1930 of the NSR's Canals Department available as a download [BR0001D].

NSR employees may also have worked for the Midland Railway Company, which operated trains in and through the Peak District. The Midland Railway Study Centre in Derby is a specialist archive relating to this company assembled from various collections. The website has a staff index and online catalogue (**www.midlandrailwaystudycentre.org.uk**).

Inquisitions and assessments for compensation for land acquired by railway companies are in Quarter Sessions records. There may also be references in the personal or estate papers of the families concerned. For example, the Sutherland Papers at the SSA contain details of property of the Duke of Sutherland in Trentham and Barlaston affected by the building of the Pottery Line [D593/H/9/67].

The Library of Birmingham has a major collection of railway material, including over 5,000 books and periodicals, timetables (including Bradshaw's), maps, architectural drawings and plans, and over 20,000 photographs and postcards of locomotives. It also houses the Wingate Bett Transport Ticket Collection, comprising over 1 million tickets from all over the world.

ROADS, TRAMS AND BUSES

For centuries the people of the Potteries relied on the sparse network of roads left by the Romans. Their main thoroughfare was Rykeneld (or Ryknield) Street linking Chester and Derby. The route is not entirely clear, but it is believed to have run through Chesterton (site of a Roman fort), Wolstanton, Fenton, Lane Delph and Blyth Bridge. During the medieval period it became common practice for potters to dig clay from the roads to use in their wares, leaving 'potholes' on the surface. Severe fines for this offence were imposed after 1604 but did little to quell the practice. Many roads were little more than ancient trackways that connected small villages and hamlets and were used primarily for the movement of livestock.

As the pottery industry developed raw materials from outside the locality were brought in by packhorse. Finished vessels were taken out in the same manner but the condition of the roads resulted in many wares being broken. As the volume of raw materials and products increased carts were used instead but often the local roads were impassable. Extra demands imposed by the growing stagecoach traffic (the main route from London to Carlisle ran through the Potteries) only exacerbated the situation. Something had to be done.

In 1762 local industrialists and gentry petitioned Parliament to be allowed to build a turnpike road from the Liverpool and London Road at Lawton to Stoke-upon-Trent. There it would join the Newcastle to Uttoxeter turnpike which had recently been improved. The petitioners drew attention to the increasing demand for their wares which were being 'exported in vast quantities' and the obstacle created by the poor condition of the roads:

This road, especially the northern road from Burslem to the Red Bull, is so very narrow, deep, and foundrous, as to be almost impassable for carriages; and in the winter, almost for pack-horses; for which reason, the carriages, with materials and ware, to and from Liverpool, and the salt-works in Cheshire, are obliged to go to Newcastle, and from thence to the Red Bull, which is nine miles and a half . . .

The burghers of Newcastle objected to this proposal since they stood to lose out by the diversion of carriages and travellers. Parliament passed the Act but with an abridgement of the road at its southern end, meaning it terminated at Burslem instead of proceeding onward to Cliff Bank, Stoke. Turnpiking brought great benefits for the local economy and North Staffordshire was soon criss-crossed by a network of turnpike roads, some new, others improvements of existing routes. The Turnpikes.org website has details of routes as well as information on the gates and tollhouses used to collect tolls from road users (**www. turnpikes.org.uk**).

The records of turnpikes relate mainly to those involved in establishing and managing turnpike trusts, who were generally drawn from the upper classes. Each trust required its own Act of Parliament, which had to be renewed roughly every twenty years. The Act included a list of the trust's subscribers, who were effectively shareholders investing in the scheme for a commercial return. These ranged from the local aristocracy and gentry, to prominent landowners, farmers and merchants. Once established, each turnpike trust had to issue regular reports on its activities, which were reported at the Quarter Sessions [SRO: Q/Rut]. Fines imposed on stage-coach drivers for various infringements on turnpikes would also be levied there [SRO: Q/RLb].

The limited nature of the road system influenced the development of the Six Towns as a sprawling, linear conurbation. Houses tended to be built along the line of the roads. The owners of the growing potbanks and mines sought to house their workers within easy travelling distance and built on any available spare land.

Creeping urbanization during the nineteenth century brought the need for short-distance transport options. George Train, an exuberant

A Potteries Motor Traction bus, c. 1960. (Courtesy of thepotteries.org)

American, opened the first tramway in the Potteries in January 1862. His 'street railway' ran from the Town Hall in Burslem to Foundry Street, Hanley, horse-drawn trams running every hour or half-hour at a fare of 3*d*. The system encountered technical difficulties and was expensive to operate and although the company remained in operation for twenty years, horse-drawn traction never really took off.

In 1881 an extension from Stoke to Longton was built as a steam tramway and the following year the original horse tramway line was converted to steam traction. A further extension from Stoke station to West End brought the total length of tramway in operation to 7 miles. For a while the service relied on open-top double-decker trailer cars: these were extremely uncomfortable and were soon replaced by more comfortable single-decker units. People complained that the steam trams showered them in dust and ashes, but they were better than 'Shanks's Pony'.

The steam trams, too, were short-lived. The British Electric Traction Company Ltd acquired control of the North Staffordshire Tramways Company in 1896 and despite carrying almost 4 million passengers per year, by the end of the century steam traction had disappeared. In its place was a network of electric tramways that was being developed by the British Electric Traction Company's subsidiary, the Potteries Electric Traction Company Ltd. Having electrified the existing tramways, from 1899 a number of extensions were added, including from Burslem to Goldenhill through Tunstall (part of the so-called Main Line), and up a very steep gradient from Burslem to Smallthorne. With the extension at its southern end from Longton to Meir, the Main Line now ran for almost 11 miles linking all the Potteries towns.

The first two decades of the twentieth century were the high point for trams in Stoke-on-Trent. By 1919 a new sight could be seen on the roads: motor buses. The City Council paid no regard to the number of operators to whom it issued licences and competition for the Potteries Electric Traction Company's routes became intense. At the height of the craze in 1924, no fewer than eighty-one bus operators were licensed to enter the city. Many of them concentrated on the tramway's Main Line from Tunstall to Longton, where the easiest pickings were to be found. In the face of such stiff competition and an unsympathetic council, the writing was on the wall for the Potteries Electric Traction Company. The last tram ran in the Potteries on 11 July 1928.

The Potteries Electric Traction Company was reconstituted as the Potteries Motor Traction Company Ltd and focused on regaining market share. The large number of local independent operators remained a problem, however, and after the Second World War the company decided that the best approach was to buy them out. Accordingly, the bus fleet became extremely mixed during the 1950s and reflected the complete lack of standardization. Smith (1977) provides a comprehensive history of the PMT and Cooke (2009) documents the many passenger vehicles that have been used on North Staffordshire's roads.

A little-known episode in Stoke-on-Trent's history is that it once had a car manufacturer. The Menley Motor Company was set up in Etruria Road, Basford by John Riley and Clement Mendham in 1920.

			WHETHER		
			4		
Number of Licence.	Full Name of Licensee.	Postal Address of Residence of Licensee.	To drive a Motor Car. (a)	Limited to driving Motor Cycles. (b)	Date of Grant
1	2	3			5
464	Samuel Massey	Boothen Road, Stoke-on-Trent	Yes	x	20 May
465	Charles Walter Bloor	5 Gordon Street, Hartshill, Stoke-on-T.	Yes	x	20 May
466	Stanley Goodwin	Wharf House, High Street West, Stoke	Yes	x	20 May
467	Thomas Sadler	130 Etruria Vale, Hanley	Yes	x	21 May
468	Joseph Hopwood	28 Edmund Street, Hanley	Yes	x	23 May
469	William Eli Arthur Marks	150 Moston Street, Birches Head, Hanley	Yes	x	23 May
470	Walter Edwin Bennett	London Road Inn, Occupation St. Stoke	Yes	x	26 May
6	Wilfred John Myatt	45 Stone Road, Longton	x	Yes	20 May
471	Albert Thorley	31 Belgrave Road, Longton	Yes	x	20 May
472	Frederick Spicer	29 Trentham Road, Longton	Yes	x	25 May
473	Herbert Bell	Fenton Manor Cottage, Fenton	Yes	x	25 May
474	Frank Henry Davies	5 Wellington Street, Fenton	Yes	x	26 May

Register of Stoke-on-Trent Drivers and Vehicles Licences, 1910–13. (Courtesy of Staffordshire & Stoke-on-Trent Archives, SA/MT/1)

The company produced a cyclecar with an air-cooled 999cc V-twin engine. Only sixteen of these cyclecars were made before the company went into liquidation that same year.

The Albert Huxley Collection at the STCA comprises material on the Potteries Motor Traction Company, including drivers' licences, identity cards and ration books from the Second World War [SA/AH/18-29 and 35-37]. Unwin (2011 and 2013) presents histories of commercial haulage companies operating in North Staffordshire during the mid-twentieth century.

An unusual record series is a list of driver and vehicle licences issued in Staffordshire between 1904 and 1960 [STCA: SA/MT]. It covers both cars and motorcycles, with the driver's name, address and details of any endorsements and is indexed. The drivers' licences run until November 1930 and the vehicle taxation registers continue into the 1960s.

The tyre companies Michelin and Dunlop were major employers in the Potteries and were especially important during the Second World War. The STCA has the Michelin archive collections, *c.* 1905–2013

[SD 1680]. Part of this archive, an index to the Michelin UK staff magazine 1936–51, is available on Staffordshire Name Indexes.

FURTHER INFORMATION

Casewell, Mark, *Index to Mining Deaths in North Staffordshire 1756–1995* (Audley & District FHS, 2015)

Cooke, John, *A Century of North Staffordshire Buses* (Horizon Press, 2009)

Davies, Robert, *Midlands Canals: Memories of the Canal Carriers* (History Press, 2006)

Deakin, Paul, *Collieries in the North Staffordshire Coalfield* (Landmark Publishing, 2004)

Dean, Richard, *Canals of North Staffordshire (Historical Canal Maps)* (M&M Baldwin, 1997)

Drummond, Di, *Tracing Your Railway Ancestors* (Pen & Sword, 2010)

Edwards, Mervyn, *Potters in Pits* (Churnet Valley Books, 1998)

Hardy, Frank, *My Ancestor was a Railway Worker* (Society of Genealogists, 2009)

Hawkings, David T., *Railway Ancestors: Guide to the Staff Records of the Railway Companies of England and Wales, 1822–1947* (History Press, 2008)

Jeuda, Basil, *Memories of the North Staffordshire Railway* (Cheshire Libraries, 1986)

Leigh, Fred, *Most Valiant of Men: Short History of the North Staffordshire Mines Rescue Service* (Churnet Valley Books, 1993)

Smith, Geoffrey K., *The Potteries Motor Traction Co. Ltd* (Transport Publishing Company, 1977)

Stone, Richard, *The Collieries and Coalminers of Staffordshire* (Phillimore, 2007)

Unwin, Ros, *North Staffordshire Hauliers, Volumes 1 & 2* (Churnet Valley Books, 2011 and 2013).

Wilkes, Sue, *Tracing Your Canal Ancestors: A Guide for Family Historians* (Pen & Sword, 2011)

Chapter 4

CHURCH AND POLITICS

THE ESTABLISHED CHURCH
Principal Churches

St Peter ad Vincula, the ancient parish church of Stoke-upon-Trent, stands on one of the oldest sites of Christian worship in Staffordshire. There is thought to have been a church here since at least the seventh century. Early buildings were replaced by a stone church around AD 805, which was then altered and enlarged on several occasions. During medieval times the church and its rectory stood more or less on their own, somewhat removed from the main centres of population in Penkhull and Newcastle. Over the years, St Peter's became the mother church of a huge parish, which included chapelries at Bagnall, Bucknall, Burslem, Clayton and Seabridge, Fenton, Hanley, Lane End, Newcastle and Norton-in-the-Moors. Several of these eventually became parishes in their own right.

Like many industrial towns, space in the pews grew short as the population expanded. A new church was begun in 1826 and consecrated in 1830. The interior features a large number of Minton Victorian memorial tiles around the walls, commemorating parishioners and others of note. The interior was remodelled in 1888, doing away with the three-decker pulpit and square family pews. The churchyard contains many memorials and the graves of several famous potters. Josiah Wedgwood was buried beneath the porch of the old church in a vault also containing the remains of his wife and son. A plain memorial marks his resting place. Re-erected fragments of the old church can still be seen in a garden to the south of the present building.

In 2005 St Peter ad Vincula was granted the status of a minster by the Bishop of Lichfield in recognition of its historic and civic status as the principal Anglian church of the city of Stoke-on-Trent.

Illustration of old Stoke church, which was demolished in 1829, from John Ward's 'The Borough of Stoke-upon-Trent', 1843. (Courtesy of thepotteries.org)

There are only a handful of pre-1700 churches remaining within the Potteries. The west tower of St John the Baptist, Burslem dates from Tudor times and is the only complete Pre-Reformation structure in the area. First mentioned in 1297, St John served as a chapel-of-ease to Stoke-upon-Trent until 1809. Originally of timber, the nave was rebuilt in brick and tile in 1717 after a serious fire. In 1788, the church was extended by the addition of a chancel to create more seating, including a magnificent window in the Venetian style. Josiah Wedgwood was born in a nearby cottage and baptized at St John on 12 July 1730. Two other famous potters, William Adams and Enoch Wood, are both buried in the churchyard. Inside, a modern tablet commemorates members of the Adams family. Although still standing, St John's no longer functions as an Anglican church.

Among other early churches, St John's, Barlaston has a tower dating from the twelfth century with the remainder of the church having been rebuilt in 1888. St Mary & All Saints, Trentham also dates from the twelfth century and was extensively rebuilt in 1844. St Peter's, Caverswall was founded in the thirteenth century and was subject to a major restoration scheme in 1880. St Bartholemew's, in the once isolated village of Blurton, is one of the few English churches to be built during the reign of Charles I.

The eighteenth century saw the first great period of church building in the Six Towns, with the erection of St Bartholemew's, Norton-in-the-Moors (1738), St John's, Hanley (1737 and rebuilt 1788), and St John's, Longton. At Longton, Anglicans used a chapel built in 1762, although it was initially registered as being for Protestant Dissenters. This became too small for the growing congregation and fell into decay before being rebuilt, as the Church of St John the Baptist, in 1795. The original red-brick nave and tower were supplemented by a new chancel in 1828.

Even with this additional capacity there was concern that large numbers of the urban poor and working class were not catered for by the Established Church. Like other industrial towns, the Potteries received substantial government funding during the 1820s and 1830s to found new places of worship. Arguably, the aim was also to pacify the new urban masses and dissuade them from revolution. Among these so-called Commissioners' churches were St Mark's, Shelton, St James the Less, Longton, Christ Church, Tunstall, and St Paul, Longport. Other churches were funded, either in whole or in part, through the generosity of local benefactors. Notable examples here are Holy Trinity, Hartshill (funded by Herbert Minton and designed by George Gilbert Scott in 1842, making it one of his earliest works) and St Thomas, Penkhull (also built by Scott at the expense of the Revd Thomas Webb Minton).

Fenton was the last of the Six Towns to receive its own Anglican place of worship. Until the mid-nineteenth century Fenton lay within the parish of Stoke. Christ Church, in what is now called Christchurch Street, was built in 1838–9, to a Gothic design by Henry Ward who also designed Stoke Town Hall. However, it had to be demolished because of subsidence and in 1890 was replaced by a second church, also called Christ Church.

GENUKI's Staffordshire pages have photographs and old postcards showing many of the county's churches (**www.genuki.org.uk/big/ eng/STS/ChurchPhotos**).

Anglican Records

Staffordshire and Stoke-on-Trent Archives is the main repository for registers from Staffordshire parishes. Registers and other parish chest documents are listed by parish in the Gateway to the Past online catalogue. Original registers are available to view on microfilm at Stoke-on-Trent City Archives, with duplicates at Staffordshire Record Office. A full list of parish register holdings for Staffordshire, including registers held elsewhere is given in *SSA Guide to Sources No. 1: Parish Registers and Bishops' Transcripts*. Bishops' Transcripts were copies of parish registers made for the local bishop, in this case the Bishop of Lichfield. These records were at the Lichfield Record Office and can now be consulted at the SRO.

Under licence from the SSA, virtually all Anglican parish registers for Staffordshire are available online as part of the Staffordshire Collection at Findmypast. Approximately 200 parishes are covered, including all those within North Staffordshire. Coverage comprises baptisms, marriages and burials from 1538 (or whenever the individual registers commenced) through to 1900, and 1653–1900 for marriage banns, with digitized images of the original registers.

This online collection also includes marriage licences. These were administered by the church courts, the same bodies that handled wills and probate. A marriage licence could be obtained for a fee if a couple wished to waive the customary reading of the banns. There are several reasons why a couple might want to do so, such as the need to expedite the wedding date or if they were Nonconformist or Roman Catholic and did not attend the parish church. An allegation and bond had to be submitted in support of such an application. An allegation was a sworn statement prepared by the groom: it may state where the intended marriage was to take place and the groom's occupation. The bond was intended to assert the authenticity and legality of the allegations, pledging a sum that would be forfeited if the documents proved inaccurate. The Staffordshire Collection on Findmypast has the Dioceses of Lichfield & Coventry Marriage Allegations and Bonds, 1636–1893 based on original documents held by the SSA.

Many registers for Staffordshire parishes may be accessed free of charge through the FreeREG project (**www.freereg.org.uk**). All of the Six Towns and most surrounding parishes are covered. New records, including for Nonconformists are continually being added.

Midland Ancestors maintains a series of marriage and burial indexes for Staffordshire including the Potteries, namely:

- Staffordshire Burial Index: Complete from the beginning of registers to 1837, containing all known recorded burials. See website for search procedures and fees. This is not to be confused with the similarly named Staffordshire Burial Index (which is actually a cemetery index) hosted by Midland Ancestors on behalf of the SSA (see below).
- Staffordshire Marriage Index: 1500s to 1837 including some Roman Catholic registers. See Midland Ancestors website for search procedures and fees.
- Staffordshire Monumental Inscriptions: See Midland Ancestors website for coverage (many parishes now available to download).

The Staffordshire Parish Register Society transcribes and publishes registers from Staffordshire parishes. Founded in 1901, its activities have been curtailed only by the two world wars and it is one of the few societies in existence still regularly printing parish registers in book form. Registers may be purchased via its website (**www.sprs.org.uk**) or the Midland Ancestors shop.

Other documents within the parish chest may name or have lists of parishioners. Those for Audley parish, for example, include a late eighteenth-century pew plan with the names of families [D4842/15/2/35-38].

ROMAN CATHOLICS
Catholicism in the Potteries
The Protestant Reformation of the sixteenth century caused a schism in English society. While some accepted the new Protestantism and its

Six of the thirty-two stained glass windows in St Joseph's, Burslem. The windows were designed by Gordon Forsyth and made by church members. (Friends of St Joseph's, courtesy of thepotteries.org)

tenets – such as the Book of Common Prayer and the abolition of the Mass – others refused to comply. The West Midlands was one area where the Old Faith was kept alive. The Gunpowder Plotters of 1605 were famously led not by Guy Fawkes, as many believe, but by Robert Catesby, who is thought to have been born in Warwickshire. When the plot was discovered, Catesby and his co-conspirators (many of whom were from the Midlands) fled London and made a stand at Holbeche House in Staffordshire.

After a brief respite under the Catholic James II, the eighteenth century brought further oppression. Although the Toleration Act of 1689 guaranteed freedom of worship for dissenting groups, Roman Catholics were expressly excluded and Catholic repression continued. Some ceremonies were held in secret during this period but most Catholics were baptized and married in Anglican churches and buried in Anglican churchyards. It was not uncommon for the Anglican minister to mark an entry in the register with 'papist' or 'recusant'. In the event of a Catholic marrying outside the Church of England, the authorities could prosecute the offending parties through the ecclesiastical courts.

The Catholic Relief Acts of 1778 and 1791 allowed new churches to be built. In the Potteries the first sign of resurgence was at Cobridge, where the Warburton and Blackwell families helped to finance the construction of a small Catholic chapel at the end of what is now Grange Street (then the lane leading to Rushton Grange Farm). This was in 1780, the same year as anti-Catholic protests in London that became known as the Gordon Riots. The disturbances so alarmed the congregation of Cobridge that they suspended construction for several months. The chapel was enlarged in 1816, at which time it was estimated to accommodate about 150 people.

This Catholic church, dedicated to St Peter, served the north of the district. Eventually, in 1895, a separate mission including Burslem, Smallthorne and Wolstanton was formed out of the Cobridge church operating from a building in Hall Street dedicated to St Joseph. The present Church of St Joseph was later built on an adjoining site.

Under the Catholic emancipation measures of the 1820s Roman Catholics were able to worship freely and more new churches began to appear. At Stoke, a mission was founded in 1838 by the priest from St Gregory's, Longton, who had begun to say Mass at the home of a Mr Maguire in Whieldon Road. By 1841 Mass was being celebrated in a joiner's shop in Liverpool Road, and in 1843 the venue was transferred to a new chapel in Back Glebe Street, dedicated to St Peter in Chains. The chapel continued to be served from Longton until the appointment of a resident priest in 1850. About this time the average attendance at Sunday Mass was 144, and by 1852 the Catholic population of the Stoke area was estimated at more than 500.

This chapel was structurally poor and far too small to accommodate the rapidly increasing membership. In 1852 the congregation purchased a new site at Hartshill and in 1854 the adjoining plot was acquired by Dominican nuns who had been searching for a suitable site in the Potteries for a new convent. Work began on the church and convent in 1856. Built in the Gothic style and dedicated to Our Lady of the Angels and St Peter in Chains, the new church opened its doors in Hartshill Bank the following year, at which point the old chapel in Back Glebe Street was sold. It is now a listed building.

Another notable Catholic church in the district is Sacred Heart, Jasper Street, Hanley, completed in 1891.

Catholic Records

Staffordshire falls within the Catholic Archdiocese of Birmingham, established in 1911 (formerly the Diocese of Birmingham). Records from Staffordshire parishes (missions) are held at the Birmingham Archdiocesan Archives (BAA) at Cathedral House, Birmingham, next to St Chad's Cathedral.

The BAA holds the episcopal and administrative records of the Midland District (1688–1840), the Central District (1840–50), the Diocese of Birmingham (1850–1911), and the Archdiocese of Birmingham (1911 to present). It is also the repository for all parishes in the Archdiocese, which comprises the ancient counties of Oxfordshire, Staffordshire, Warwickshire and Worcestershire. As well as baptisms, marriages and burials, these holdings include congregational records, showing whether an ancestor received confirmation or was a church benefactor. The BAA's registers, including those for Staffordshire, have been digitized and are available on Findmypast (search under 'England Roman Catholic Parish Registers').

Other collections at the BAA cover the activities of a wide range of Catholic charities, societies and organizations. Of particular note are the records of the Catholic Family History Society (Midlands Branch), which was disbanded in 2007. There is an online catalogue (**www. birminghamarchdiocesanarchives.org.uk**). The registers of certain missions remain with their incumbents (details on the website).

Catholic Missions & Registers 1700–1880. Volume 2, The Midlands and East Anglia, compiled by Michael Gandy, gives details of Staffordshire Catholic mission registers (and sixteen other counties) and includes date coverage and location of registers.

The persecution of Dissenters (both Catholics and Nonconformists) from the sixteenth to eighteenth centuries generated various genealogical records. Recusant Rolls list Dissenters and show the fines and property or land surrendered by the accused. Surviving lists have been published in the journal *Staffordshire Catholic History* at various dates and some original records are in the Quarter Sessions series [Q/RRr]. Returns of Papists are records from audits of Roman Catholics taken nationwide at various times, arranged in dioceses by town or village. Some returns simply record the numbers of Catholics and not their names. Again these have been published in *Staffordshire Catholic History* and its successor journal *Midland Catholic History*. Returns of Papists' Estates are registers of Roman Catholics who refused to take oaths of loyalty after the Jacobite Rebellion of 1715 [Q/RRp].

The Midland Catholic History Society promotes the study of post-Reformation Catholic history and recusants in the Midland counties and issues a regular journal (**http://midlandcatholichistory.org.uk**). A detailed account of early Catholics, based on papers from the Bagot family collection, is given in 'Roman Catholicism in Elizabethan and Jacobean Staffordshire' by Anthony Gretano Petti (*Collections for a History of Staffordshire*, Fourth Series, Vol. IX).

THE CRADLE OF METHODISM

The Potteries can claim to be one of the cradles of Methodism in Britain, having been associated with this Nonconformist tradition since its inception. John Wesley first preached in Newcastle-under-Lyme as early as 1738, the year of his conversion, and returned to the area many times. He had a great affection for North Staffordshire and was astounded by the economic and social changes unfolding before his eyes. In his journal for 8 March 1781, he noted: 'I returned to Burslem. How is the whole face of this country changed in about twenty years! Since which, inhabitants have continually flowed in from every side. Hence the wilderness is literally become a fruitful field. Houses, villages, towns, have sprung up: and the country is not more improved than the people.'

During Wesley's first visit to Burslem in 1760 a convert, Abraham Lindop, opened his cottage for services. The first Methodist chapel in the Six Towns was built at Hill Top four years later and Wesley preached there on six occasions. The entry in Wesley's diary for 31 March 1784 records: 'I reached Burslem, where we had the first society in the county, and it is still the largest, and the most earnest.' By 1789 the Hill Top Chapel was the centre of a circuit with around 1,300 members.

In Hanley, Wesleyans opened their first chapel in 1783 in the area known as Chapel Fields, later Chapel Street, between Bryan Street and St John's Anglican church. The pulpit was said to be too high for the building and only those at the front could see the minister's face. For all its shortcomings, Wesley himself preached from that pulpit on

Interior of the Bethesda Methodist Chapel, Hanley. Bethesda was the Conference Church for the whole of the Methodist New Connexion movement. (Courtesy of thepotteries.org)

30 March 1784. In Stoke, a small group began to meet in an upper room in London Road around this time and went on to build their own Methodist chapel on land bought from master potter Thomas Wolfe. In 1801 the Burslem Methodists built Swan Bank Chapel and moved there from Hill Top and in 1804 the Newcastle circuit, which initially included Stoke, was formed.

Despite the burgeoning support, all was not well within the Methodist movement, however. In 1797 disagreements within the Wesleyan body nationally led some followers to secede and set up the Methodist New Connexion. Hanley's society was devastated as many influential leaders left taking much of the congregation with them. As a result, membership of the Hanley Wesleyan society was reduced from 150 to 8 people almost overnight.

Several of this group went on to found the Bethesda New Connexion Methodist Chapel in Albion Street, Hanley, known as the 'Cathedral of the Potteries'. The first chapel, erected in 1798, seated 600 and in 1811 a semi-circular rear extension was added to bring the capacity up to 1,000. The whole building was demolished in 1819 and a new chapel was built. Local architect Robert Scrivener added a stuccoed Italianate frontage with Corinthian portico in 1859. By this time Bethesda was one of the largest Nonconformist chapels outside London, attracting huge congregations and seating up to 2,000 people. The building is no longer used as a place of worship but The Friends of Bethesda hold regular open days (see **www.bethesda-stoke.info**).

It was against this background that a preacher called Hugh Bourne addressed a 'camp meeting' at Mow Cop, an isolated village on the Cheshire–Staffordshire border, 6 miles north of Stoke, on 31 May 1807. People had travelled from as far as Macclesfield and Warrington to hear him. For 14 hours Bourne preached and discussed, concluding only at 8.00 p.m. as darkness closed in on the proceedings. A second meeting was held at the same location three months later.

Bourne, a lowly born man from Bucknall who had quit his job as a wheelwright to become a roving preacher, rattled the Methodist authorities. They condemned the proceedings at Mow Cop as 'highly improper in England' and excluded Bourne from the Methodist circuit. Undeterred, Bourne and his followers organized under the name Camp Meeting Methodists. In 1811 Bourne was joined by another evangelist called William Clowes and his followers, and together the two communities adopted the name Primitive Methodists. This was intended to show that they wished to get back to Wesley's primitive ways for street and field evangelism. The first Primitive Methodist Chapel was built in Tunstall that same year.

By 1820 the Primitive Methodist movement had over 7,000 members and held its first conference in Hull. Churches were established up and down the country, as well as overseas. In 1841 a chapel was built on Mow Cop, which was subsequently given up in favour of a larger building nearby.

Hugh Bourne, founder of Primitive Methodism. (Wikimedia, Creative Commons)

In the Potteries, nineteenth-century Methodism – in its various strands – appealed just as much to working class folk as to the prosperous middle classes. Miners, canal boatmen, shop assistants and potbank workers of every description attended the chapels and brought their children to be baptized there.

Although other forms of Nonconformism had a presence in the Potteries, none could rival the various strands of Methodism. Chapels run by other denominations known to have existed in the area include the Presbyterians at Newcastle-under-Lyme (1690, Unitarian from 1804); Baptists at Hanley (1789) and Burslem (1791); Independent (Congregationalists) at Hanley (1784); and Independent Methodists (not related to other chapels) at Burslem in 1837. A group known as the Sandemanians registered a building in Tunstall in 1812 and is said to have met for some time.

This popularity brought great wealth, allowing the construction of chapels that were not just places of worship but buildings of high architectural quality. In addition to Bethesda, notable examples are (or were): the Old Methodist Chapel, Epworth Street, Stoke (now demolished); and the Swan Bank (rebuilt in 1971), Bethel and Hill Top chapels, all in Burslem.

Following the schisms of the early 1800s, the theme during the early twentieth century was reunification. In 1907 the Methodist New Connexion joined forces with two smaller groups, the United Methodist Free Churches and Bible Christian Methodists to form the United Methodist Church. Then in 1932 the United Methodist Church merged with the Wesleyan Methodists and the Primitive Methodists to form the Methodist Church of Great Britain.

The Methodist Heritage Handbook provides information on historic Methodist locations in Britain, including Bethesda Chapel, Mow Cop & Methodist Chapel, and Swan Bank Chapel, Burslem (**www. methodistheritage.org.uk**). One of the sites listed, Englesea Brook Chapel and Museum, Crewe, tells the story of Primitive Methodism (**www.engleseabrook-museum.org.uk**).

Nonconformist Records

Prior to 1754, Nonconformists could marry in their own chapels. Under Hardwicke's Act of 1753 marriages had to take place in a licensed Anglican parish church before an Anglican minister. Quakers (as well as Jews) were exempt from the new law. After the introduction of civil registration in 1837, all religious denominations were free to hold legal

Primitive Methodist Centenary Meeting at Mow Cop, 1910. (Public domain)

marriage ceremonies and to keep their own registers. As very few chapels had their own burial grounds, individuals were either buried in the local Anglican churchyard or cemetery (some had areas set aside for Nonconformists) or were sent further afield to an independent chapel which did have a burial ground.

The SSA holds the registers for many, though by no means all, Nonconformist places of worship in the county. At present, these registers are not in the Staffordshire Collection on Findmypast. The complexities in tracing Nonconformist places of worship are considerable. Nonconformist churches proliferated in huge numbers during the nineteenth century. In many Potteries communities it was not unusual to find a Wesleyan, a New Connexion/United Methodist and a Primitive Methodist chapel co-existing, probably with at least one other denomination as well. Many operated only for a few years, while others merged at later dates. Meanwhile, the same registers may have been used across a wide geographical area. *SSA Guide to Sources No. 2: Non-conformist Registers* lists those held by the county archive service.

The STCA has an especially rich collection of Methodist chapel and circuit records, 1799–1986 [SA/SM]. In addition to chapel registers, materials include minutes, financial records, Sunday school attendance lists, photographs and magazines: see the catalogue in the STCA Search Room for details. There is an additional series for the Bethesda Methodist Chapel that includes lists of church members, *c.* 1830–60 and of Sunday school attendees [SA/BE].

As with Catholic chapels, not all registers were surrendered to the Registrar General under the Non-Parochial Registers Commissions of 1837 and 1857. Across Staffordshire as a whole seventy-seven chapels deposited their registers. These are now available at TNA [in Classes RG 4 and RG 8] and through the BMD Registers (**www.bmdregisters. org.uk**), Ancestry and TheGenealogist websites. Staffordshire Record Society has published a list of dissenting chapels and meeting houses in Staffordshire between 1689 and 1853, compiled from the Return made to the General Register Office Under the Protestant Dissenters Act of 1852 (*Collections*, Fourth Series, Vol. III).

Other Nonconformist records which may be of value include minute books (some denominations had to apply to leave and re-join the church when they moved area), account books (records of payment for burial), lists of members, Sunday school admissions, monumental inscriptions, and magazines, newsletters and year books (which may include obituaries).

Methodist records are held at the John Rylands University Library, Manchester. These do not include local chapel registers but may be of help to those whose ancestors were Methodist preachers or prominent lay persons. The My Methodist History website has useful information and resources for tracing Methodist ancestors (**www.mymethodist history.org.uk**), with links to associated sites for Wesleyan Methodists, Primitive Methodists and Bible Christians. Its new resource, the Methodist Missionary Register, documents people who went to preach the gospel overseas. The very dated but still active North Staffordshire Methodist Heritage website contains a wealth of information on the Methodist movement in the area, including histories and photographs of chapels (**www.rewlach.org.uk**).

The Library of the Religious Society of Friends, at Friends House, Euston Road, London, is the main repository for researching Quaker ancestors and publishes several research guides (**www.quaker.org.uk**). Some copies are held locally at the SSA and at the Friends Meeting

House (Bull Street, Birmingham); details at the Quaker Family History Society (**www.qfhs.co.uk**). The Library of Birmingham holds and is cataloguing the archives of the Society's Central England Area Meeting, 1662–*c.* 2000.

For other Nonconformist sources see specialist guides such as Ratcliffe (2014) and Milligan & Thomas (1999).

THE JEWISH COMMUNITY

During the nineteenth century a small Jewish community established itself in the Potteries. Initially, Hebrew services, in the Ashkenazi Orthodox tradition, were held in a private house in Marsh Street, Hanley. The community made efforts to find a more permanent and suitable home, leading to the purchase of an old Welsh Chapel in Hanover Street in 1873. In 1900 there were around thirty-five seatholders.

At a general meeting of the Congregation in 1902 the Chief Rabbi, Dr Alder, called for the erection of a new synagogue. Two adjacent properties in Birch Terrace, Hanley, were purchased and a new synagogue opened there a few years later. This remained in use until 2004, when the site was sold and the Congregation relocated to London Road, Newcastle-under-Lyme.

The latter is the location of the Jewish cemetery serving both Stoke-on-Trent and Newcastle. The land was given to the Jewish community in the 1850s by the Duke of Sutherland. Under Hebrew law land that is used as a burial ground must be bought, so a fee of £1 was charged. The first burial took place in 1886. In 1974 the cemetery chapel was demolished to make way for a road-widening scheme and in 2004 the replacement chapel was demolished to accommodate the relocated synagogue from Hanley.

Records of the Stoke-on-Trent and Newcastle-under-Lyme Congregation, as well as articles and other material relating to the Jewish community in the Potteries, may be accessed through the Jewish Communities and Records website, **www.jewishgen.org/jcr-uk/ Community/stoke/index.htm**. The STCA does not hold any Jewish registers of life events, however the general minutes of the Hebrew Congregation in Hanley, 1889–1916 and of the Stoke-on-Trent

Congregation, 1948–73 on microfilm may contain the names of some members.

CEMETERIES AND BURIAL GROUNDS
Principal Cemeteries
By the middle of the nineteenth century the burgeoning population was outgrowing the churchyards and calls were made for separate, municipally owned burial grounds.

In Hanley the issue got caught up in proposals to provide a public park. However, the Shelton-based potter John Ridgway argued that provision of a cemetery was more pressing. When the Borough of Hanley was incorporated in 1857, Ridgway was elected its first Mayor and helped to form a Burial Board Committee. The following year the Committee secured a site in Shelton and a competition was launched for the laying out of the cemetery grounds and the design of new chapels. Hanley Cemetery opened in 1860 and the populace had to wait until 1897 for the opening of Hanley Park.

Longton launched a design competition in 1872, prior to the opening of Longton Cemetery in 1878. The original site covered approximately 7.4 hectares (about 21 acres) and has been extended several times. Tunstall Cemetery was also laid out during this period, on part of Tunstall Farm, and opened in 1868. Burslem Cemetery opened in 1879 and covers approximately 11.4 hectares (about 28 acres). It was intended as 'a recreation park, to be used for walking, riding and driving', as well as a cemetery, and at least a third of the land was taken up with the lodges, chapel, walks and drives. Only about 5½ acres was laid out for burials.

Stoke Cemetery, known as Hartshill, opened in 1884. The site chosen was not a popular one because it was so far away from the town, between the villages of Hartshill and Penkhull. There was also public disquiet about the choice of architect and the number of chapels. Without consulting ratepayers, the Council accepted a petition from leading Anglicans that there should be one chapel 'for church people' and another for 'dissenters' and agreed to build two chapels.

The last of the Six Towns to get its own cemetery was Fenton. This was laid out in 1887 on a 16½-acre site in the north-east of the town, on sloping ground at the rear of Fenton Park. This too had separate chapels for Anglicans and Nonconformists.

Today, there are nine cemeteries administered by Stoke-on-Trent City Council. Opening times are given on the Council website, which also has a list of closed churchyards across the Six Towns (**www.stoke. gov.uk/directory/26/cemeteries_and_churchyards**). Other municipal cemeteries in the district include those at Newcastle-under-Lyme (opened 1866), Silverdale (1886) and Knutton (1888).

Cemetery and Burial Records

Burial records from all of the city's cemeteries are kept at Carmountside Cemetery and Crematorium. These are arranged in date order and there is no name index. Enquiries and search requests should be sent to the Carmountside Cemetery Office at the address given in Appendix 2.

 Staffordshire Burial Indexes

BMSGH

Stoke on Trent Archives

Introduction

These indexes were created from images provided by the Staffordshire and Stoke on Trent Archive Service. These images may be viewed in the searchrooms of the Archive Service only and not online.

In each case it is advisable to book space on a computer before you visit and contact details for all three offices can be found on the General Enquiries Archives page.

Staffordshire Record Office:	All cemeteries
Stoke on Trent City Archives:	Stoke-on-Trent City and Newcastle Borough cemeteries
Lichfield Record Office:	All cemeteries

The information recorded in the registers differ from cemetery to cemetery. No burial register entries will record the cause of death: this information is on the death certificate only. Some registers record a grave location, others simply provide a grave number.

The Archive Service's ACRE project to film cemetery registers was funded initially by the Heritage Lottery Fund and subsequently by the County Council and the Friends of the Staffordshire and Stoke on Trent Archive Service. The filming was carried out by Worcester Record Office.

Search the Burial Indexes

Cemetery Maps

- Audley Cemetery
- Attwood Street Cemetery
- Burslem Cemetery
- Carmountside Cemetery
- Chesterton Cemetery
- Eccleshall Road Cemetery
- Fenton Cemetery
- Hanley Cemetery
- Keele Grave Layout
- Knutton Cemetery
- Longton Cemetery
- Lonsdale Street Cemetery, Stoke
- Madeley Cemetery with phase 2
- Newcastle Cemetery
- New Stone Road Cemetery
- Rugeley Stile Cop Cemetery
- Rugeley Wolseley Road Cemetery
- Silverdale Cemetery
- Smallthorne Cemetery
- Stoke Cemetery
- Stone Cemetery
- Tixall Road Crematorium
- Trentham Cemetery
- Tunstall Cemetery

The Staffordshire Burial Index website.

Midland Ancestors maintains the Staffordshire Burial Index, an index of burials created from cemetery registers held by the SSA. The transcripts may be searched online at **www.bmsgh.org/burialsearch/** and the original images may be viewed in the search rooms at the STCA or SRO. The information recorded in the registers differs from cemetery to cemetery: some record a grave location, others simply provide a grave number.

Parish and cemetery burials in Staffordshire are listed in the National Burial Index from indexes compiled by Midland Ancestors; it is available as a DVD and online at Findmypast. The Federation of Family History Societies website has a list of burial grounds covered (**www.ffhs.org. uk/burials/sts3.php**).

Monumental Inscriptions

Over the last forty years Midland Ancestors volunteers have transcribed the monumental inscriptions (MIs) from graves, tombstones and memorials across Staffordshire. These transcriptions have been published and many are now available either on CD-ROM or as downloads. The indexes are also open to postal and/or email enquiries. Copies of these MIs may be consulted at the Midland Ancestors Reference Library (Birmingham), the SSA search rooms, and the Society of Genealogists in London.

Other sources for information on deaths include newspaper announcements and obituaries, and wills (see Chapter 1).

CHARTISM AND TRADES UNIONS
Chartism in the Potteries

The Potteries' association with the labour movement goes back to the very beginnings of organized labour and the political reform movement known as Chartism. Under the Reform Act of 1832, Stoke-upon-Trent became a Parliamentary Borough and was able to return two Members of Parliament. However, the Act only went part of the way to meeting the demands of political reformers and during the 1830s a grassroots movement evolved around a wider campaign for political and social reforms. They unveiled their demands in a 'People's Charter', launched in London in 1838, and hence became known as the Chartists.

The People's Charter had six main demands: the vote for all men aged over 21, the abolition of a property qualification, secret ballots, fixed elections, equal sized constituencies and salaried Members of Parliament. A national petition in support of the Charter attracted over 1 million signatures. Mass rallies were held across the country, some of which became violent. The Hanley & Shelton Political Union, established in 1838, was one of many organizations to espouse the Chartist cause. It organized a Grand Meeting in the Potteries on 17 November 1838.

The Potteries avoided the more severe expressions of discontent over the Reform Act seen elsewhere. However, the election of John Davenport, the Longton pottery manufacturer, as one of the first MPs did not prove popular. He was not enthusiastic about the Reform Act and was a severe employer. A contemporary account recorded that 'on the day of nomination, at Stoke, whilst Mr Davenport was addressing the electors, missiles were profusely thrown into the hustings, which inflicted some severe contusions on several gentlemen, and drove the candidates and their friends to seek shelter in the adjoining Town Hall'. There was further trouble in 1837, when Davenport was again elected to Parliament. In 1841, the crowd directed its ire towards Mr Copeland, another pottery manufacturer who was standing for the Conservative Party. According to historian John Ward: 'The Liberal populace then seized and destroyed the banners of the opposite party, routed them in all directions and proceeded to Stoke to demolish the windows of Mr Copeland's manufactory, which they effectively accomplished, as well as the windows of several of his new houses adjacent'.

The most notorious Chartist-related incident in North Staffordshire was in August 1842. A group of workers in the potteries and pits around Hanley were involved in an industrial dispute with their employers and this situation became caught up in wider calls for a general strike in support of the Charter. On Monday, 15 August, Chartists and miners declared that they would join together and 'all labour cease until the People's Charter becomes the law of the land'. The following day, 16 August, the strikers marched on Burslem amid an increasingly inflamed situation. Soldiers were called from Newcastle to disperse the mob, resulting in more than 270 arrests. At their trials the following

October, 54 North Staffordshire men were sentenced to transportation and a further 146 to imprisonment with hard labour. The episode scared working class communities in the Potteries for many years.

One of those imprisoned was Joseph Capper, a blacksmith and preacher from Tunstall. Although he preached a message of peaceful resistance and had not been present at the riot, he was widely seen as one of the ring-leaders and so singled out by the authorities. He served two years in prison and is recognized as one of the key figures in both Chartism and Primitive Methodism in North Staffordshire.

For further details of Chartism see Anderson (1993) and the specialist website **www.chartistancestors.co.uk**.

Growth of Trades Unions

The earliest record of trades unionism among the pottery workers of North Staffordshire can be found in a 1792 newspaper report that records their efforts to combine for better wages. This was a short-lived endeavour and it would take another eighty years for trades unions to become fully established within the pottery industry.

Many of workers' early efforts to form unions were small, specific to particular specialist trades and often brief. The Union of Clay Potters was started to represent the skilled workers handling the early stages of manufacture, and the Pottery Printers Union spoke for those decorating the finished product. In 1825, these two unions called the first official strike in the Potteries but it was soon defeated and the union destroyed. A further attempt to create a China and Earthenware Turners Society in 1830 fared no better.

The following year the National Union of Operative Potters was established, with the aim of recruiting all those working in the industry, including in other parts of the country. A key cause of complaint was the truck system, whereby employees were paid in vouchers or tokens that they could only spend in their employers' shops. Although membership grew to 8,000, the union was again defeated in strikes in 1834 and 1836 and ceased to operate. During the 1840s, such trades unionism as existed in the industry was largely non-confrontational. The United Branches of Operative Potters, founded in 1843, opposed strikes, but proved no more resilient than its predecessors, declining over the following decade to a small local organization. It was revived briefly as the National Order of Potters in 1883 but lasted only a few years. By mid-century, trades-union activity had subsided.

Enduring trades-union organization arrived in the Potteries with the revival of the industry in the 1870s. Yet many of the organizations established over the following twenty years were limited in both numbers and ambition. Among those that formed and quickly disappeared during this period were the Amalgamated Society of Pottery Moulders and Finishers, founded in 1893 and dissolved in 1900; the China Earthenware Gilders Union, which lasted just three years from 1891–4; and the Cratemakers Society, founded in 1872 but no longer in existence by the end of the decade. Many pottery unions struggled to recruit, especially away from their Staffordshire heartlands.

At the beginning of the twentieth century workers' representation was still highly fragmented. There were more than seventy major pottery manufacturers in Stoke-on-Trent, each with hundreds of unique trades and each trade having its own worker representative. In 1906 the three biggest unions merged to form the National Amalgamated Society of Male & Female Pottery Workers. By 1921 most of the remaining unions had joined the renamed National Society of Pottery Workers (NSPW). It had around 60,000 members throughout the country, most of whom worked in Stoke-on-Trent. Many of them had been recruited by the Society's charismatic general secretary, Sam Clowes. In 1970 the NSPW became the Ceramic & Allied Trades Union, which has since been absorbed into the modern trades-union movement.

Trades-Union Records
The Hobson Collection at the STCA comprises a wide range of materials relating to the history of trades unionism in the pottery industry assembled by researcher Stephen Hobson [PA/HOB]. While there are few records relating to individuals, the collection provides valuable social context on working and welfare issues in the sector from the late nineteenth century. Materials include industry wages and prices agreements, papers of unions and employers' organizations, and newspaper cuttings.

The Working Class Movement Library in Salford holds the archives of the Ceramic & Allied Trades Union and its predecessor organizations, including membership returns, newspaper cuttings and wage agreements (**www.wcml.org.uk**).

The Modern Records Centre at the University of Warwick has substantial collections of trades-union and labour movement archives. These files may include details such as membership lists, contributions books, minutes of branch meetings, wage rates, company files, and accident and mortality reports. The holdings range from long-defunct local organizations; to Midlands branches of early national unions; to the national archives of current-day trades unions.

Crail (2009) and that author's specialist website **www.union ancestors.co.uk** have further details on tracing trades-union ancestors.

FURTHER INFORMATION

Anderson, Robert, *The Potteries Martyrs: Chartism in North Staffordshire* (Military Heritage Books, 1993)

Burchill, Frank and Richard Ross, *A History of the Potters' Union* (Ceramic & Allied Trades Union, 1977)

Crail, Mark, *Tracing Your Labour Movement Ancestors* (Pen & Sword, 2009)

Greenslade, Michael, *Catholic Staffordshire* (Gracewing, 2006)

Milligan, E.H. and M.J. Thomas, *My Ancestors Were Quakers* (Society of Genealogists, 1999)

Ratcliffe, Richard, *Methodist Records for Family Historians* (Family History Partnership, 2014)

Chapter 5

CIVIC SOCIETY

WORKHOUSES AND THE POOR LAW
The Workhouse System
The use of workhouses to house the poor began with the introduction of the Poor Law Act of 1601 and witnessed a rapid growth during the eighteenth century. Each parish maintained its own workhouse, which in general was able to accommodate between 30 and 100 inmates. Penkhull workhouse was built in 1735, for the parish of Stoke, opposite St Thomas's Church and could accommodate 80 paupers. Burslem's 1780s workhouse was at Greenhead and was extended in 1835 to hold 300 people. Wolstanton workhouse was at the north-east end of the Marsh, near the church and village, and could accommodate around 100. Often inmates from these establishments were provided with work at local manufactories, with the bulk of their earnings going to the parish.

Under the Poor Law Amendment Act of 1834 responsibility for administering poor relief passed to new Poor Law unions (PLUs). The Act had been passed in response to the rising costs involved in providing poor relief, and allowed parishes to group together in order to tackle the problem jointly. These inter-parish collaborations were known as PLUs and their formation led to a building boom as small parish workhouses were either expanded or replaced by larger institutions. Often the new workhouses were built outside the existing centres of population, creating isolated communities for people who might already have been displaced from their home parish. In certain cases outdoor relief was offered to paupers within their own homes, so avoiding the expense of being taken in as a workhouse resident.

Due to its large population, Stoke-upon-Trent formed its own PLU

Chell workhouse with the superintendents Mr and Mrs Burden. (Public domain)

and did not need to join with other parishes. At that time Stoke-upon-Trent PLU covered Hanley, Stoke, Fenton and Longton. The 1834 Act came at a crucial time for Stoke as the existing workhouse was mired in crisis. Two of the officers had been convicted of embezzlement, while at the same time the Potter's Union had declared its intention to take over the administration of relief and use the rates to support industrial action. An investigation by the Poor Law Commission led to the setting up of a new Stoke-upon-Trent PLU governed by an elected Board of twenty-four Guardians.

The original Penkhull workhouse was replaced in 1832 by a new and remote one on London Road, known as the Spittals. This soon grew from its original two blocks. In 1842 a school house, hospital and vagrants' wards were added; followed by a new school block and chapel in 1866, with further additions through into the early twentieth century. Capacity was increased to 500 people after 1836 and to 800 people by 1855. Similar investments in new workhouses were made at Wolsanton & Burslem PLU in 1838 (for a site on Turnhurst Road, Chell able to accommodate 400 inmates); and at Newcastle-under-Lyme PLU in

1838–9 (for a site in Keele Road with 350 beds). The latter replaced nine smaller parish workhouses within the Newcastle-under-Lyme area.

Under the post-1834 regime more work was provided within the premises, which was part of the aim to make workhouses repellent to the poor. They became self-sufficient, even to the extent of having a wharf on the canal over the road to bring in stone for the vagrants to break. As numbers increased so did the facilities necessary to supply all aspects of life. Strict principles of segregation were enforced, in particular to differentiate between the 'deserving' and 'undeserving' poor. Not only was there separation between men and women, but also between the elderly/infirm and those who were deemed fit enough to work.

Outdoor relief continued, however, in the Potteries more than elsewhere. When in the 1870s the Local Government Board campaigned against outdoor relief at a series of meetings in Staffordshire, the chairman of Stoke's guardians led opposition to the plan. Between 1871 and 1876 the number of recipients of outdoor relief in Stoke fell by 9 per cent, compared with 33 per cent for England and Wales as a whole. The Wolstanton & Burslem Union also resisted the campaign, having one of the highest proportions of paupers on outdoor relief in the country: 92 per cent in 1870 and 89 per cent in 1885, at a time when some unions had less than 30 per cent.

Boards of Guardians were elected by ratepayers and made up of respectable traders, businessmen and the local gentry. The Guardians employed a master and matron, as well as medical officers, nurses, teachers and other staff. They oversaw a regime that was grim and unforgiving. On admission, inmates were stripped of all their clothes and given a bath, for many the first of their lives. They would then be put into workhouse clothes (it was an offence to abscond while wearing them) and segregated by age and gender. The daily routine was hard work, with education or training for the children, interspersed by innutritious, unappetizing meals.

The workhouse struck fear into all who came into contact with it. Charles Shaw, who entered the Chell workhouse in 1842 as a 10-year-old boy, wrote of his experiences in his autobiography *When I Was a Child*:

I had heard of workhouse skilly but had never before seen it. I had had poor food before this, but never any so offensively poor as this. By that rare culinary-making nausea and bottomless fatuousness it could be made so sickening I never could make out. Simple meal and water, however small the amount of meal, honestly boiled, would be palatable. But this decoction of meal and water and mustiness and fustiness was most revolting to any healthy taste. It might have been boiled in old clothes, which had been worn upon sweating bodies for three-score years and ten. That workhouse skilly was the vilest compound I ever tasted.

Shaw's account inspired Arnold Bennett in his *Clayhanger* trilogy, where Darius Clayhanger, father of the book's protagonist Edwin Clayhanger, experiences a very similar episode as a child in the local workhouse: 'the Bastille'. The workhouse remained a feature of life until the early twentieth century. In the case of Chell, the city council acquired the building in 1930: it later became the Westcliffe Institution and then the Westcliffe Home for the Aged, prior to demolition in 2010.

Higginbotham (2007), as well that author's excellent website (**www.workhouses.org.uk**), and Baker (1984) have further information on workhouses in North Staffordshire.

Workhouse Records
Workhouses were a feature of daily life before the welfare state and most people's ancestors would have come into contact with them at some point in their lives.

The Board of Guardians generated an enormous amount of records. Admission and discharge registers generally show full name, date of admission, date of birth, abode, occupation and marital status, and date of discharge. Creed registers were a way of ensuring inmates' religious needs were met. Apprenticeship records document those indentured to local tradesmen and servants registers show who was put as hired hands to factories or farms, or into domestic service. Punishment books include name, date, offence, punishment and often a comment on character. Other records cover the administration of the workhouse and those who worked there. Minutes of meetings were produced and often

Creed register for Wolstanton & Burslem Poor Law Union, 1887. (Courtesy of Staffordshire & Stoke-on-Trent Archives, SA/CW/8)

reported verbatim in the local newspaper. There are also reports from sub-committees formed to investigate and report back on various subjects, and details of tenders received from local traders and who was awarded the job.

Most of the Potteries was covered by the Stoke-on-Trent, Wolstanton & Burslem and Newcastle-under-Lyme unions. Adjacent authorities, which might also be worth consulting, were: Stone PLU, covering Trentham, Hanford and Blurton (workhouse at Stafford Road in Stone); Cheadle PLU, covering Caverswall (workhouse at Bank Street, Cheadle); and Leek PLU, covering Norton-in-the-Moors (workhouse on the Ashbourne Road, south of Leek).

Unfortunately the survival of workhouse registers across Staffordshire as a whole is very poor. Of eighteen PLUs, workhouse admissions and discharge registers have survived for just six. Stoke-upon-Trent is the sole representative from North Staffordshire and those records relate to the period 1836–8 only. These are covered within an online index of admissions and discharges for Staffordshire workhouses between 1836 and 1900 at Staffordshire Name Indexes (**www.staffsnameindexes.org.uk**). The survival rate for birth, death, creed and other registers is better: Stoke-on-Trent Union, Wolstanton

& Burslem Union and their successor the Stoke & Wolstanton Union are all represented, although some records are still subject to the 100-year closure rule. The Gateway to the Past online catalogue lists what is available (select PLUs as Collection Type) and there is also a handlist in the STCA Search Room.

Before 1834 poor relief was overseen by the parish, either through poorhouses or through out relief for those at home. Records for both, where they survive, are most likely to be found among the papers of the parish overseer: as for example with Norton-in-the-Moors [STCA: SA/C-C/5].

CHILDREN'S HOMES

By the late nineteenth century there was increasing recognition that the workhouse was not an appropriate environment for orphaned or destitute children. New institutions were set up away from the workhouse in airy rural locations, organized along the lines of a village community. These so-called 'cottage homes' provided accommodation for pauper children from age 3 upwards.

Cottage homes came rather late to North Staffordshire compared with elsewhere. It was not until 1901 that the Stoke Guardians built Penkhull Cottage Homes on land adjacent to Grindley Hill Farm in Newcastle Lane. The original development comprised twelve homes, a receiving block and a house for the superintendent, Mr Till, whose wife was the homes' matron. Each home accommodated around a dozen children under the care of a house 'mother'. By the time of their official opening the homes were already full with 140 children in residence aged from 1 upwards. The children's natural mothers were allowed to visit once a week. The addition of a further ten homes in 1924 increased the total capacity to 300 children. The homes continued in operation until the 1980s; actor Neil Morrissey is a former resident. There were similar cottage homes at Cheadle and Alsagers Bank, operated by the Cheadle and Newcastle-under-Lyme unions respectively.

In addition to the Penkhull Cottage Homes, the Stoke & Wolstanton Union operated a number of scattered homes. In 1924, these were located at: Basford Hall, Basford; Oxford Road, Basford; and 2 Stanley Street. The latter had been inherited from the Wolstanton & Burslem

PLU at its merger with the Stoke-upon-Trent PLU in 1922. These homes appear to have ceased operating by about 1930.

A new type of establishment emerged in the 1850s, in response to the creation of the Reformatory School system by an Act of 1854. Reformatory Schools were places of detention for convicted juvenile offenders who were first required to spend two weeks in an adult prison. When a campaign to remove this requirement proved unsuccessful, an alternative institution was proposed, the Certified Industrial School, which was aimed at younger and less serious cases, and omitted the prison element. Further Acts in 1857 and 1861 defined the categories of offences in greater detail.

The Stafford County Industrial School for Boys was established at Werrington, about 4 miles to the east of Stoke-on-Trent in 1868. Pupils were first admitted in January 1870, there being accommodation for 107 boys aged 10 years or over. Mr Benjamin Horth and his wife Emily were appointed as superintendent and matron, with James Horth as schoolmaster and assistant. The School originally had 7 acres of land attached and a further 26 acres were rented in 1873, with field and garden work providing the boys' main industrial employment in its early years. Training in tailoring, shoemaking and basket-making was provided.

In 1933, Werrington became an Approved School, one of the new institutions introduced by the 1933 Children and Young Persons Act to replace the existing system of Reformatories and Industrial Schools. It accommodated up to 120 boys aged under 13. In 1955 the site was taken over by the Prison Service and now forms the basis for Werrington Young Offenders Institution. Staffordshire Record Office has various records, including admission and discharge books, dating mainly from the 1890s.

North Staffordshire Training Home for Girls, Cliffe House, Hill Street, Stoke was a Certified School for young women, similar to the Industrial Schools. At Hanley, there were several Magdalen Homes, operated by various Christian and charitable organizations. Other institutions in the area included: North Staffordshire Blind School at The Mount, Greatbach Avenue, Stoke-on-Trent; and North Staffordshire Hostel for Mothers and Babies, 2 Enderley Street,

Newcastle-under-Lyme. During the twentieth century many of these institutions were taken over by Stoke-on-Trent Borough Council or equivalent local authorities.

Peter Higginbotham's Children's Homes website has lists of homes, with some histories, together with bibliographic references where available (**www.childrenshomes.org.uk**).

The STCA has records for certain homes including an admission register for Penkhull, 1908–16 [SA/PCH]: check the Gateway to the Past online catalogue for details. Such records are classed as highly sensitive and are subject to the 100-year closure rule.

HOSPITALS

The Potteries' transformation into an industrial centre during the late eighteenth century brought a need for organized medical provision. The first hospital, known as the 'House of Recovery', opened to the public in 1804 at Etruria, on land donated by Josiah Wedgwood II. Construction was undertaken by Francis Coxon of Hanley, who delivered a handsome, good-quality brick building, three storeys high. During the first 9 years over 5,000 patients were treated and by 1814 demand was such that an extension began to be discussed.

The House of Recovery's cramped position made expansion difficult and it was decided to build a second hospital instead. The Wedgwoods again provided the land (this time through sale), a site being chosen at Wood Hills, on the turnpike road from Etruria Wharf to Cobridge. The new facility opened on 22 April 1819, with another representative of the great pottery families, Josiah Spode, as chairman of the governors. This, too, was gradually expanded as demand rose. Among the additions were new wards for the treatment of burns and scalds, many of the casualties coming from the nearby Earl Granville's ironworks.

In 1861 experts reported that the whole hospital was threatened by subsidence. Moreover, Etruria itself was becoming more and more polluted. An infamous mound of refuse from the Slippery Pit colliery and ironworks, known as Tinkersclough tip, grew by the day and came within 150yd of the building. The tip burned and smouldered continuously and was the cause of many children being burnt or overcome by fumes. William Yates of Eastwood, Hanley offered £5,000

North Staffordshire Infirmary, c. 1915. (Public domain)

for the building of a new Infirmary on another site, provided he was paid £250 per annum for life. The Governors decided to accept. The offer proved extremely timely: Yates died a few days after signing the cheque and the Infirmary received the full benefit.

The Potteries' third hospital, the North Staffordshire Infirmary, opened at Hartshill in 1869. It was one of the first English hospitals to be built on the pavilion system favoured by Florence Nightingale, meaning that all the buildings were positioned around a large central courtyard. Known later as the North Staffordshire Royal Infirmary and Eye Hospital, it remained the district's principal general hospital for over a hundred years, before merging with the nearby Orthopaedic Hospital and City General Hospital to form the University Hospital of North Staffordshire. As a result, new facilities were built and all services were transferred to the new single site in 2012.

Other hospitals within the Potteries included: Longton Hospital (founded in 1867); Haywood Hospital, Burslem (founded in 1881); and the Orthopaedic Hospital of the North Staffordshire Cripples' Aid Society (founded in 1916 and mentioned above).

Alun Davies's *The North Staffordshire Royal Infirmary, 1802–1948* (Churnet Valley Books, 2006) charts the history of the NSRI from its inception through to the formation of the National Health Service. Lawley (2011) offers a pictorial history of Stoke-on-Trent's hospitals. The Voluntary Hospitals Database has detailed time series and statistics on the growth of individual hospitals from the mid-nineteenth century, such as number of beds, number of nurses and expenditure on in-patients and out-patients (**www.hospitalsdatabase.lshtm.ac.uk**).

Although local repositories have substantial holdings relating to hospitals, individual patient records seldom survive and those that do are subject to strict confidentiality conditions. Patient records are closed for up to 100 years but close relatives may be able to gain access by filing a Freedom of Information Act request to the relevant authority. The Wellcome/National Archives Hospital Records Database is the best finding aid: it documents the existence and location of the records of UK hospitals, based on information provided by the repositories concerned (**https://data.gov.uk/dataset/hospital-records**). For some establishments staff records may also be available.

Staffordshire and Stoke-on-Trent Archives holds records for North Staffordshire (Royal) Infirmary and predecessor institutions, 1742–1975 under numerous headings and split between the STCA and SRO. Name-rich series include an admissions and discharge book from the early 1880s [SD 1321/36]; a subscriptions book for 'Hospital Saturday', 1935–48 (a pre-NHS care scheme) [D6140]; nursing staff records, 1913–82 [D6020]; and general staff records, 1900–79 [SD 1611].

Other health series are: the records of Westcliffe Hospital, Chell, *c.* 1930–74 [SD 1552]; registers of tuberculosis and infantile mortality for North Staffordshire, 1934–92 [D5786]; pre-NHS medical records for Norton-in-the-Moors [SD 1633]; and materials from the Hanley Nursing Society, 1895–1982 [SD 1260]. There are also miscellaneous health-related photographs from the 1960s [SD 1624]; and notes, photographs and cuttings from a television documentary about City General Hospital made in 1985 [SA/CGH]. The Potteries Museum Collection has some registers of pottery workers found to be suffering from silicosis and asbestosis in the 1930s and 1940s [SD4842/1/61]. Local authority series include the records of the Commissioners and

Boards of Health for each of the Six Towns but these are mainly administrative.

For professional registrations of doctors see the *UK Medical Registers, 1859–1959* dataset and of nurses the *UK & Ireland, Nursing Registers, 1898–1968*, both on Ancestry.

ASYLUMS

While the welfare of the general populace was of widespread concern, the same could not be said for that of the mentally ill. Only during the second half of the nineteenth century did adequate provision start to be made for those suffering various forms of mental illness.

The Victorians had a rather sweeping definition of the term 'insanity': many of the patients ('inmates' would probably be a better term) were suffering from post-natal depression, epilepsy, alcoholism or other minor afflictions. From 1871, the census returns made special provision for those with mental health problems, describing patients as either 'idiots', 'imbeciles' or 'lunatics'. The distinctions are somewhat vague and overlapping but those suffering from dementia were mostly described as 'imbeciles'.

A number of asylums are likely to have taken patients from the Potteries. The main facility was the North Staffordshire Asylum, Cheadle Road, Cheddleton, near Leek. It was designed and built between 1893 and 1897 by Giles, Gough & Trollope, who designed many such establishments. The water tower is credited as being 'the highest structure in Staffordshire Moorlands'. It became Staffordshire Mental Hospital in 1948, then St Edward's Mental Hospital, and later St Edward's Hospital, Near Leek. In 1979 it had around 900 patients but closed in 2001 and was subsequently converted into a series of apartments and houses. Chadwick & Pearson (1993) provides a more detailed history. Kivland (2001) is a collection of four books of memoirs of this hospital, including maps and drawings by patients and references to the rules and regulations that applied to staff.

Prior to the opening of Cheddleton, patients would have been sent to the Staffordshire County Asylum at Stafford. This opened in around 1818 and initially had accommodation for up to 120. By 1844 there were 245 patients, of whom 183 were paupers and 62 were private.

The sprawling Cheddleton Asylum, Leek, later known as St Edward's Hospital. (Public domain)

Conditions had recently been improved due to an outbreak of dysentery. In succeeding years demand for its services was eased by the opening of new asylums at Coton Hill, Stafford, in 1854 and Burntwood, in the south of the county, in 1864. Coton Hill catered for private patients from the middle and upper classes. It closed in 1976 when, apart from the chapel and the lodges, it was demolished and the new Stafford District General Hospital was built on the site. The A Turn of the Key website documents its history and memoirs (**https://aturnof thekey.com**).

The history of asylums and the treatment of mental illness are chronicled on Andrew Robert's website (**http://studymore.org.uk**), which includes a comprehensive list of such institutions across England and Wales.

Probably the most useful and widely available asylum records are the admission registers which show that patients were often admitted and discharged within a short space of time. As with hospital records, these are closed to the public for 100 years but may be accessed by close family members. The authorities had little respect for patients' identities and it is not uncommon to find just initials or first names listed in institution registers and census returns. Documents within the SSA catalogue for Cheddleton County Lunatic Asylum are limited to the building itself and no patient records are listed [see under 'Lunacy', series Q/AI]. There is a limited run for other asylums, including Stafford, 1858–9 [Q/AIc/1/3/2] and SpringVale (a private asylum), 1833 [Q/AIp].

Many asylums, or former asylums, are included in the Wellcome/ National Archives Hospital Records Database (see above). Some patient lists from county asylums can be found at TNA (Class MH).

SCHOOLS, UNIVERSITIES AND COLLEGES
The Growth of Education

It is difficult to believe that not many generations ago few children received a full-time education, and of those who did most were unable to continue their studies beyond elementary level unless they were exceptionally bright or of wealthy backgrounds. In the first half of the nineteenth century it was not uncommon for local children over the age of 5 to work 60 hours a week in the potbanks and mines. The harsh conditions they experienced there have already been noted (see Chapter 2). Urged on by poverty and improvidence, parents had little choice but to put their children to work at the earliest opportunity.

The first attempts to rectify the situation came from the Church. Both Anglicans and Dissenters ran Sunday schools where children received a moral education as well as some instruction in the 'three Rs'. One such was the Bethesda Schoolrooms in Hanley, opened by the New Connexion Methodists in 1818. This hugely impressive two-storey building with Flemish bond brickwork and a stuccoed gable provided for more than 1,000 children, who were taught to read and write, and also instructed in religious and general knowledge. Teachers and scholars had access to its extensive library (known as the 'Bethesda General and Juvenile Libraries'), which also served a large number of external subscribers.

Besides the Bethesda School, the New Methodists had four other chapels and schools at Eastwood Vale, Etruria, Hanley Upper Green and Shelton. Meanwhile, the Wesleyans had schools alongside their chapels at Etruria and Old Hall Street; and the Independents had three schools at the Tabernacle, Hanley; Hope Chapel; and Brunswick Chapel, Shelton. Not to be left out, the Baptists catered for 200 at their Sunday school and the Primitive Methodists taught 180 alongside their chapel at Shelton. The Burslem Ragged School in Greenhead Street was for destitute children who could not afford even the small charge at the Hill Top Sunday School, which was only a few hundred yards away.

As the nineteenth century progressed different types of schools emerged, divided broadly between private and charity. Many were funded by the National Society for Promoting the Education of the Poor in the Principles of the Established Church, founded in 1811, and were known as 'National Schools'. Having close links to the Church of England, the Society aimed to provide a basic education while stemming the influence of Nonconformists. National Schools opened in Lichfield Street, Hanley, in 1815, for 300 day scholars, and St Mark's, Shelton, for 150 day scholars. The British & Foreign Schools Society, largely supported by Nonconformists, had schools at Hanley, Cobridge, Tunstall and Burslem. By 1842, there were only 2,831 day school places in the Potteries and not all of those were filled. By contrast, attendance at Sunday schools approached 18,000.

The Education Act of 1870 introduced compulsory state education for children aged 5–13 inclusive. Many new schools were built to house the sudden upsurge of pupils. The school leaving age steadily increased, from age 10 in 1893, to 12 in 1918, to 14 in 1944 as a result of the Butler Education Act. Following the Six Towns' Federation, responsibility for schools passed to the new Stoke-on-Trent Education Committee.

School Records
Records from many nineteenth-century schools have survived and are available online or via local archives. Staffordshire school admission registers to 1914, held by the SSA, have been published on Findmypast as part of the National School Admission Registers Project. The SSA website has a list of the registers that are included (**https://tinyurl.com/y773xvkj**). Log books for schools that were the responsibility of Stoke-on-Trent City Council are held at the STCA with a handlist in the search room [SA/ED/LOG]. These relate mainly to the management of the school and few children's names are mentioned. There are also a few punishment books, for example, for Eastwood Vale Infants School, 1888–1911 [SD 1532]. Burslem Ragged School records are filed

The log book for Middleport Girls School, 1907. The entry for 25 November notes: 'A day's holiday is granted today in consequence of a vote of the ratepayers being taken on the Federation of all the Pottery towns'. (Courtesy of Staffordshire & Stoke-on-Trent Archives, SD1241/2/1)

separately [SD 1395], as are those for Middleport Schools, 1877–2001 [SD 1241]; and there is a long series for Dr Hulme's Educational Foundation, 1708–1952.

Many school records fall within the 100-year closure rule and may not be accessible. More general files relating to education within the city (both pre- and post-Federation) are also under reference SA/ED, including a Staff Register for 1900–8 from the Staffordshire Potteries Pupil Teachers' Centre [STCA: SA/ED/73].

Adult and Higher Education

Children were not the only ones recognized as being able to benefit from education. Adult education for working men, particularly in technical subjects, was seen as a means of 'self-improvement'. Mechanics' Institutes catered for this adult working class, providing them with an alternative pastime to gambling and drinking in pubs. Often they were funded by local industrialists, who recognized the benefits from having more knowledgeable and skilled employees.

114

The Mechanics' Institution, Hanley, was founded in 1826 for 'the promotion of useful knowledge among the working classes' at the instigation of Benjamin Vale, then curate of Stoke and later Rector of Longton, and with the support of Josiah Wedgwood and other leading local men. Its origins can be traced back to The Pottery Philosophical Society, which was established at the Red Lion Inn, Shelton in 1820, with a largely middle-class membership. The Institution prospered, especially the library, and in 1861 it moved from Frederick Street to new premises in Pall Mall. In 1887, most of the building was acquired by the Free Library, with the Mechanics' Institution museum becoming the nucleus of the Borough Museum.

Later the Workers' Educational Association grew up to provide continuing education to the working class and was particularly strong in North Staffordshire. The STCA has a long series of records, 1929–94 [SD 1665].

Free public libraries were another innovation of the Victorian age. Until then, access to libraries, like education, had been restricted to those who could pay. James Straphan, a bookseller, founded the Pottery Subscription Library at Hanley in 1790. By 1840 the library, consisting of some 3,000 volumes, was housed in the shop of Thomas Allbut, who had succeeded Straphan as librarian and treasurer. Members were elected and paid an entrance fee of 2 guineas and an annual subscription of 1 guinea. The library was still in existence in 1860. A similar facility, the Shelton Subscription Library, was founded in 1814 and housed in the Bethesda Schoolroom. Prior to the establishment of the free Borough Library in 1887, there was a subscription newspaper room at Hanley Town Hall.

From the mid-nineteenth century new technical, vocational and arts colleges were set up to meet the growing needs of the local pottery, mining and construction industries. Foremost among these were the Stoke School of Science & Art, London Road (1860); the Sutherland Institute, Longton (1898); and Burslem School of Art, Queen Street (1907), all of which were housed in suitably grand buildings. Alumni from Burslem included the ceramicist Clarice Cliff (1899–1972); the artist William Bowyer (1926–2015); and Arnold Machin (1911–99), who designed the classic 'plain' British postage stamp and served as headmaster at the Burslem School of Art during the 1940s. Later these institutions were united as Stoke College of Art, which in turn became the Faculty of Art and Design within the new North Staffordshire Polytechnic in 1970 (now Staffordshire University).

Keele University was founded as the University College of North Staffordshire in 1949 and admitted its first 159 students the following year. It was the first new university to be established in Britain following the Second World War. The University is situated on an estate with extensive woods, lakes and parkland, formerly owned by the Sneyd family, and includes Keele Hall. Until the 1990s most students followed a unique four-year course, beginning their studies with a Foundation Year.

Both universities have alumni offices which maintain registers of their graduates. They may be willing to pass on enquiries and requests to former students, subject to data protection regulations.

COURTS, PRISONS AND CRIMINALS
The Court System
Historically, the judicial system in England and Wales relied on Assize Courts and Quarter Sessions, a system that dated back to the twelfth century. Judges rode on horseback from one county town to the next, trying all those charged with more serious criminal offences that could not be dealt with by magistrates or the Quarter Sessions. By the middle of the sixteenth century six assize circuits had developed, each under the control of a Clerk of the Assize. The assizes were normally held twice a year in Lent and Summer. In some counties the assize was an annual event and therefore people could spend many months in prison awaiting trial. Staffordshire was part of the Oxford Circuit, with assizes held at Stafford.

Quarter Sessions were the lower of the two courts and dealt with the lesser, non-capital crimes. As well as dispensing justice, these courts originally collected taxes and other monies due to the Crown. The courts were presided over by knights, called Keepers of the Peace, later known as Justices of the Peace. A statute of 1388 required that these sessions should be held in every quarter of the year – Easter, Trinity, Michaelmas and Epiphany – to be presided over by three Justices of the Peace, and

116

hence they became known as the Quarter Sessions. Justices of the Peace were appointed at the start of each reign by the new monarch, and had to swear an oath of allegiance. They were required to possess 'justice, wisdom and fortitude', and latterly to have a private income in excess of £100 a year.

Changes in Tudor times saw the Quarter Sessions administering the Poor Law and therefore replacing the Sheriff as county administrator. In the centuries that followed they acquired a whole range of other administrative responsibilities, from registering boats and barges, to licensing gamekeepers, printing presses and county militia. Thus, Quarter Sessions records cover much more than petty crime and are a key source for the family historian.

The Potteries was served initially by the Staffordshire Quarter Sessions at Stafford until the establishment of a separate court at Hanley in 1880. In 1846 County Courts, dealing with civil cases, were created. In 1894, many of the administrative functions of the Quarter Sessions, including the Poor Law, were transferred to the new County Councils, although they retained responsibility for licensing, betting and gambling.

Regular Petty Sessions courts began in the eighteenth century, due to the increase in workload for the justices of the Quarter Sessions. These met far more often – daily by the nineteenth century – and dealt with minor crimes, licensing, juvenile offences and civil offences such as bastardy and child maintenance. Under legislation of 1839, a stipendiary magistrate was appointed for the pottery communities, with lock-ups in each of the Six Towns.

Assizes, Quarter Sessions and Petty Sessions were abolished by the Courts Act of 1971 and replaced by the present arrangement of High Courts, Crown Courts and Magistrates Courts.

Court Records

The SRO holds the records for Staffordshire Quarter Sessions under series Q. The best place for family historians to start is with the Order Books [Q/SO] or Printed Order of Court [Q/SOp], which summarize the outcomes of individual cases. From there it may be possible to find supporting documentation in other series. 'Indictments' were charges brought against an accused as a means of beginning criminal proceedings, while 'presentments' were reports by parish officials noting offences in a particular parish [both are catalogued under subseries Q/SPi]. Testimonies given by the accuser and witnesses prior to the case coming to court are found in the depositions [Q/SBd], while examinations of this evidence once the court was in session are contained in the session rolls (also referred to as session bundles or files) [Q/SB, Q/SR]. Petitions to the justices may also be found here but are sometimes catalogued separately.

The most common document – making up the majority of all surviving Quarter Sessions records – was a 'recognizance', which was a bond or obligation entered into between the court and an accused or witness [Q/SPr]. The recipient could be required to attend court either to give evidence or answer a charge. They could also be required to keep the peace (*pace ferund*) or to be of good behaviour (*de se bene gorend*). The principal was required to find two sureties or guarantors, who were bound for £10 each. The idea was that those bound with an offender would act as a restraining influence upon them. If a recognizance was broken and the offender could not pay they would go to gaol.

Further record series deal with appeals and transfers of cases to and from higher and lower courts (the Assizes and Petty Sessions respectively) [Q/SPa, Q/SPk, Q/SPt], and with calendars of prisoners held awaiting trial (see below).

Petty Sessions were held initially in town halls, country houses or public houses. Returns of Petty Sessions convictions are found in the Quarter Sessions bundles, mainly 1850s–70s. There is a separate series for convictions before magistrates sitting in Petty Sessions under series Q/RC, divided into: Convictions [Q/RCc]; Notices of convictions of habitual drunkards [Q/RCd]; Convictions under Juvenile Offenders Act [Q/RCj]; and Registers [Q/RCr]. The SRO has a few surviving records from Petty Sessions held at Trentham Hall, mainly from the period around 1805 [classified under 'Petty Sessions for Pirehill North Hundred'].

Later Petty Sessions records (1886–1939) are under D1123 and there are separate series for the Staffordshire Potteries Stipendiary Magistrates Court, 1871–1939 [D1142 and D3612]. These include court registers,

registers of convictions and orders, juvenile court registers, licensing convictions, bastardy orders, married women orders, and orders of judicial separation. Other series cover petty session cases at Leek, Tunstall, Newcastle, Longton, Cheadle and elsewhere compiled from police records covering various periods, some of which are still closed [series C/PC/].

The records of the Assize courts are at TNA. For the Oxford Circuit these comprise Minute books, 1657–1971 [ASSI 1-3], Indictments, 1627–1971 [ASSI 5], Depositions and Case Papers, 1719–1971 [ASSI 6], Pleadings, 1854–90 [ASSI 8], and Miscellaneous, 1660–1888 [ASSI 4, 9 & 89]. These records are very formal in style, were written mainly in Latin until 1733 and may have gaps. The William Salt Library holds a collection of around 200 Staffordshire Assize Calendars covering the period 1746–1861 with many gaps [WSL: s600/1], with separate volumes for the period 1860–1903 [WSL: D1905] plus some other years. A transcript of four Assize Calendars from 1842–3 has been published in the Fourth Series, Vol. XV (1992) of *Collections for a History of Staffordshire*.

Criminal Cases on the Crown Side of King's Bench in Staffordshire, 1740–1800, in *Collections*, Fourth Series, Vol. XXIV (2010), presents the records of all cases in the Court of King's Bench arising in Staffordshire between those two dates. King's Bench was the supreme court of criminal law for England and Wales, and this is the first publication of its records for the eighteenth century for any English county.

Prisons and Prisoners

In the days before the regular police force, responsibility for local law enforcement fell to the parish. Parish constables acted as law enforcement officers, usually on an unpaid and part-time basis. They were expected to monitor trading standards and public houses, catch rats, restrain loose animals, light signal beacons, provide local lodging and transport for the military, perform building control, attend inquests and collect the parish rates. Most offences could be dealt with by fines, or referral to the Petty or Quarter Sessions (see above). But many parishes maintained their own local lock-up as a place of detention. These were used to detain vagrants and local drunks, as well as more

Irish nationalists interred at Stafford Gaol following the Easter Rising, 1916. (An Post Museum, Dublin)

serious offenders prior to being sent to the nearest gaol. In Leek, for example, the lock-up was part of the Old Town Hall on Market Place.

North Staffordshire had no substantial gaol of its own and, like the rest of the county, relied on the county gaol at Stafford. There has been a gaol at Stafford since the end of the twelfth century. By the eighteenth century there was both a Gaol and a House of Correction, both located near to the town's North Gate. Executions were carried out at Sandyford Meadow along the Stafford to Sandon Road. The new Staffordshire Gaol opened in May 1793 and was substantially enlarged during the nineteenth century. This huge edifice dominated the county town for decades, striking fear into all who saw it, not least because it was the designated site for executions.

Prisoners were put to work on treadwheels, pin-heading or stone-breaking, forms of punishment that also enabled the prisoner to earn his keep. The treadwheels, introduced in 1817, powered the corn mill and pumped water from wells within the prison grounds.

Stafford Gaol grew into a huge complex. The gatehouse stood on Gaol Road and contained the reception ward and a room for the warders. Its roof was used as the place of execution until 1817, when new gallows were built on a cart and brought out before the gatehouse when required. The prison infirmary was originally located in rooms above the governor's house, but was later moved to a new building in the prison grounds to help prevent the spread of infectious diseases. A women's prison was added in 1852 with a separate female infirmary. The most visible landmark was two imposing towers which stood on the corner of Crooked Bridge Road and Gaol Road. These were built in the mid-nineteenth century as accommodation for prison warders and their families. They were found to be unsafe and were demolished in 1953.

In a notorious case in 1820, three young men from the Potteries were convicted of rape, a crime which then carried the death penalty. William Toft was a 21-year-old painter on china; John Walklate, aged 24, was a potter's printer and was known as a good, steady workman; and Daniel Collier, aged 18, worked as a miner. They had been found guilty of raping Hannah Bowers of Sneyd Green. A large crowd travelled from Stoke-on-Trent to Stafford, where the execution was due to be carried out on Saturday, 15 April. Many of them had walked through the night to make sure of their place in front of the gallows. The *Staffordshire Advertiser* of 18 April 1820 carried this account of their execution, as the chaplain started to address the crowd: 'During this address, the prisoners prayed devoutly; and while they were expressing, "Lord, remember me", the drop fell, about five minutes past eight. Walklate died instantly, Toft struggled a little, but Collier was much convulsed. After hanging for the usual time their bodies were cut down, and delivered to their friends.' John Taylor, the Hanley town crier (known as 'Tambourine John'), was charged with retrieving their bodies and they were buried in Hanley churchyard the following day.

The William Palmer website, dedicated to the notorious 'Rugeley Poisoner', has details of other prisoners executed at Stafford (**http://staffscc.net/wppalmer/**), while Standley (1993) documents 200 years of the prison's history. The Capital Punishment website (**www.capitalpunishmentuk.org**) has listings of all known British executions back to 1735, together with information on the methods used.

The SRO has early records for gaols and houses of correction within the Staffordshire County Quarter Sessions [Q/AG]. The individual series are:

- Stafford Bridewell Register, 1792–1806 [D(W)1723/1].
- Stafford House of Correction Register, 1806–15 [D(W)1723/2].
- Stafford Register of Debtors, 1793–1807 [D(W)1723/3].
- Stafford Register of Felons, 1793–1816 [D(W)1723/4-5].
- HM Prison, Stafford, Registers, Admission and Discharge Books, 1878–1964 [D5112].

SNI has an extensive list (known as a calendar) of prisoners who appeared at Staffordshire Quarter Sessions, 1779–1900. The Stafford Gaol Photograph Albums Index, 1877–1916 on the same site comprises around 6,300 entries of prisoners compiled from surviving photograph albums [D5112 and 6957].

The Discharged Prisoners Aid Society, North Staffordshire branch has a list of those donating to the charity, 1865–1917 [P(L)/6/4].

Other Judical Records

Every year parish officers drew up new lists of those qualified for jury service at the Quarter Sessions. The list was then displayed in the parish so that objections could be made. Under the Act for Better Regulation of Juries, 1730, jury panels were selected from the jury lists by lot, with the intention of preventing eligible jurors of higher social status from evading their responsibilities through undue influence with local officials.

Jury lists are found in the Quarter Session records. They generally show: surname and forename(s), place of residence, parish and hundred, and title/nature of qualification. Staffordshire Jurors' Lists, 1811–31 are on SNI; survival is good for North Pirehill hundred, the area covering most of the Potteries, as well as for North Totmonslow hundred (Leek and the Staffordshire Moorlands).

Although an ancient office dating back to Norman times, the Coroner's system as we know it today stems from the Victorian era. There was growing concern that, given the easy and uncontrolled access to numerous poisons and inadequate medical investigation of the actual cause of death, many homicides were going undetected. Under the

Coroners Act of 1887, coroners lost many of their earlier fiscal powers and became more concerned with determining the circumstances and the actual medical causes of sudden, violent and unnatural deaths.

The Coroner's involvement in investigating a death will be shown on the death certificate. If a post-mortem were held (but no inquest), this will be indicated in the 'cause of death' section on the certificate as: 'Certified by [coroner's name] . . . after post mortem without inquest'. If an inquest was deemed necessary, the certificate will give the date it was held and the verdict: 'accidental death', 'natural causes', 'murdered', 'took own life', etc.

Coroners' records are generally held in the Quarter Sessions archives. In North Staffordshire coroners reported initially to the Quarter Sessions for the Borough of Newcastle-under-Lyme, and later also for the Borough of Hanley. A limited run of nineteenth-century coroners' reports survive and are listed in the Quarter Sessions Coroners' Reports, 1850–61 index on SNI. These derive from police reports relating to coroners' cases rather than the court's own records. Case papers can be consulted at the SRO under reference Q/APr/7. Coroners' inquests would almost certainly be reported in the newspapers and this may be the only source of information for cases outside the period covered by the SNI indexes.

CHARITIES AND FRIENDLY SOCIETIES

The juxtaposition of avid social reformers alongside conditions of grinding poverty made the Potteries a natural breeding ground for charitable efforts. Outraged by the plight of the urban poor, people of a charitable disposition – many though not exclusively Nonconformists – banded together to perform social works. Their targets were numerous. Women and families were frequent recipients, in particular children and unmarried mothers; the elderly and infirm, prostitutes and drunkards were cared for too. Some operated their own homes, refuges and schools, while others sent volunteers out into the communities. Missions overseas were also supported, especially by church groups.

A prominent charity was the North Staffordshire Cripples' Aid Society which ran the Cripples' Hospital at Hartshill. It was founded by Sydney Malkin, a prominent businessman and Mayor of Burslem. The

Society was initially located at Hanchurch, before moving to Wodehouse Street, Stoke, where mothers would bring their disabled children for treatment. Demand was such that new premises had to be found and Malkin acquired Longfields at Hartshill, which had belonged to the Minton family. He established the Cripples' Hospital there in 1918. It later became the Limes Maternity Hospital.

A similar organization was the Mount School for the Deaf, founded by A.J. Story at the Mount, Hartshill in 1897. Originally known as the North Staffordshire School for the Blind and Deaf, it was the first residential school for deaf children founded under the Elementary Education (Blind and Deaf Children) Act, 1883. Fresh air was considered to be stimulating and many of the lessons were taken outside.

The SSA holds the records of many charitable organizations, including: North Staffordshire Cripples' Aid Society, 1802–1948 [SD1321 and D5188/E]; Mount School for the Deaf, 1896–c. 2000 [SD1224]; Potteries Association for the Blind, c. 1841–2006 [SD 1557]; the Chatterley Dole Charity, 1886–1974 [SD 1507]; and the Hanley and Shelton Anti-Slavery Society, 1829–39 [SD 1121]. The Old Nortonian Society was a charitable society in Norton-in-the-Moors with records at the SSA under various references. University College London has records from the North Staffordshire Society for Promoting Spiritual and Temporal Welfare of the Adult Deaf & Dumb and of the Blind, 1868–1911 and related organizations (**http://blogs.ucl.ac.uk/library-rnid/2012/04/13/stoke-story-staffs/**).

Various non-political mutual societies were established to assist members financially in time of illness, old age and hardship. By law, society rulebooks had to be submitted to the Quarter Sessions and sometimes these include membership lists as well. There are separate series for charities and trusts [Q/RSb], friendly societies [Q/RSf] and savings banks, building societies and loan societies [Q/RSb, Q/RSl, Q/RSs]. The Ancient Order of Foresters is one example: it had 'courts' (branches) at Biddulph and Knypersley. Under the Unlawful Societies Act of 1799 freemasons also had to register with the Clerk of the Peace of the local Quarter Sessions [Q/RSm]. TNA holds some society records.

LOCAL GOVERNMENT
The Path to Federation

At the beginning of the nineteenth century the Potteries had no discernible form of local government. Local powers, such as they were, were vested in the parishes, which were loath to burden their rate payers with anything that might be considered unnecessary expenditure. The area had no representation in Parliament and did not even have an authorized market. The situation contrasted sharply with nearby Newcastle-under-Lyme: it had been a borough since medieval times, a position that brought significant power and privileges (see Chapter 8). As early as 1783 there had been calls for the creation of a corporation for the whole of the Potteries. It came to nothing and meanwhile the need for local government increased.

What filled its place was competition between under-developed and ill-equipped authorities. Burslem, Hanley and Stoke each tried to assert leadership over the district. Civic rivalry played out in many forms, most

Fenton Town Hall, completed in 1889, in a pen drawing by Neville Malkin. (Courtesy of thepotteries.org)

visibly through ever more ambitious municipal building programmes. As a result, the Potteries ended up with probably the highest concentration of nineteenth-century municipal buildings in the country. Libraries, public baths, markets, mechanics institutes, water works: all proliferated as the Six Towns vied to outdo one another in shows of civic power. The situation was exacerbated as the towns became boroughs, a status that was acquired in turn by Hanley (1857), Longton (1865), Stoke (1874) and Burslem (1878). Tunstall and Fenton remained urban districts only, though still had their complement of municipal buildings.

Nowhere was this one-upmanship more evident than in town halls. Each of the pottery towns had established a town hall as a seat of local administration; often these were alongside and/or grew out of the market. But from the mid-nineteenth century town halls began to take on a new meaning as statements of power. At one point there were thirteen sites within the Six Towns that were or had been functioning as town halls. In Burslem, for example, a new town hall in an elaborate baroque style was built in 1854–7 to replace the existing eighteenth-century building. Following its incorporation as a borough, and as part of an attempt to retain its autonomy, a third town hall was built on a new site in 1911. In Hanley, a town hall was built in Town Road in the early 1800s, followed by a second in 1845, twelve years before incorporation. This, in turn, was superseded by a third town hall, which was formerly a hotel, in 1884. In Stoke, the plan involved not just the building of a new town hall but the creation of a whole new town centre. Under a scheme led by local personalities including Josiah Spode, the modest settlement set around the ancient church was to be significantly enlarged in order to establish Stoke as the municipal as well as ecclesiastical seat of power. Among other developments, it resulted in Stoke Town Hall on Glebe Street, a massive edifice that was (and remains) the largest of the Potteries' old municipal buildings.

By the beginning of the twentieth century the case for federation was becoming irresistible. Despite the support of the Duke of Sutherland, a further attempt failed in 1901, the existing towns still believing that they had too much to lose. Federation, as the County Borough of Stoke-on-Trent, was finally achieved on 31 March 1910. The new borough covered some 11,139 acres and had a population of 234,000. Its first Mayor was Cecil Wedgwood. In 1925 the County

Borough was raised to city status and the title of Lord Mayor was conferred in July 1928. In common with other cities around the country, Stoke-on-Trent moved to a system of elected Mayors in 2002 but this was subsequently abolished after a local referendum.

Electoral Records

Parliamentary representation dates back to the thirteenth century with English counties and most English boroughs electing two or more Members of Parliament. However, it was not until the Representation of the People Act 1832, also known as the Great Reform Act, that the franchise was extended and electoral registers were first created.

Before 1832, Staffordshire was represented by two MPs for the county and two for each of four parliamentary boroughs: Stafford, Lichfield, Newcastle and Tamworth. The county MPs were elected by males aged 21 and over, owning freehold land worth £2 net per annum, while the boroughs had various different systems for electing MPs. Approximately 1 per cent of the adult population was entitled to vote. Reforms during the nineteenth and early twentieth centuries led to the increased representation of manufacturing towns such as Stoke-on-Trent, and in the decision to create constituencies roughly equal in population. Large-scale maps of parliamentary constituencies from 1885 as well as borough maps of Newcastle-under-Lyme, Hanley and Stoke can be found online (**www.londonancestor.com/maps/bc-staff-th.htm**).

The Representation of the People Acts of 1832, 1867 and 1884 extended the franchise (right to vote) to more and more of the male population, although it was always based on the ownership or tenancy of land of a specified annual value. Despite these changes, by 1911 only 58 per cent of adult males were registered as electors. In 1918 the franchise was extended to all males aged 21 and over, and to women aged 30 and over who were, or whose husbands were, local government electors. Eventually, in 1928 all women aged 21 and over were given the vote.

Electoral registers are lists of persons entitled to vote compiled annually. Before 1918 they include the nature of the qualification of each person that entitled them to vote. Draft registers were compiled by parish overseers and town clerks, and later by electoral registration officers. Anyone might then object to someone's name appearing on the list, or appeal against their name not being included. Other sources were also checked so that persons having died or moved from the area could be removed from the register.

The STCA has electoral registers for the original Stoke-upon-Trent constituency, 1857–63; for certain wards within the new post-1885 Stoke-upon-Trent constituency up to 1918; and for the Hanley constituency (which included Burslem), 1885–1915. There is good coverage for all Potteries constituencies post-1918. Registers for the county constituencies (1832–67) within the Pirehill and Totmanslow hundreds are also at the STCA, with some duplicates at the WSL. The SSA's *Guide to Sources No. 9: Electoral Registers 1832–2001* provides detailed coverage of all these holdings.

Newcastle Library has occasional series for Newcastle-under-Lyme. Certain registers are available on microfiche at the SRO and on microfilm at the British Library, London.

FURTHER INFORMATION

Baker, Diane, *Workhouses in the Potteries* (City of Stoke-on-Trent Historic Buildings Survey, 1984)

Chadwick, Max and David Pearson, *The History of St. Edward's Hospital, Cheddleton* (Churnet Valley Books, 1993)

Davies, Alun, *The North Staffordshire Royal Infirmary, 1802–1948* (Churnet Valley Books, 2006)

Gibson, Jeremy and Colin Rogers, *Coroners' Records in England and Wales* (3rd edn, Family History Partnership, 2009)

Gibson, Jeremy, Else Churchill, Tony Foster and Richard Ratcliffe, *Quarter Sessions Records for Family Historians* (5th edn, Family History Partnership, 2007)

Higginbotham, Peter, *Workhouses of the Midlands* (Tempus Publishing, 2007)

Kivland, Sharon, *Memoirs* (Staffordshire University, 2001)

Lawley, Ian, *If Walls Could Talk: Images of the North Staffordshire Royal Infirmary and the City General Hospital, Stoke-on-Trent* (Phillimore & Co., 2011)

Standley, A.J., *Her Majesty's Prison Stafford: Sentenced to 200 Years* (n.p., 1993)

Chapter 6

MIGRATION AND HOUSING

RURAL AND IRISH MIGRATION

The growth of the Potteries as one of the country's pre-eminent industrial regions was driven by migration. As a product of the Industrial Revolution, the pottery industry demanded workers and lots of them: some were skilled, others less so. Industry pioneers such as Wedgwood, Spode and Adams looked initially to their Staffordshire backyard. The Staffordshire Moorlands, rural parishes around Newcastle-under-Lyme and the south of the county were all sources of workers, as was the wider area from Cheshire in the west to Derbyshire in the east.

This is not to say that the rural economy was in decline; far from it. Although farming experienced a depression after the Napoleonic wars, Staffordshire escaped the worst effects because of demand from its growing industrial towns. Early moves towards enclosure gave the county one of the most efficient agricultural economies in the country and both landowners and tenant farmers prospered. With a high concentration of mixed farms, there were plenty of labouring jobs, many of them seasonal. The rural population found this work increasingly unattractive, however, and people left the land to get better paid work in urban areas such as Stafford, the Potteries and the Black Country. In the 1830s across Staffordshire as a whole nearly 600 more people left the countryside than settled. Out-migration continued to grow, reaching a peak of over 1,100 in the 1860s.

As domestic workers moved from the land to the potbanks, landowners were forced to look further afield to meet the labour shortage. From the 1820s, migrants from Ireland began to be seen in North Staffordshire. At first they were seasonal workers, who came to work on the farms, but after the Potato Famine of the late 1840s many stayed and took more permanent jobs. The Irish continued to come to Staffordshire in large numbers until at least the 1860s. At this point, increasing mechanization in agriculture started to destroy seasonal jobs and farm work became less of a draw.

In the Potteries the number of Irish immigrants never reached the concentrations seen in other Midlands towns. Figures are hard to come by: best estimates, based on census data, are that during the mid-nineteenth century Irish-born migrants accounted for around 2 to 3 per cent of the population.

Herson (2015) and associated website provide an account of Irish emigrants to Stafford during this period (**https://divergentpaths stafford.wordpress.com**).

Settlement records are one way of tracking rural migration. Settlement laws required incomers to possess a certificate issued by the parish they had left, which undertook to support them if they needed help within forty days of arriving in their new parish. To assess whether or not a person or family was entitled to legal settlement, an examination (interview) was conducted and based on this, either a certificate or a removal order was issued. These records can provide a detailed account of how the person came to be in the parish.

Settlement and removal records are found in several sources, depending on the period in question. Before 1836 settlement was a parish matter, so the records will be in the parish overseers' papers at the SSA. After 1836, responsibility passed to the PLUs (see Chapter 5). If a removal order was issued, the receiving parish may hold a copy of the original order. Decisions on removals had to be ratified at the Quarter Sessions, where appeals were also heard. The relevant records are included either in the courts' general proceedings or under a separate heading.

Census records should be the first port of call where Irish origins are suspected. Unfortunately, birthplaces for settlers are often not recorded as precisely as those born in Great Britain. An ancestor's entry may simply say 'Ireland' without mentioning a county or village. As most (though by no means all) Irish settlers were Roman Catholic, church records at Findmypast should be consulted (see Chapter 4). Workhouse records (Chapter 5) and settlement records (see above) may also be useful. For research within Ireland see specialist guides such as Paton (2013).

Apprenticeship, religious and workhouse records may all be useful in establishing the vital link between the Potteries and an ancestor's parish of origin and are dealt with in other chapters.

COMINGS AND GOINGS: POTTERY INDUSTRY MIGRATION

The success of the pottery industry in Staffordshire was built on assimilating the most up-to-date knowledge and innovations wherever they were to be found. Much of this know-how was brought by migrant workers. The role of the Dutch-born Elers brothers and of the early pioneers' appetite for intelligence on developments in Europe have

The pottery kiln built by Staffordshire-born potter James Bennett on the Ohio River in 1840. Bennett & Bros produced yellow ware and Rockingham ware in East Liverpool before moving to the Pittsburgh area. (Public domain)

already been described (see Chapter 2). Later the tide turned and the Potteries became the supplier of skilled workers to locations within the British Isles, North America and beyond. For anyone anywhere in the English-speaking world wishing to start a pottery industry, the first place they would look for workers was the Staffordshire Potteries. Some went on short-term contracts, sometimes marrying and/or having families while they were away; others never returned.

Incomers, such as the French-born Leon Arnoux, continued to play an important role in the development of the Staffordshire Potteries into the nineteenth century. Born in Toulouse, Arnoux came to Britain in 1848 to study manufacturing techniques, Herbert Minton offering him the job of art director. He was responsible for Minton's display at the Great Exhibition of 1851 and his new majolica coloured glazes won a reputation for both Minton's and himself. His acclaim inspired other French and Continental artists to migrate to Minton's. Arnoux encouraged local artists to familiarize themselves with Continental styles and productions, while his engineering background enabled him to effect several technical improvements in pottery making, including the down-draught oven.

By 1800 between 15,000 and 20,000 people were employed in the pottery industry in North Staffordshire. There was job security for all who had the necessary skills. Indeed, skilled labour was so scarce that a system of annual hiring was instituted, enabling employers to contract potters for a period of twelve months: this way employers could be sure they had enough skilled workers for the year ahead. Compared with conditions elsewhere, this made ceramics an extremely attractive industry. Some sought opportunities outside the Potteries. For instance, it is known that the pottery industry around Llanelli, south Wales, recruited many workers from Staffordshire (Bridge, 2004).

From the late 1820s, some of the more skilled potters began migrating to factories in Continental Europe. Both the Dutch and Swedish industries are known to have benefitted in this way (De Groot, 2002) and it is likely that others did too. The number of British potters per European firm was relatively small, tens at the most, but their expertise meant they made a significant impact. Their scarce skills and knowledge enabled them to command high wages compared with the local potters. Some even became managers or part-owners of the factory they worked for.

Edwin Abington, a former china painter from Stoke, became director of the Dutch company De Sphinx, which produced porcelain, in 1856. In turn, he recruited Richard Cartwright, an engraver from Burslem to work in the printing department. Together they reorganized the decorating of wares according to the 'English system' (meaning employing more women). Cartwright stayed for more than forty years, only returning to Staffordshire in 1899.

By the middle of the nineteenth century many in the Potteries were facing hardship. Mechanization and a depressed economy had led to an over-supply of workers and people's thoughts turned to seeking a new life abroad. The Potters' Emigration Society, started in around 1844 by trades unionists, was a short-lived attempt at organized emigration to the United States (see box below). Others went under similar schemes sponsored by organizations such as the British Temperance Society or of their own accord. A notice of 1852 refers to a tea meeting being held at the Primitive Methodist School Room in Tunstall for three young men ('esteemed friends') who were leaving for Australia. The reason for their departure is not stated but the timing fits that of the Victoria gold rush.

British potters, primarily from Staffordshire, played a major role in the growth of the American pottery industry. In his landmark work on this subject, economic historian Frank Thistlethwaite studied the careers of 100 British emigrant master and journeymen potters (Thistlethwaite, 1958). He found arrivals during every decade of the nineteenth century, with peaks between 1839 and 1850 and between the American Civil War and 1873. These emigrants established industries at East Liverpool, Ohio and Trenton, New Jersey, as well as other locations, with Rockingham ware as one of the principal products.

THE POTTERS' JOINT STOCK EMIGRATION SOCIETY

In the 1840s, working and living conditions in the Potteries led some to seek a new life abroad. The scheme was instigated by William Evans, a Welshman who settled in the Potteries and became a prominent agitator for workers' rights. As editor of the *Potters' Examiner* newspaper, the mouthpiece of the United Branches of Operative Potters, he advocated organized emigration as a way of overcoming potters' ills. As Evans saw it, emigration would relieve pressure within an overstaffed industry, allowing wages and sale prices of pottery to rise for those that remained.

> ### TO THE SHAREHOLDERS OF THE POTTERS' EMIGRATION SOCIETY.
>
> *The First General Meeting of this Society, will take place on Monday Next, May 20, 1844,*
>
> ### AT MR. WILLIAM BERRY'S,
> # TALBOT INN, HANLEY,
>
> *When individuals will be put in nomination to fill the different offices of the company. Every Shareholder is respectfully requested to attend and to take into his serious consideration, and investigation the character of every individual put in nomination; the election of whom will take place on the next General Meeting Night.*
>
> By Order of the Central Committee of the United Branches of,
>
> OPERATIVE POTTERS

Notice to the 'Shareholders of the Potters' Emigration Society' in the Potters' Examiner and Workman's Advocate, 18 May 1844. (Public domain)

The Potters' Joint Stock Emigration Society and Savings Fund was founded in 1845 to promote the idea. The plan was to raise enough money to buy 12,000 acres of farmland in the United States. Once the land had been bought each shareholder was entered into a draw, with the successful ticketholders each winning a 20-acre holding. The initial draw was made in Hanley's Meat Market, amid great excitement, with eight families being successful.

Evans used the *Potters' Examiner* to promote the scheme. He published general information to prospective migrants and specific details about the Upper Mississippi area. Letters from migrants in Illinois, Ohio and Wisconsin to families back home were printed to demonstrate the benefits of migration. Rather than give money to the strike fund, readers were encouraged to donate to the savings fund that aimed to assist potters to emigrate.

Enough money was raised to purchase land in Wisconsin, where a new settlement called Pottersville was founded. But the immigrants were not prepared for the poor land and harsh frontier conditions. It is not known how many families made the journey: certainly fewer than 100. By 1850 the scheme was cancelled and its demise brought down the United Branches of Operative Potters. Many of the emigrants returned home, though others stayed and continued to build their lives in Wisconsin and elsewhere.

The Hobson Collection at the STCA has material related to William Evans and the Potters' Joint Stock Emigration Society within its trades-union series [PA/HOB/1-4]. Goodby (2003) offers a detailed account of this doomed venture.

For some the emigration was involuntary. Justice was harsh during the seventeenth and eighteenth centuries and a sentence of transportation could be handed down for relatively minor offences such as stealing a sheep or a pair of breeches. Crimes such as rioting were even more likely to attract harsh punishment. In 1842 more than fifty potters and miners from across the Potteries were transported to Van Diemen's Land (modern-day Tasmania) in the wake of Chartist unrest (see Chapter 4). Overall, more than 16,000 convicts from the West Midlands were transported to Australia between 1788 and 1852, the majority from industrial areas such as the Potteries and the Black Country.

Religious conviction was another motivation for people to leave their Staffordshire homeland. For example, around 1,200 Mormons from Staffordshire are thought to have emigrated to the United States during the middle years of the nineteenth century (Arrowsmith, 2003). Government assistance was available for those wishing to travel as free settlers. Between 1876 and 1879 more than 1,000 assisted migrants from the Midlands settled in Queensland alone. Of these around 430 came from Staffordshire, many of whom were miners.

JONATHAN LEAK: THE CONVICT POTTER

Jonathan Leak, a potter from Burslem, arrived in Australia as a convict in 1819. He had been convicted with two others of breaking into the home of Mrs Chatterley of Shelton and stealing a quantity of silver. Having initially been given a death sentence, this was commuted to transportation to Australia for life. He arrived at Sydney in the Colony of New South Wales on board the brig *Recovery* on 18 December 1819.

Earthenware bottles made by Jonathon Leak in New South Wales and a contemporary newspaper advertisement. (Public domain)

Before his conviction Leak had run his own pottery works in Commercial Street, Burslem. While working in the Government Pottery in New South Wales, he realized the potential for setting up his own business. Permission for this was granted, as well as for his wife and children to have free passage from England. He was given a ticket-of-leave, meaning he was permitted to spend the rest of his sentence working for himself provided he stayed within the colony.

In July 1823 Leak successfully obtained two land grants close to the Government Pottery, which enabled him to establish his own workshop. By 1828, Leak's pottery was employing over twenty free men and he was the only potter operating in the colony. Newspaper articles refer to the production of 40,000 bricks weekly, while advertisements show a variety of goods for sale including tiles, bricks, ginger beer and other bottles, stone jars for pickling and preserving, and earthenware of all sorts.

Jonathan Leak was eventually granted a conditional pardon which gave him citizenship of the colony but no right to return to England. He is remembered as the most successful potter in the early history of Australia.

HOUSING

Like most towns in the nineteenth century, housing conditions in the Potteries varied markedly according to social class. Certain groups tended to congregate within specific areas, leading to a form of segregation according to class, occupation and ethnicity. Thus, miners would cluster together in rows of terraced houses situated close to the mines where they worked; the middle classes often lived in their own (sometimes suburban) estates; and the small Irish community tended to live close to one another in the poorer parts of town.

It had not always been like this. Given the Potteries' rural origins, early eighteenth-century housing was in cottages and farms next to and between the potbanks. As the manufactories proliferated, workers' housing, too, developed in a random, unplanned manner. Josiah Wedgwood's model village alongside his factory at Etruria – which opened in 1769 – broke the mould, providing his workers with houses and gardens within a rural setting. But it was motivated as much by commercial necessity as philanthropy: Etruria was some distance from established centres of population and Wedgwood needed (by the standards of the day) large numbers of people to staff his new works.

At Etruria the houses were built along one street and had earth floors. According to the historian E.J. Warrillow: 'They were roomy and well lit, with quaint windows of small panes of green glass . . . The front door steps were of iron, six inches wide, and were always kept beautifully polished . . . By 1865 there were approximately 125 numbered and 65 un-numbered houses in the village.' While the concept was original, the houses themselves appear to have been similar to those

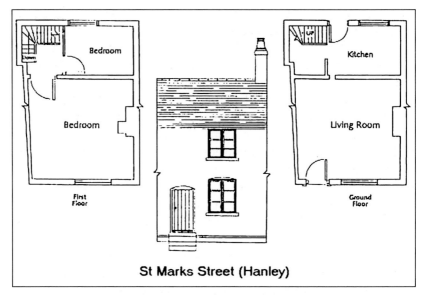

St Marks Street (Hanley)

Plan of a worker's house in St Mark's Street, Hanley, built around 1840. The layout was typical of much working class housing of the time. (Stoke-on-Trent Historic Building Survey)

being built elsewhere in the area at the time, albeit probably of superior quality. In general, workers' properties comprised either one or two rooms downstairs, plus two upstairs. Few had water supplies or sanitation.

Roden (2008) discusses housing developments that occurred within the jurisdiction of the manor courts (known as copyhold areas) during the early stages of the Industrial Revolution. It shows that while a few famous potters were responsible for a handful of the developments, the majority were orchestrated by property speculators who were seeking to take advantage of the economic boom brought about by the pottery industry.

By the beginning of the nineteenth century many areas were beginning to be developed in a more systematic manner. Estates were laid out to rigid specifications. Although water and sewerage were still elementary, this was compensated to some extent by relatively low-density building, often with small gardens attached. Overall, the

Potteries avoided the back-to-back dwellings and dense courts of the kind found in Birmingham and elsewhere, most likely because land for development was relatively abundant. The fact that some housing initiatives were financed by cooperative societies composed of artisans concerned about such matters may also have been a factor.

Estates often contained a church or chapel, a school, beerhouses and shops. Normally several grades of houses were built so that there was some mixing of classes and occupations. As most housing was built to rent, financiers and contractors were very aware of the need to attract the best custom. Features such as a hall (also called a 'lobby') or separate parlour were marks of superiority. In the Potteries, perhaps more than other area of the country, decorative detailing such as tiles and terracotta architraves were used across the housing stock. Numerous examples are still to be found, often in surprising places. In the better quality terraced housing room sizes increased and better provision was made for kitchens and lavatories. But at the same time, amenities such as front and rear gardens often disappeared.

By the mid-nineteenth century substantial detached and semi-detached houses for the middle classes became more numerous. Such households had, by definition, one or more live-in servants, which had significant implications for the layout of a house. As well as separate sleeping accommodation (usually very cramped), the design had to ensure that servants were kept out of sight as much as possible. Unsolicited collisions between mistress and servant, gentleman and tradesman were to be avoided at all costs. In the larger houses there was even gradation between the servants, so that the 'upper' servants were separated as much from the 'lower' servants as they were from the 'family'.

One of the most notable examples of an estate of middle-class detached houses is The Villas, Stoke. This development of twenty-four dwellings was built in the early 1850s by the Stokeville Building Society to designs by the architect Charles Lynam. Herbert Minton was one of the main influencers behind the scheme. Predominantly following the Italian style, the houses all had clear differentiation between service and family areas. The Villas district was the first designated conservation area in Stoke-on-Trent and a number of the houses are listed.

Of course, housing of this quality was the exception rather than the norm. Indeed, over the course of the nineteenth century housing conditions for much of the working population actually deteriorated. Government inspectors commented on the conditions on frequent occasions. A report in 1848 expressed particular concern about common lodging houses. Conditions at a house in Stafford Street, Longton, kept by a Mrs Tomlinson, were typical:

> In one house there are two rooms, four beds in one, and two in the other; they charge 9d. per night for adults, and 1d. for children. There are three houses: and six bed-rooms, eleven beds in the three front rooms, and five in the back rooms, making in all: sixteen beds in six rooms. These rooms are about ten feet square, and one window in each room. The back yards are confined, and the privy and cesspool broken and filthy.

The situation was not much improved by the end of the century, despite a number of reports and inquiries. The piecemeal nature of development led to a situation where the middle classes often lived cheek by jowl with housing of the very poorest quality and overcrowding was rife. An inquiry published in 1901 reported how:

> at the rear of one of the best residential quarter, I found a house with three rooms rented at 4/- a week. I went straight upstairs here, keeping as far as possible from the filthy walls. The room I entered was about eleven feet square. It contained two bedsteads standing close together. A little boy and a woman were the only persons at home. They told me that the father, mother, and seven brothers and sisters occupied the apartment at night. The elder brother was fifteen years of age, and the youngest child was three. There was no bed covering; the place was over-run with vermin; and there was no ventilation, for the windows would not open. Consequently the air in the place was heavy and sickening.

Visiting the area in the 1930s, J.B. Priestley described housing conditions in the Potteries as 'Victorian industrialism in its dirtiest and most cynical aspect'.

While the problem was clear for all to see, the authorities were slow to act. Not until the interwar period did the corporation begin a programme of house building. Between 1921 and 1939 over 8,000 council houses were built around the city. Estates constructed during this period include Bentilee, Abbey Hulton, Carmountside, High Lane and developments around Trent Vale. Further expansion followed after the Second World War, but years of undermining meant that the high-rise development that came to characterize other urban centres was, on the whole, avoided.

HOUSING RECORDS

Rate books, held at Stoke-on-Trent City Archives, may provide an insight into your ancestor's housing circumstances. Rates were collected in each parish for support of the sick and poor, and other local purposes such as highways, sewers, lighting and gaols. These can be used to establish whether your ancestors were tenants or property owners, while the rateable value of the property can be used to gauge the status of the occupant. The STCA has a good collection of municipal rate books from across the Six Towns [SD 1452] plus valuation lists for the period 1913–56 [SD 1214]; see search room handlists for both series.

Newcastle-under-Lyme Reference Library has microfilm copies of municipal rate books from 1840, intermittently to 1892. These cover the whole town by street, listing owners and occupiers. Rate books and valuation lists from urban and rural districts now covered by Staffordshire Moorlands are at Staffordshire Record Office [D4627].

Before incorporation, rates were paid to the parish. Under the Poor Relief Act of 1601 the inhabitants of a parish had to contribute, according to their ability to pay, towards the maintenance of the poor. From this the local taxation system, based on rates, grew and evolved. The STCA has a parish rate book for Stoke covering Penkhull, Boothen, Clayton and Seabridge, Shelton and Hanley and dated August 1807. There is also a rate collector's ledger for St Paul's parish, Burslem, 1817–1926 [SD 1592]. Other parish rate books may be found at the SRO but comparatively few have survived for North Staffordshire.

The so-called '1910 Lloyd George Domesday Survey' was a property revaluation that took place at the end of the Edwardian period at the instigation of David Lloyd George, who was then Chancellor of the Exchequer. The resulting records link individual properties to extremely detailed Ordnance Survey maps used in 1910, which are coupled with the accompanying books containing basic information on the valuation of each property. The registers for Stoke-on-Trent are available at the STCA [D3573] and are now online for the whole country at TheGenealogist website (**www.thegenealogist.co.uk**).

The Stoke-on-Trent Historic Buildings Survey in the 1980s recorded all housing then surviving in the Potteries and built before 1914, and made detailed plans of over 100 buildings. This archive is now deposited at the Potteries Museum & Art Gallery. The City Surveyor's Collection at the STCA has plans of Harpfield, Meir and other housing schemes, as well as files on aspects such as water supplies and sanitation [SA/CS].

Roden (2008) is a highly detailed and scholarly account of early housing developments in the Potteries during the period 1700–1832. The tenancies in this book are listed online at Staffordshire Name Indexes as 'Copyhold Tenants of the Manor of Newcastle-under-Lyme, 1700–1832'. Rural properties may be covered by the Tithe Commutations of the 1830s and 1840s (see Chapter 8).

FURTHER INFORMATION

Arrowsmith, Stephen G., *The Unidentified Pioneers: An Analysis of Staffordshire Mormons 1837 to 1870* (Brigham Young University, 2003); available at https://scholarsarchive.byu.edu

Bridge, Brian, *Leaving Llanelli: Potters Returning to Staffordshire 1871–1881* (Llanelli WEA journal, 2004)

de Groot, Gertjan, 'British Potters in Swedish and Dutch Pottery Industries in the 19th Century', conference paper (2002); available at www.researchgate.net/publication/319245599

Goodby, Miranda, 'Our Home in the West: Staffordshire Potters and Their Emigration to America in the 1840s', *Ceramics in America* (2003); available at: www.chipstone.org/article.php/75/Ceramics-in-America-2003/

Herson, John, *Irish Families in Victorian Stafford* (Manchester University Press, 2015)

Paton, Chris, *Tracing Your Irish Family History on the Internet* (Pen & Sword, 2013)

Roden, Peter, *Copyhold Potworks and Housing of the Staffordshire Potteries, 1700–1832* (Wood Broughton Publications, 2008)

Thistlethwaite, Frank, 'The Atlantic Migration of the Pottery Industry', *Economic History Review*, 11, 264–78 (1958)

Chapter 7

EVERYDAY LIFE IN THE POTTERIES

LITERATURE AND THE ARTS

Although he only spent a little over twenty years in the Potteries, Arnold Bennett's time there framed his world view and provided inspiration for many of the characters, events and places in his writing. In his novels and plays, this son of a Hanley solicitor sketched in graphic detail life in 'the five towns', highlighting many of the pressure points and injustices in late Victorian society (see box below). The cruelty of the Chell workhouse; the bawdy behaviour in the public houses; the avarice of the factory owners; the drudgery of life in the potbanks and down the mines: all were captured in Bennett's writings and always with a poignant sympathy for the working class.

Bennett was not unique in writing about the Potteries. A succession of writers has sought to disentangle the area; some more sympathetically than others. Visiting in 1884, Charles Dickens observed that although not a pleasant sight, the area was not 'in any way spoilt by its potworks, grotesque and ugly though many of them are', as they provided the basis for 'busy towns and thriving settlements'. But by 1908 J.F. Foster saw the Potteries as a byword for the ultimate industrial desolation, referring to its 'inch-thick greasy mire beneath the tread', 'small and wizened houses' and 'everthing [sic] sombre, wretched, blighted'. George Bernard Shaw and George Orwell in the 1920s and J.B. Priestley in the 1930s all found little to appeal and sought to blacken the Potteries in print.

Artists who have worked in conventional media include: Charles

William Brown (1882–1962), an acclaimed amateur painter who spent his working life in the mines; and Reginald Haggar (1905–88), who taught at the Stoke and Burslem Schools of Art.

It is, of course, in ceramics that local artistic expression is most readily found. Much of the ware was decorated by hand and those employed to do the work had to be not just skilled technicians but highly accomplished and creative artists. Women could make their mark in this field just as well as the men, and could even use design as a route to management positions. The success of Clarice Cliff in this respect has already been noted (see Chapter 2). Charlotte Rhead followed a similar route. Born in Burslem in 1885, she worked for several pottery firms before joining H.J. Wood, where she brought out a number of designs. One of these, Florentine, is still to be found in quantity. She later became a director of the successor company, Wood & Sons. More often than not, however, all that is known about these highly talented people – male or female – is their name. Potteries.org profiles the work of leading companies, including some individual artists. The Barewall Gallery in Burslem has collections by twentieth-century North Staffordshire artists and ceramicists (**www.barewall.co.uk**).

The North Staffordshire Field Club provided a focus for many early photographers, both amateur and professional, including William Blake and J.A. Lovatt. It was founded in 1865 to study the natural history, geology, industrial history, folklore and local history of North Staffordshire. Its first president was industrialist and banker James Bateman, FRS. The organization made a significant contribution to the intellectual life of the area, in particular through making an early photographic record of the changes affecting the Potteries in the late nineteenth and early twentieth centuries (see Chapter 1). Its records and publications, including membership lists, are held at Staffordshire Record Office [D6104] and other libraries.

Stoke-on-Trent City Archives, Staffordshire County Museum and Keele University all have substantial collections by local photographers (see Chapter 1). GENUKI has a list of professional photographers working in Staffordshire (**www.genuki.org.uk/big/eng/STS/Stsphots.html**). Other sources for information on photographers (often little more than lists) are: **www.earlyphotographers.org.uk**; and **www.victorianphotographers.co.uk**.

ARNOLD BENNETT: SON OF THE POTTERIES

Arnold Bennett was born in May 1867 in Hanley, where his father Enoch Bennett became a solicitor. After working for his father for a short while, he went to London as a solicitor's clerk and experimented with journalism. After winning a literary competition in 1889, he was encouraged to take up journalism full-time and joined the editorial staff of *Woman* magazine. After 1900 he devoted himself entirely to writing, dramatic criticism being one of his foremost interests.

Arnold Bennett, 1867–1931. (Public domain)

His first novel, *A Man from the North*, was published to critical acclaim in 1898, followed in 1902 by *Anna of the Five Towns*, the first of a succession of stories set in the Potteries and displayed his unique vision of life there. Many of the locations in *Anna of the Five Towns*, *Clayhanger* and other Bennett novels correspond to actual locations in and around the district. There was 'Bursley' (Burslem), 'Hanbridge' (Hanley), 'Knype' (Stoke), 'Longshaw' (Longton) and 'Turnhill' (Tunstall). The 'forgotten town' was Fenton, which has no literary twin in Bennett's prose.

From 1903 to 1911 Bennett lived mostly in Paris, producing many novels and plays as well as working as a freelance journalist. During this time he continued to enjoy critical success. On a visit to America in 1911 he was acclaimed more than any visiting writer since Dickens. He returned to England to find the *Old Wives Tale* (published in 1908) being hailed as a masterpiece.

By 1922 he had separated from his French wife and taken up with the actress Dorothy Cheston, with whom he lived until his death from typhoid in 1931. His ashes are buried in Burslem Cemetery.

Although Arnold Bennett spent most of his life outside the Potteries, he never forgot the debt he owed to his birthplace. It gave him a unique setting for so many of his novels, a setting which he enhanced with his penetrating description of people and places. He is commemorated by a plaque at his childhood home in Waterloo Road, Cobridge; and by a statute outside the Potteries Museum & Art Gallery.

Keele University has a substantial Arnold Bennett archive, including many of his personal papers, literary manuscripts and pictorial material (**www.keele.ac.uk/library/specarc/collections**).

THEATRE, VARIETY AND CINEMA

For such a small area, the Potteries has had a surprisingly large number of theatres and other entertainment venues over the years. With the exception of Fenton, by the late nineteenth century each of the Six Towns had at least one theatre. As with other aspects of Potteries history, this is at least partly explained by competition between the towns, each attempting to outdo the other with larger and ever more expensively appointed venues.

The first permanent theatre in the area is thought to have been the Theatre Royal in Newcastle-under-Lyme which opened in 1788. Josiah Spode and Josiah Wedgwood were among the shareholders. Having been successful for many decades, it closed towards the end of the nineteenth century and later found use as a cinema.

A permanent venue within the Six Towns took much longer to establish. Several attempts by local businessmen to form theatres during the 1820s came to nought. Instead, local people relied on travelling theatres that toured the country. Entertainment was also found in the public

Poster for Laurel and Hardy's appearance at the Theatre Royal, Hanley, 1952. (Staffordshire Past Track)

147

houses. The Sea Lion in Hanley, for instance, is said to have had a large yard behind the inn that played host to plays and circuses. Music was a prominent feature inside the pubs and inns of the time and eventually spawned the music hall. Larger concerts and performances are known to have been held in the old Hanley Market.

Eventually, in 1852 the Royal Pottery Theatre opened in Pall Mall, Hanley. It had been converted for theatre use from a lecture hall known as The People's Hall, which in turn had previously been a Methodist chapel. It soon became known more generally as the Theatre Royal.

This was the first of many theatre, concert and music hall venues opened in the area during the last half of the nineteenth century. Neale (2010) lists 28 such venues in the Six Towns during this period: 13 in Hanley; 5 in Burslem; 5 in Longton; 4 in Stoke; and 1 (the Prince of Wales Theatre) in Tunstall. Some of these many theatres were successful; others were financial disasters bringing bankruptcy or worse on their owners. Several have mysteriously burnt down and only a very few can be seen in the city of Stoke-on-Trent today.

The opening of a new theatre or music hall was the cause of much civic pride. The grand opening of the Empire Varieties Theatre, New Street, Hanley, in 1892 was attended by aldermen, county councillors and officials from neighbouring towns. Addressing the audience, the manager, Fred Gale, as quoted in the *Era*, 19 March 1892, explained that:

> It was intended to bring before their audiences some of the best talent it was possible to secure. No expense would be spared to attain this object. The entertainment they meant to bring before the Hanley public from week to week was one to which any man might bring his wife, sister, or mother, without fear of being chastened on his return home. The management would make it their business to put down severely anything in any way objectionable.

The opening programme featured: The Voltynes, clever bar performers; Turner and Atkinson, tenor and baritone vocalists; Miss Carlotta Davis, a burlesque actress and skipping rope dancer;

Percival and Breeze, sketch performers; Howlette's Marionettes, described by the *Era* as 'extremely diverting'; and Mr Sam Jesson, a singer. The scene would have been repeated, week after week, at venues across the Potteries, providing all-too-brief moments of light relief for industrious workers.

Neale (2010) surveys the history of Stoke-on-Trent's theatres, concert and music halls, and information on the main venues is presented at Matthew Lloyd's website, **www.arthurlloyd.co.uk**, dedicated to the music-hall star Arthur Lloyd. Local newspapers carried notices and reviews of performances similar to those quoted above, which may mention theatrical ancestors (see Chapter 1). These, as well as specialist theatrical newspapers such as the *Stage*, the *Era* and *Music Hall & Theatre Review*, are available at the British Newspaper Archive (**www. britishnewspaperarchive.co.uk**).

The STCA has an extensive collection of historic theatre and concert programmes. As well as the major theatres, the collection includes smaller, informal venues such as amateur productions put on in church and village halls. A handlist is available in the STCA Search Room. Of particular note are the collections relating to the Theatre Royal and Grand Theatre, Hanley [SD 1145, SD 1259, SD 1326] and the Mitchell Memorial Theatre, *c.* 1943–50 [SD 1662].

Collections with a musical orientation include: North Staffordshire Symphony Orchestra, 1904–2006 [SD 1352, 1384 and SA/COPE]; City of Stoke-on-Trent Choral Society, 1928–82 [SD 1579]; Potteries Gramophone Society, 1930–47 [SD 1695]; and the English Folk Dance & Song Society, North Staffordshire Branch, 1921–76 [D5104].

Potteries.org has a history of the Porthill Players, an amateur dramatic and musical society founded in 1911.

HOLIDAYS AND RECREATION
Wakes Weeks

In the eighteenth century there was no entitlement to paid holidays. Time off was limited to certain festivals and saints days which were recognized by the Church. In the Potteries these eventually evolved into a week-long annual holiday known as The Wakes. Shops closed and people took off on foot, by train or other means to enjoy the festivities.

Wakes week at Trentham swimming pool, c. 1950.

At Trentham Park the Duke of Sutherland threw open the gates of his estate and laid on entertainment (another episode referred to by Charles Shaw in *When I Was A Child*). In 1850 as many as 30,000 people visited the Park on the annual 'Trentham Thursday'. The revelry often lasted for the first four or five days of Wakes Week, or until the workers ran out of money. Even then, many chose not to return to work.

Initially there were three separate Wakes celebrations. Burslem Wakes was held during the week following the Nativity of St John the Baptist on 24 June. Tunstall Wakes was held in late July to celebrate St Margaret, to whom Wolstanton parish church is dedicated; and the Stoke Wakes focused on the first Sunday in August. Around 1880 it was decided that a single Wakes Week for the whole district would be less disruptive and the timing of the Stoke Wakes was adopted. By the early 1900s Wakes Week had turned into an annual fortnight holiday.

Although some people respected the religious origins, for most the Wakes were a time of fun and jollity, offering escape from the drudgery of everyday life and work. Boxing rings, music, acrobatics and gambling were all in evidence, as well as wheelbarrow races and team games. Dog and cock fighting were popular and continued to be organized furtively long after they were outlawed. The prevalence of alcohol and the inevitable drunkenness that followed led the Church to complain that the Wakes were nothing but an excuse for hedonism. Employers were not happy at the disruption to production. Temperance groups, Sunday schools, Church leaders and manufacturers organized alternative activities – galas, tea parties, picnics and trips to the countryside – in an attempt to bring the Wakes under control.

It was social progress rather than prescriptive regulation that curtailed the Wakes' worst excesses. From the 1840s the railways allowed Potteries' workers to travel further afield, opening up new locations such as Rudyard Lake in the Churnet Valley. This was promoted by the North Staffordshire Railway Company following the opening of the Churnet Valley line in 1849. During Stokes Wakes Week in August 1850 nearly 200 people arrived at Rudyard Lake by train to enjoy boating and picnic parties. Within a few years grand regattas were being held on the lake. One of those making the trip in 1863 was John Lockwood Kipling, a pottery designer from Burslem. He met his future wife, Alice Macdonald, there and they named their son, the novelist and poet Rudyard Kipling, after their meeting place.

Another beauty spot brought within easier reach by the railway was Mow Cop, which became a tourist attraction and not just a place of religious pilgrimage (see Chapter 4). Annual fetes at places such as Keele Hall and Leek were also popular.

Public Parks

While the annual Wakes Week provided welcome respite, demands were also growing for open spaces closer to home. In 1879 the Duke of Sutherland advocated a public park on land he was developing around Longton. The plan was opposed initially but in 1887, after the election of a new Mayor, was eventually accepted. The Duke donated 45 acres for the scheme, to be known as Queen's Park, and a public subscription was launched to meet the set-up costs. At the opening ceremony in July 1888, the Duke observed: 'We all know how necessary lungs are for the human frame. Open spaces are quite as necessary to those who toil much indoors and in a smoky town.' In the Potteries, with its slagheaps and smoke-laden atmosphere, fresh air was increasingly recognized as a precious commodity.

As so often in the Potteries, the other towns followed suit. Hanley unveiled the first section of a 100-acre site in 1894, though the park was not fully opened until Jubilee Day 1897. Burslem Park, complete with ladies' and gentlemen's reading rooms, was opened in 1893. Other civic parks opened at Etruria (1904), Northwood (1907), Tunstall (1908) and later at Fenton (1924).

The popularity of public parks during the Victorian and Edwardian periods is difficult to comprehend today. It was not uncommon for crowds of 10,000 or more to visit Burslem or Hanley park on a Sunday. Boating, fishing and skating (during winter months) were all popular, as well as simply 'promenading' in front of one's peers. Organized activities had to be paid for, however, so the poorer sections of society still found themselves excluded.

Sports Clubs

Sport provided a welcome, albeit brief, release for those who worked in the mines and the potbanks. Men and boys would kick a ball around in the street or on waste ground, and later in the blossoming public parks. As in many working class towns, there was a fierce rivalry for fans' affections between local football teams. In the Potteries the rivals were 'City' (Stoke City, otherwise known as 'the Potters') and 'Vale' (Port Vale, known as 'the Valiants'). For much of their existence the two clubs have played in different leagues and so have rarely met, but the rivalry was (and remains) real nonetheless.

The origins of Stoke City FC are deep and not entirely agreed upon. Some accounts say it was founded in 1863 by apprentices from Charterhouse School while serving as apprentices at The Knotty (North Staffordshire Railway Company). The first recorded match was in

Stoke City FC, 1877–8. (Public domain)

October 1868 when a team called Stoke Ramblers and consisting largely of railway employees played at the Victoria Cricket Club ground. In 1878 the Ramblers amalgamated with the Stoke Victoria Club to become Stoke FC and moved to a new athletics ground nearby. In 1888 the Potters were heavily involved in the formation of the Football League and were founder members for its inaugural season. The Potteries connection was further strengthened by the siting of the League's office at 8 Parkers Terrace, Etruria (later to become 177 Brick Kiln Lane). Port Vale is almost as old, having been formed – according to club records – in 1876 in Burslem.

STANLEY MATTHEWS: THE POTTER WITH THE GOLDEN TOUCH

No one has come to immortalize the Potteries' sporting prowess like Sir Stanley Matthews. The first professional footballer to be knighted, Matthews is one of the most renowned players of modern times. His professional career covered some thirty-three years, much of it playing for Stoke City.

Matthews was born in 1915, in a terraced house in Seymour Street, Hanley, the third of four sons of local boxer Jack Matthews (who was known as 'The Fighting Barber' of Hanley). He first played for the Potters in 1932 and remained with the club until 1947. After fourteen years at Blackpool, he returned to city in 1961 until his retirement as a player in 1965, by which time he had made almost 700 League appearances. He helped Stoke to the Second Division title in 1932–3 and 1962–3. Following a short stint as Port Vale's general manager between 1965 and 1968, he then travelled the world coaching enthusiastic amateurs.

During his career Matthews gained respect and admiration far beyond regular football supporters. When in 1938 it was mooted that he might be moving to another club, there was a public outcry in the Potteries. Employers complained that their workers 'were so upset at the prospect of losing Matthews that they could not do their work!'. Despite playing in nearly 700 league games, he was never booked. The plaque outside his birthplace at 89 Seymour Street denotes him as 'Footballer and Gentleman'.

He died in February 2000, just after his 85th birthday, and his ashes were buried beneath the centre circle of Stoke City's Britannia Stadium. He is commemorated in a statue outside the ground.

Horse-racing was another popular pastime. The first properly laid out racecourse in the area was on Knutton Heath near Newcastle. Having failed to come to an agreement to hold their own races on the Newcastle course, in 1823 race-goers in the Potteries set about organizing their own race meeting. This was to be held on the

Thursday and Friday of Stoke Wakes Week and 47 acres of land was leased from the Wedgwood family to establish a new course. A thousand pounds was spent laying out the course and building a large stand for spectators. The first race meeting was a huge success. The *Staffordshire Advertiser* reported that the committee had put on a varied programme, which included a foot race and a prison bar match as well as horse races. By the early 1830s the races at Etruria were attracting over 30,000 spectators and competitors from across the Midlands.

Finney Gardens in Bucknall became an important sporting venue in the late nineteenth century. Originally a 16-acre market garden flanking both sides of the railway track, from the 1860s grand galas and horse races began to be held there. By the 1890s a cricket ground and athletics ground had been established.

Edwards (1996) has further details on boxing, horse-racing and professional football within the Potteries.

Sport is not well represented in the SSA catalogue. Record series that may throw light on family members' sporting endeavours are: North Staffordshire Referees Club, 1913–2005 [SD 1466]; Longton Swimming Club, 1929–36 [SD 1455]; Burslem Working Men's Club, 1906–97 [SD 1706]; and North Staffordshire and District Cricket League (recent) [SD 1714]. The National Football Museum in Manchester holds extensive archives of Football Association and Football League records and is able to answer enquiries relating to relatives who have played the game at amateur or professional level (**www.nationalfootball museum.com/collections**).

PUBS, INNS AND BREWERIES

Pubs and inns have always played an important role in the life of the Potteries. Initially these were rural alehouses and inns: an 'alehouse' was an ordinary dwelling where the householder served home-brewed ale and beer, whereas an 'inn' was generally purpose-built to accommodate travellers. By the mid-eighteenth century larger alehouses were becoming common, while inns beside the major highways grew in grandeur and new ones sprang up to serve the stage coaches.

Very early photograph of the George Hotel, Swan Square, Burslem, the site of the Chartist riots. (Courtesy of thepotteries.org)

The sixteenth-century Greyhound Inn at Penkhull is one of the oldest in the district: for many years it hosted the Court of the Manor of Newcastle-under-Lyme. The Castle Hotel was one of many coaching inns in Newcastle. The origins of the Pack Horse at Longton go back to the time when Longbridge was a scattered hamlet in the Fowlea Valley between Newcastle and Burslem. Later, on the opposite side of Newcastle Street, the Duke of Bridgewater was built alongside the Trent & Mersey Canal when the former hamlet, its name changed to Longport, was expanding rapidly as a result of the new waterway. Josiah Wedgwood and others are known to have met at the Leopard (another coaching inn) in Burslem in 1765 when planning the canal.

Public houses reflected the communities they served and in the nineteenth century this meant there was strict stratification. Charles Shaw, writing in the 1890s, recalled that, in Tunstall, beerhouses were 'for the common heard [*sic*], but, the [Sneyd Arms] hotel and the Lamb were for the gentlemen'. The Colliers Arms beerhouse in Moorland Road, Burslem was noted, in 1864, as being 'a house of resort for the loose characters of the town', while around the same time another beerhouse in High Street was known to harbour prostitutes. The Coachmakers Arms, Lichfield Street, Hanley is probably the best surviving example of a nineteenth-century Potteries beerhouse.

Victualling has always been a highly regulated trade. From 1522, a person wishing to sell alcoholic drinks had to apply for a licence from the Quarter or Petty Sessions, and from 1617 licences were required for those running inns, hence the term 'licensed victualler'. A loosening of regulations during the 1820s and 1830s led to a significant increase in the number of licensed premises, as a result of which drinking in public houses became much more acceptable. From the 1880s a more ostentatious form of public house design began to emerge. One of the best examples is the Golden Cup Inn, in Old Town Road, Hanley, which is now Grade II listed.

The temperance movement was born in reaction to what many saw as 'the demon drink' affecting the working classes. Many such initiatives were led by Nonconformists who saw the fight against the evils of alcohol as part of their Christian mission. One of its leaders in the Potteries was Jeremiah Yates, a well-known Chartist, who ran a temperance coffee house (also referred to as a temperance hotel) at Mile's Bank, Hanley. Wherever they could, campaigners took over beerhouses and public houses and converted them into temperance halls, as happened with the Sutherland Arms at Longton during the 1870s. The temperance movement persisted into the twentieth century. *The Potteries, Newcastle and District Directory* of 1907 lists three temperance societies in Burslem alone: Church of England Temperance Society (Burslem Auxiliary), Burslem Temperance Society and Sons of Temperance, Wedgwood Sub-Division.

Grindley (1993), Edwards (1997) and Edwards (2014) all survey the history of pubs in the area. Potteries.org has extensive listings, photographs and pub histories. The Stoke-on-Trent Historic Buildings Survey, available at the PMAG, provides details of many of the more notable pub buildings in existence at the time the study was made in the 1980s.

Licensing Records

Victuallers' documentation is to be found in various categories of Quarter and Petty Sessions records. Landlords had to declare that they would not operate a disorderly pub and to enter into certain obligations before the court could issue a licence; these oaths are generally catalogued as 'recognizances' or 'bonds'. Landlords that failed to adhere to these requirements would appear on charges of 'keeping a disorderly house' and so appear under the criminal headings of the court's records. The SRO has a limited series of licensed victuallers registers from the period 1628–1792 [Q/RLv]. Later licences and related hearings are listed in the general Quarter Sessions or Petty Sessions series (see Chapter 5). Stoke, Burslem and Fenton came under the Pirehill North Magistrates Court for licensing purposes and that court's records contain a long series of licensing applications (1872–1984) [SRO: D5272/1/3].

There are not many temperance-related records for North Staffordshire. The SRO has a small collection relating to the Newcastle-under-Lyme Methodist Temperance League, 1877–83 [D6275/1], as well as plans for Old Temperance Hall, Union Street, Leek, 1921 [6474/1/1]. General record series relating to Nonconformist congregations may also detail their activities in this regard.

Other sources for records of pubs and publicans include newspapers (e.g. brawls, festivities), land records (deeds, tithes, enclosures), rate books, fire-insurance records and apprenticeship agreements. Information on tied pubs and their owners can be found in the records of brewery companies, and in photographic collections.

MARKETS, SHOPS AND FOOD

Being a product of the industrial era, markets came relatively late to the Potteries. Historically, Newcastle-under-Lyme had been North Staffordshire's main commercial centre. A market had been held there since the twelfth century and the burghers of Newcastle gained much power as a result (see Chapter 8). With the rise of the Potteries, markets were established within the Six Towns from the mid-eighteenth century. As with other areas of civic life, the nature and extent of the markets became a source of rivalry between the towns.

In Stoke a market was held in the original town hall, erected in 1794. Built by subscription and administered by trustees, it was a typical building of the period, with an arcaded market below and a meeting room above. By 1818 there was a Saturday market, but in 1834 this was overshadowed by the market at Hanley, so, in 1835, a new market hall was built. In Burslem, a covered meat market opened in Market Place, next to the town hall, also in 1835, where it remained for many years. Longton market has operated from sites in or near Market Square (now Times Square) since 1802.

Large-scale 'retail experiences' came late to the Potteries. For much of the nineteenth century shops were limited to the traditional trades – bakers, chemists, haberdashers, ironmongers, etc. Michael Huntbach opened the district's first department store in Lamb Street, Hanley in 1876, having bought up the surrounding properties. By the time of his death in 1910, Huntbach's store occupied more than 20,000ft² and employed 300 staff. Other emporiums were Bratt & Dyke at the corner of Stafford Street and Trinity Street, and McIlory's in Hanley.

Like many working class areas, the co-operative movement, which advocated the principles of self-help, was an important feature of trading in the Potteries. One of the first stores opened in Newcastle Street, Burslem in 1901. It became the basis for the Burslem Co-operative Society, Stoke-on-Trent's most successful mutual commercial enterprise. Initially 200 joined, each subscribing 4s. By 1932, the Burslem & District Industrial Co-operative Society had 50,000 members, 112 shops and capital of more than £1 million.

Oatcakes are a type of pancake made with oatmeal that has been a staple for the working classes in Staffordshire for over 200 years. Although not unique to Staffordshire (they are found also in Cheshire, Derbyshire and parts of North Wales), oatcakes have become synonymous with the county and especially Stoke-on-Trent. In the nineteenth century they were sold from the front rooms of the Potteries' terraced houses. Some of these houses evolved into more permanent shops, with a hatch through which the oatcakes were sold on the street.

The Staffordshire oatcake looks nothing like its Scottish cousin. It is made from a batter comprising oatmeal, flour, milk and water that is ladled on to a griddle. The final result resembles a French crepe. Today all manner of exotic fillings are added to the modern oatcake, though the purists will tell you that cheese and bacon are the original and best. Sausage, eggs and tomatoes are also popular fillings. Sambrook (2009) provides an authoritative history of this local delicacy.

Lobby, a type of thin stew, was another Potteries staple. Often it comprised little more than potatoes and was served in an ironstone bowl with a cloth tied tightly round the top. This, too, is not unique to Stoke-on-Trent, but a version of the lobscouse recipe that is supposed to have been introduced to these shores by the Vikings. Writer Paul Johnson mentions it in his childhood memoir of Stoke in the 1930s (Johnson, 2004). Referring to The Sytch, a huge polluted waste ground populated by potbanks, mines and iron furnaces, he describes how the workers:

> used to take their midday 'dinner' with them. It was called Lobby and was a thin stew . . . It seemed to me a horrific kind of meal but it was no doubt nourishing and they liked it. All carried their supply of Lobby to work and never thought of eating anything else. There were no canteens. The master potters said, 'Can't afford 'em. Dust want to send us down Carey Street?' [meaning bankruptcy]

Key sources for shop-owning ancestors include trade directories (look for advertisements as well as directory listings), rate books, and property records such as deeds. Commercial disputes may have ended up in court and be reported in the newspapers. Shop-owners frequently went bankrupt and so ended up in the civil courts or in debtors prison. Photobooks, such as *Hanley Then and Now* (History Press, 2012), serve to show not only the shops and their owners, but the diversity of products sold.

ORAL AND COMMUNITY HISTORY

The Potteries' mode of speech is sufficiently distinct in terms of grammar, pronunciation and vocabulary to qualify as a dialect rather than just an accent. In days gone by, the fact that people spent most of their time in close proximity with others in the same social class – either in the potbanks or the mines – is likely to have helped to reinforce and preserve the dialect. In these days of global media and Estuary English it is less pronounced than it used to be, but any visitor to the area is still sure to notice.

Experts believe that the North Staffordshire dialect may derive from Old English, as spoken by the Anglo-Saxons. This may explain the very round vowel sounds: for example, the vowel 'o' followed by an 'l' is pronounced 'ow' as in towd (told), owd (old), cowd (cold), and gowd (gold). The local word 'nesh' – meaning soft, tender or to easily get cold – is derived from the early English, 'nesc', or 'nescenes'; and 'slat' – meaning to throw – is from the Old English 'slath' (moved). 'Mithered' means to be worried about something; 'sneaped' is to be upset; and 'famished' is to be very hungry. Other dialect words are: 'surry', meaning friend; 'brazzle', meaning hard (and/or hard-faced); 'farrantly', meaning good or amiable; and 'clemmed', meaning starving. One of the most noticeable phrases for the visitor is use of the term 'duck' as a greeting (for a man or woman), although this is found in other areas of the north and east of England and is not unique to North Staffordshire.

Wilfred Bloor's 'Jabez' character by artist W. Walker. (Keele University)

In recent years, archives and heritage institutions have placed increasing emphasis on so-called 'community history', collecting and documenting ordinary people's recollections and experiences of their communities. The Staffordshire Dialects Project on the BBC Stoke & Staffordshire website has accounts of people's accents and dialects in use across the county, collected under a 2005 project called Staffordshire Voices (**www.bbc.co.uk/stoke/voices2005**). Unfortunately, the audio links from this site no longer function. Potteries.org has a guide to the North Staffordshire dialect, as well as memories of life in Stoke-on-Trent based on interviews with local people and published accounts (**www.thepotteries.org/memories**).

Wilfred Bloor (1915–93) was born and bred in the Potteries and spent his working life researching the effects of dust in the pottery industry. His interest in different dialects, and especially that of North Staffordshire, led to his creation of the character Jabez. Under the pseudonym 'A. Scott' he wrote over 400 Jabez tales in Potteries dialect for the local *Sentinel* newspaper. The Wilfred Bloor Papers at Keele University comprise his manuscript and typescript articles, cuttings, correspondence and audio cassettes from the 1960s to the 1990s (**www.keele.ac.uk/library/specarc/collections/**).

The *Sentinel* maintains an extremely popular 'nostalgia' section, offering a look back at times gone by in Stoke-on-Trent, North Staffordshire and South Cheshire from the 1890s to the 1990s (**www.stokesentinel.co.uk/all-about/way-we-were**). It has spawned an active Facebook group (**www.facebook.com/sentinelwaywewere**). *Nostalgic Memories of Stoke on Trent and the Potteries* (True North Books, 2015) is one of many books that aim to capture such memories. Cockin (2010) is a collection of folklore and 'oddities of human life and character' from the Potteries and surrounding area.

FURTHER INFORMATION

Booth, John, *Hanley Then and Now* (History Press, 2012)

Cockin, Tim, *Did You Know That . . . 6: Facts About The Potteries, Stone, Newcastle* (Malthouse Press, 2010)

Edwards, Mervyn, *Potters at Play* (Churnet Valley Books, 1996)

Edwards, Mervyn, *Potters in Pubs* (Churnet Valley Books, 1997)

Edwards, Mervyn, *Potters in Parks* (Churnet Valley Books, 1999)

Edwards, Mervyn, *Stoke-on-Trent Pubs* (Amberley Publishing, 2014)

Gibson, Jeremy and Judith Hunter, *Victuallers Licences: Records for Family and Local Historians* (3rd edn, Family History Partnership, 2009)

Grindley, Joan-Ann, *A Pint-sized History of Stoke-on-Trent and District* (Sigma Leisure, 1993)

Johnson, Paul, *The Vanished Landscape: A 1930s Childhood in the Potteries* (Weidenfeld & Nicolson: 2004)

Neale, William A., *Old Theatres in the Potteries* (Lulu.com, 2010)

Sambrook, Pamela, *The Staffordshire Oatcake: A History* (Palatine Books, 2009)

Chapter 8

BEFORE THE POTBANKS

MEDIEVAL STAFFORDSHIRE

The Domesday Survey of 1086 contains little evidence for the settlements that form modern-day Stoke-on-Trent. Stoke is mentioned as part of the royal manor of 'Pinchetel' (Penkhull), over 1,000 acres of arable land that covered much of present-day Newcastle-under-Lyme, Hanley, Shelton, Stoke and Boothen. It is likely that Tunstall is accounted for within the manors of Thursfield and/or Chell. Fenton-Vivian or Little Fenton was at that time a separate manor to Fenton Culvert or Great Fenton, which appears to have been attached to Buckenhall Eaves (hence 'Bucknall'). Longton is believed to have been part of the manor of Wolstanton. Only Burslem ('Barcardselim') is recorded as a separate manor at that time, held by Robert of Stafford. It was assessed for a third of a hide and was worth 10s. a year (meaning it was very poor).

Domesday Book shows that Staffordshire as a whole was sparsely populated compared with other counties, with extensive woodlands and largely uninhabited uplands. The Normans had ravaged the area in the effort to exert their authority after the Conquest. Rebellions were put down mercilessly, motte and bailey castles were built at Chester, Stafford, Dudley and Tutbury, and large areas of Staffordshire including Cannock Chase were designated for royal hunting. Hemmed in by the landscape and oppressed by a tyrannical regime, the populace had to rely on subsistence agriculture.

Penkhull is probably the earliest inhabited place within the Potteries district, its hill-top position having attracted, in turn, the Celts, Romans and Anglo-Saxons. Its situation afforded easy access to wooded hunting grounds, clear views over the surrounding countryside and proximity to streams in the Lyme Valley to the west, and the Trent Valley to the east. But in the twelfth century the Normans built a 'new castle' to the west of Penkhull and from this point its influence began to decline.

A market town quickly grew up within sight of this castle and by the year 1173, the Borough of Newcastle-under-Lyme ('New Castle under the Elm Trees') had been established. By the mid-1230s many of the manors in the area had become closely associated with Newcastle. In the centuries that followed, Newcastle-under-Lyme grew to be the largest centre of population and leading market town. It would dominate the history and economy of North Staffordshire for the next 600 years, until the arrival of the Potteries in the eighteenth century.

Apart from the burghers of Newcastle, the other force in North Staffordshire in the medieval period was the Church. The Cistercians settled in the moorlands regions, establishing houses at Croxden in 1179, Dieulacres (near Leek) in 1214 and at Hulton in 1219. An Augustinian priory was founded at Trentham in 1150. These religious houses wielded considerable power. They operated large estates, managed through dependent farms and granges, and were not averse to clearing existing villages and hamlets to make way for new farms. Hulton and Trentham, in particular, depended on wool for a large part of their income and on occasion disputes broke out between them over pasture rights.

The medieval period saw a boom in church building and restoration. St Peter ad Vincula, Stoke, St John the Baptist, Burslem, St Giles, Newcastle, and St Edward the Confessor, Leek, were all either established or expanded during this period, as well as many others.

What were to become staple industries were beginning to develop. Coal was being mined at Tunstall by 1282, Shelton by 1297, Norton-in-the-Moors by 1316 and Keele by 1333. Drift mining or shallow excavation with bell pits would have been used. Iron ore was being mined in the Tunstall area by the thirteenth century and spread to Longton, Knutton, Chesterton and Talke. Newcastle's Ironmarket suggests that it was a centre for the buying and selling of the resulting ore. At that time the ore would have been smelted in small furnaces that served the local market.

Until relatively recently archaeological evidence for pottery-making

Abbey Hulton mill, from 'Ten Generations of a Potting Family' by William Adams. (Courtesy of thepotteries.org)

in the region during this period was scant. But in 2000 large quantities of late medieval pottery were discovered during building work at the Burslem School of Art, where William Moorcroft and many other famous ceramic artists learned their trade. The trove included large pottery bowls and jugs from the 1400s in styles known as Cistercian ware (a brown glazed earthenware made from clay rich in irons) and white ware (another form of earthenware made from white-firing clays with low levels of iron). Other evidence comes from Sneyd Green, where excavations have revealed a series of small-scale kilns. Overall, however, the industry appears to have still been a domestic sideline at this time.

Medieval Records

The Manorial Documents Register, administered by The National Archives, is a centralized index to manorial records for England and Wales. It provides brief descriptions of documents and details of their locations in both public and private hands. The index is now largely computerized (including Staffordshire) and forms part of the TNA Discovery Catalogue (**http://discovery.nationalarchives.gov.uk/ manor-search**).

Manorial records include court rolls, surveys, maps, terriers and other documents relating to the boundaries, franchises, wastes, customs or courts of a manor. Although manorial records do not record births, marriages or deaths as such, they may contain considerable information about individuals, including approximate dates of death. The key records here are those relating to changes in tenancy on the death of a tenant: presentments and admittances. Other useful records are: lists of jury members and manorial officials; presentments and orders giving the names of those who offended against local byelaws and committed minor crimes; and civil pleas brought against neighbours or others in the community in cases of debt or trespass.

Survival is patchy and as the ownership of manors changed frequently and did not necessarily remain within the local area, manorial documents can be spread far and wide. *SSA Guide No. 7: Manorial Records* is a guide to its holdings for manors in both Staffordshire and other counties. North Staffordshire manors with entries in the list from before 1500 include: Audley, Betley, Biddulph, Bucknall, Leek, Norton-in-the-Moors, Trentham and Whitmore. Use the Manorial Documents Register to identify potential holdings elsewhere.

The publications of the Staffordshire Record Society are a rich resource on medieval Staffordshire and its history (**www.s-h-c.org.uk**). The Society has published many medieval manuscripts and documents from the county in its journal *Collections for a History of Staffordshire* (referred to below as simply *Collections*). Key record series which are likely to include names from the period include pipe rolls, plea rolls and feet of fines, episcopal, cathedral and monastic records, lay subsidies and early Quarter Sessions records. These tend to be county-wide without specific reference to North Staffordshire. A key source for general history is its annotated version of Walter Chetwynd's *History of Pirehill Hundred With Notes* by Frederick Perrot Parker (in two parts: New Series, Vol. XII (1909) and Third Series (1914)). It includes the pedigrees of notable Staffordshire families. Some SRS volumes have been digitized and are available via the Internet Archive (**www.archive.org**).

The Staffordshire Historical Collections on British History Online have various plea rolls and other medieval documents (**www.british-history.ac.uk/staffs-hist-collection**).

Durie (2013) and Westcott (2014) provide further insights into interpreting and understanding early documents. The Medieval Genealogy website contains links to numerous sources, including public records, charters, manorial records, early church and probate records, funeral monuments and heraldry (**www.medievalgenealogy.org.uk**). The heraldry of Staffordshire has been discussed in various articles in the *Midland Ancestor*, the journal of Midland Ancestors.

TUDOR AND STUART PERIODS

At the beginning of the sixteenth century the religious houses continued to exert influence, even though the numbers of brethren were in steep decline. When Trentham Priory was dissolved in 1536 it possessed huge tracts of land across North Staffordshire, yet had only eight priors in residence. They were each granted annuities and either took up positions as rectors locally or moved away.

Farming prospered during this period. It was largely pastoral, with livestock being moved between upland and lowland pastures during the year and preference given to cattle over sheep. More land was brought under cultivation by clearing woodland and the use of former 'waste'. The enclosure of open fields began: Tunstall was enclosed by 1614 and visitors in the late seventeenth century commented on the quantity of enclosures around the county compared with elsewhere. Yeoman farmers such as the Fords at Ford Green Hall, Smallthorne, showed off their new-found wealth by building large timber-framed houses (**http://fordgreenhall.org.uk**).

Although Staffordshire as a whole featured prominently in the English Civil Wars, hostilities were concentrated in the south of the county, in areas such as Lichfield, Tamworth, Cannock and Stafford. North Staffordshire escaped the worst excesses, though the area was traversed frequently by both the Royalist and Parliamentary armies en route to engagements elsewhere. At the outbreak of the conflict in 1642

Ford Green Hall. (Wikimedia, Creative Commons)

the Staffordshire Moorlands was controlled for Parliament by Sir John Bowyer of Knypersley and there was a Royalist garrison at Biddulph. At Keele Hall, the Sneyds opted for the king and garrisoned their property, but it soon fell to Parliament. The nearest thing to a battle was a skirmish at Biddulph Old Hall in 1644. After winning over Cheshire, the Parliamentary forces laid siege to the hall where several Catholic families had sought refuge. Heavy artillery was used against the contingent of 150 troops and the occupants were left with no alternative but to surrender. The hall was subsequently plundered by the local population and remains a ruin today.

By this time the farmer-potters were beginning to upscale their operations. There are records of pottery being made in Penkhull by about 1600, as well as dish-making at Tunstall. In 1635 three men from Tunstall appeared before the manor court accused of digging holes in the road to obtain clay. In Burslem, a trade in the manufacture of butterpots, used in making butter, developed; these were large cylindrical pots made of unglazed material. Writing in his *Natural History of Staffordshire* in 1686, Robert Plot commented on the prevalence of pottery in the area and described Burslem as the mother town. Plot observed that the potters lived in small cottages in their own area of enclosed land, with bottle-shaped kilns adjoining: 'The greatest pottery they have in this county is carried on at Burslem, . . . for making their several sorts of pots they have as many different sorts of clay, which they dig round about the towne . . . the best being found nearest the coale'. Around this time the practice of glazing with salt was developed as an alternative to the lead glaze used previously. According to some accounts, it was introduced by two Dutch potters called the Elers brothers in their potwork at Bradwell; others attribute it to an accidental discovery in a small pottery at Bagnall. Saggars – fireclay boxes used to hold the wares during firing – were also introduced around this period (see Chapter 2).

New equipment; novel approaches to glazing and preparing the clay; innovations in firing within the oven; and markets for the resulting wares: little by little the potter's art was being assembled, ready to be kick-started in the century that followed.

Early Modern Records

In 1641–2, all males over the age of 18 were required to swear an oath of Protestant loyalty, as part of efforts to count and tax Roman Catholics. Each parish compiled protestation oath returns that were submitted to Parliament, effectively making this a census of all adult males. Regrettably, few records survive. In Staffordshire, the south of the county – Offlow hundred – is well covered but in the north only returns for Newcastle-under-Lyme and Stow (both in Pirehill hundred) survive. There are no returns at all for Totmonslow hundred (the north-east). These records are held at the House of Lords Record Office and available online (**http://digitalarchive.parliament.uk** using references HL/PO/JO/10/1/105/42 and 43 respectively for the two Pirehill series). A similar oath list from 1722, following the Jacobite Rebellion is within the Staffordshire Quarter Sessions [Q/RRo].

Following the Restoration, other taxes were introduced in order to rebuild the country's shattered economy. The hearth tax was a graduated tax based on the number of fireplaces within each household. Introduced in 1662 by Charles II, the hearth tax was collected twice a year, at Michaelmas and Lady Day. A person with only one hearth was relatively poor, whereas somebody with six or more could be considered very affluent. Persons with houses worth less than 20s. per annum were exempt, as were those in receipt of poor relief, otherwise 2s. per hearth was payable. This unpopular legislation was repealed in 1689. The SRS has published the Staffordshire hearth tax for 1666: this was released in stages between 1921 and 1927 and is denoted as part of *Collections*, Third Series. Hearth Tax Online is an academic project providing data and analysis of the hearth tax records (**www.hearthtax.org.uk and http://hearthtax. wordpress.com**).

Engraving of Staffordshire historian Walter Chetwynd by Robert White. (Wikimedia, Creative Commons)

A particularly important source for this period is a list of Stoke-upon-Trent residents drawn up in 1701. Pre-dating the modern census by more than 100 years, such lists were compiled occasionally for a variety of reasons. The Stoke list is dated 2 June 1701 and is written on the first forty pages of a seventy-two-page quarto paper booklet. The listing begins with the date and a brief description of the area included and the format of the entries. It is described as: 'A collection of the names of every particular and individual person in the parish of Stoke-upon-Trent, in the County of Stafford, as they are now residing within their respective Liberties and Families within the said parish; together with the age of every such person, as near as can conveniently be known . . .'. The whole list has been published by the SRS as *The Stoke upon Trent Parish Listing, 1701* (*Collections*, Fourth Series, Vol. XVI).

The SRS has published a long series of rolls from the Staffordshire Quarter Sessions, 1581 through to 1608, transcribed by Sambrooke Arthur Higgins Burne. These appeared in various issues of *Collections*, Third Series between 1929 and 1949. Two particularly name-rich sources transcribed from lists at Staffordshire Record Office are: *The Gentry of Staffordshire 1662–3* (Fourth Series, Vol. II) with additions (Fourth Series, Vol. XIII); and *List of Staffordshire Recusants 1657* (Fourth Series, Vol. II).

Other records from this period published by the SRS include: Muster Rolls for 1539: *Hundreds of Cuttleston and Pyrehill* (New Series, Vol. V); *Hundreds of Seisdon and Totsmonlow* (New Series, Vol. VI, Part 1); *Transcripts of Staffordshire Suits in the Court of Star Chamber* during the reigns of Henry VII and Henry VIII (various volumes, 1909–12); *A Subsidy Roll of 1640 (Pirehill Hundred)* (Third Series, 1941); *Militia Roll For Pirehill Hundred c.1685* (Third Series, 1941); *Notes on Staffordshire Visitation Families* by William Fowler Carter (Third Series, 1910); and numerous family histories, for example, *The Mainwarings of Whitmore and Biddulph* (Third Series, 1933).

The Manorial Documents Register has many documents from this period for manors across North Staffordshire; for example, surveys and rentals from the early 1600s (see above). Similar records can sometimes be found in family and personal papers, such as those for the manor of Newcastle-under-Lyme (at Penkhull) in the Adams Collection [SD1256/EMT7/801A]. The SRO has records of Freemen's Admissions for Newcastle, 1620–1906.

The heralds' visitations were enquiries by the College of Arms into those that claimed the right to bear arms (armigers) by investigating their pedigrees. Between 1530 and 1686, heralds travelled the country producing a vast number of pedigrees and family trees – many of questionable accuracy – as well as notes and other comments. The visitations for Staffordshire (1583, 1614, 1663–4) have been published by the Harleian Society and others; facsimiles are readily available online (see **www.medievalgenealogy.org.uk/sources/visitations. shtml**).

GREAT ESTATES AND HOUSES

In the absence of both a local aristocracy and large mercantile centres, the economy of North Staffordshire began to be dominated by a provincial, land-owning class.

In 1540 William Sneyd purchased a large estate at Keele from the Crown; it had belonged to the Knights Hospitallers before the Dissolution. The Sneyds were related to the powerful Audley family of

Western aspect of Keele Hall from the gardens. (Wikimedia, Creative Commons)

Cheshire and an ancestor had fought against the French at Poitiers in 1356. They became successful drapers and merchants in Chester and were even more successful at marrying wealthy heiresses. Little by little from the fourteenth to the sixteenth centuries the family grew in stature.

William Sneyd's son Ralph built the first Keele Hall in 1580. But having aligned with the wrong side during the Civil War, the family fell into decline. Its fortunes were revived when Lieutenant Colonel Walter Sneyd became a Member of Parliament from 1784 to 1790. He commanded the Staffordshire Militia, which served for thirteen years as a bodyguard to George III at Windsor (see Chapter 9), a position from which he managed to accrue many advantages. His successor, Ralph Sneyd, invested in coal mines at Silverdale and elsewhere that further increased the family's wealth. This he ploughed into managing and improving the estate, eventually rebuilding Keele Hall in 1860. In the early twentieth century, the Sneyd family's association with Keele gradually dwindled in the face of an expensive social life, economic failure and indifferent absentee ownership. The estate remained in the family until 1949, when it was acquired as the home of the newly created University College of North Staffordshire, later to become the University of Keele.

Even more powerful than the Sneyds was the Leveson-Gower family, Dukes of Sutherland. The Leveson family originated in medieval Willenhall, near Wolverhampton, as small-scale sheep farmers. Using the profits from the sale of wool, they expanded their estates in south Staffordshire and members of the family established themselves in the London wool trade. Like the Sneyds, the Levesons were quick to see the economic opportunities brought by the Reformation. Having already bought Lilleshall Abbey in Shropshire, James Leveson purchased Trentham Priory, Stone Priory and other Church estates. The family continued to live at Lilleshall until settling at Trentham in 1630.

In the late seventeenth century the Levesons' Staffordshire estates passed through the female line to the Gower (later Leveson-Gower) family, long-established in Yorkshire. They advanced through the peerage as Barons Gower (1703), Earls Gower (1746) and Marquises of Stafford (1786), until in 1833, having married the Countess of Sutherland, the 2nd Marquis was created Duke of Sutherland. At that time the Duke and Duchess were the largest private landowners in Britain.

During the eighteenth and early nineteenth centuries the Leveson-Gowers treated North Staffordshire as their personal fiefdom, which effectively it was. Earl Gower (later the first Marquis of Stafford) invested in mineral extraction and employed James Brindley to survey for the Trent & Mersey Canal. On his death in 1803 his second son Earl Granville took over the family's interests in Staffordshire. In 1839 the 4th Earl Granville established an iron works at Shelton, where he was already mining coal. The 5th Earl established new works at Etruria in 1850 and created the Shelton Bar Iron Company. Many other industrial ventures in the district were either initiated by the Leveson-Gowers or undertaken on land leased from them. At least their activities in Staffordshire brought visible benefit for the population. In Scotland, the 2nd Marquess (formerly Elizabeth, Countess of Sutherland) is remembered as one of the instigators of the Highland Clearances, effectively destroying the traditional highland way of life and resettling thousands of families and replacing them with sheep.

Trentham Hall in 1880 from 'Morris's Seats of Noblemen and Gentlemen'. The front entrance is at the left, leading into the three-storey main house. The two-storey family wing is at the right, beyond the campanile. (Wikimedia, Creative Commons)

Much of the family's wealth found its way back to Trentham. Having been expanded around 1700, Trentham Hall was again remodelled in the 1740s, including significant additions to the gardens. But even greater things were to come. In 1759 the 2nd Earl Gower commissioned the acclaimed landscape designer Lancelot 'Capability' Brown to transform Trentham. Over the next twenty-one years he had an enormous impact on the estate. The lake was enlarged; the park wall was repaired and expanded; Tunstall Fields, to the west of the hall, was turned into parkland; and two neoclassical lodges were built at the south-west end of the lake with a sunken fence to separate the lawn from the deer park. The house, too, was re-designed by the architect Henry Holland.

But even this was not enough. With money flowing into the Sutherland's coffers, the 2nd Duke instigated yet another rebuilding programme. It was led by the leading architect of the age and produced one of the largest country seats in England, with an equally elaborate and highly acclaimed garden. Yet within fifty years of its completion the whole thing had been flattened (see box below).

THE TRAGEDY OF TRENTHAM HALL

After the death of George Granville, 1st Duke of Sutherland in 1833 his successor George Granville, 2nd Duke of Sutherland, along with his wife Duchess Harriet, embarked upon an extensive rebuilding of the Trentham estate. Celebrated architect Sir Charles Barry, who designed the Houses of Parliament, was engaged to lead a £123,000 building programme. Barry extensively redesigned the hall including rebuilding the dining room and conservatory, as well as putting a belvedere tower over the old kitchen. The orangery, sculpture gallery and clock tower were added and in 1842 he remodelled Trentham church.

Perhaps Barry's greatest achievement was the Italian Flower Gardens. Divided into three terraces, the gardens were flanked on the east by a wrought-iron trellis and on the west by a shrubbery. Barry created the shape and form of the Italian Gardens but he was no plantsman and the celebrated innovative planting schemes were the work of head gardener George Fleming.

However, the Hall's proximity to the intensive industries of the Potteries did not make for a comfortable co-existence. In 1872 gardening journalist D.T. Fish reported that the River Trent was 'the foulest blot on Trentham' describing 'a foul slimy sewer, brimful of the impurities of every dirty crowded town that hugs its banks'. Sadly the Trent also provided water to Trentham's lake and its fountains, which meant the once beautiful features were ruined by the stench of brown sewage.

As pollution increased, Trentham's allure waned. In 1905 the then Duke and Duchess abandoned the house and offered it to the Borough Council. After due consideration it politely declined. Trentham Hall was sold for recovery of the materials to a local builder and promptly demolished. The contents of the house were sold off for a paltry £500.

The site re-opened to the public in the 1930s following the formation of Trentham Gardens Ltd to maintain and manage the gardens. A new ballroom was built, as well as an art deco outdoor swimming pool by the lake. After being used for war work between 1939 and 1945, post-war Trentham established itself as a venue for dances and entertainment. Several attempts at restoration during the 1970s and 1980s had to be abandoned. Eventually, in 1996, a £100 million regeneration scheme was approved that has restored the historic estate and gardens into a popular tourist and leisure destination.

The return of the estate to active use for the people of Stoke-on-Trent and the nation is to be welcomed, but the wilful loss of Charles Barry's Trentham Hall – one of the country's most notable Victorian houses – remains an enduring tragedy.

The Leveson-Gowers and the Sneyds were at the apex of a pyramid of county families. Others with influence within the district were the Bowyers family of Knypersley Hall, the Batemans of Biddulph Grange, the Foley family of Longton Hall and the Swinnertons of Butterton Hall, near Newcastle-under-Lyme. The latter passed into the Pilkington family after Mary Swinnerton married Sir William Pilkington, 8th Baronet in the late 1700s. Many of these gentry families were 'nouveau riche', having made their money in pottery or other industries. Early pioneers Josiah Wedgwood and Josiah Spode established themselves at Etruria Hall and Fenton Hall respectively (the Spodes later moved to The Mount, Penkhull). Meanwhile, the Davenports extended and transformed both Westwood Hall, near Leek, and Wootton Hall, near Ellastone. At various times, Maer Hall was owned by both the Wedgwoods and the Davenports. Other industrialists in the area included the Kinnersly family at Clough Hall, Kidsgrove, who were bankers and iron merchants from Newcastle-under-Lyme. Hardly any of these country seats survive. Walton & Porter (2006) describe the fate of the district's lost houses and the Lost Heritage website has photographs of some of them (**www.lostheritage.org.uk**).

LAND, ESTATE AND PROPERTY RECORDS
Taxation
The most important source for studying land and property during the eighteenth century is land tax. Introduced in the early 1700s, this became an annual tax levied on all landowners holding land with a

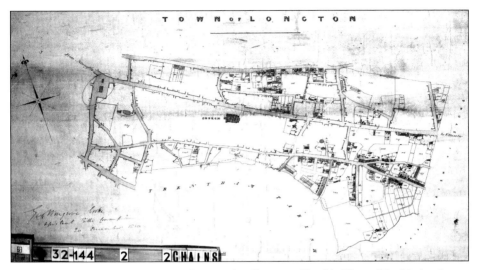

Tithe map of Longton, c. 1840, showing the allotment of land holdings. (The National Archives)

value of more than 20s. per year. The surviving documents consist of assessments and returns and show the owners of real estate in each parish. From 1772, the returns were altered to include not just the owners but all occupiers/tenants of land and property in the parish with the exception of paupers. Most documents survive from 1780 to 1832, a period when the returns were used to establish a person's entitlement to vote and were in effect electoral registers. From 1780, duplicate copies were lodged with the Clerk of the Peace and are now found among Quarter Session records [Q/RPl]; these are available at the SRO on microfilm.

From 1788 land owners were able to commute their tax payments into a one-off payment but their names were still recorded each year. As part of the process a near complete listing of all occupiers and owners for the whole country was compiled in 1798 and can be found at TNA [Class IR 23, with related records in IR 22 and IR 24]; these are online at Ancestry.

The Tithe Commutation Act of 1836 reformed the system of tithes that had been levied on farmers and landowners since the Middle Ages, whereby they paid one-tenth of their annual produce to the church. The

Act allowed tithes to be converted into cash payments, called tithe awards. New maps were drawn up to show who owned each field and property, along with a schedule (known as an apportionment) listing all the owners and tenants, and what each plot of land was worth. Tithe Commissioners administered and collected the annual payments, which were based on land values and the price of corn. Records were made in triplicate: one for the parish, one for the diocese and one for the Tithe Commission.

For Staffordshire, parish and diocesan copies, often including pre-1836 parish tithe lists, are at either the SRO or William Salt Library; those of the Tithe Commission are at TNA [Classes IR 29 and IR 30]. *SSA Guide to Sources No. 3: Tithe Maps and Awards* is a handlist of local holdings. Staffordshire Name Indexes has a searchable index of the awards themselves (1836–45): searches show information such as owner's name, occupier's name, township and parish, and plot name and number. It is proposed to digitize the tithe maps and make them available online; similar maps for the whole country are already available at TheGenealogist subscription website (**www.the genealogist.co.uk**).

Glebe terriers were surveys of the Church possessions in the parish, listing houses, fields and sums due in tithes. For Staffordshire, most surviving terriers date from the seventeenth and eighteenth centuries and are held within the former Lichfield Record Office collection. Transcripts have been published by the SRS as *Staffordshire Glebe Terriers 1585–1884. Part One – Abbots Bromley to Knutton* (*Collections*, Fourth Series, Vol. XXII (2008)); and *Staffordshire Glebe Terriers 1585–1884. Part Two – Lapley to Yoxall* (Fourth Series, Vol. XXIII (2009)).

The window tax was one of many obscure taxes levied during the eighteenth century. Introduced by William III as a replacement for the much-despised hearth tax, it imposed a flat rate tax per dwelling, initially at 2*s.* per house. Houses with between ten and twenty windows paid an additional 4*s.* and those with more than twenty paid another 8*s.* Some householders blocked up windows so as to reduce their tax liability. The tax was payable by the occupier of a property rather than the owner and those not paying the church or poor rate were exempt. From 1784 it was combined with the house tax. The SRO has returns from various dates for Trentham [D593/N/2/16], Newcastle-under-Lyme [D1798/618/227-228] and Totmonslow North [D3359/12/1/217].

Estate and Property

The enclosure of agricultural land effectively broke up the smallholding system of farming and consolidated vast open shared tracts of land in the hands of wealthy landowners. The process began in the twelfth century but became widespread from 1750. Under a legal process known as Inclosure, open land was allotted to landowners by private Acts of Parliament and later by the Inclosure Acts between 1801 and 1845. These Acts list the landowner who brought the case to Parliament, while the enclosure award details how the land was to be divided up between the landowner and others, together with the amounts of land. In addition, a map of the land under investigation as part of the enclosure process might survive with the names of the landowners written on them. The SRO has surviving records for Staffordshire under Inclosure (Awards, plans, tithe agreements and exchanges) [main series under Q/RDc]; copies are often found in family papers, parish documents, and other collections. *SSAS Guide to Sources No. 5: Staffordshire Enclosure Acts, Awards & Maps* is a guide to holdings. An academic project has produced an electronic catalogue and directory of enclosure maps for England and Wales (**http://enclosuremaps.data-archive.ac.uk**).

Staffordshire and Stoke-on-Trent Archives holds a huge collection of records and papers relating to the estates of the Leveson-Gower family. The index runs to 9,600 entries and is likely to refer to tenants or others who had dealings with the estate. Examples include: Agents' annual accounts, 1837–8, 1843–4; North Staffordshire Farm Rentals, 1812–57; Knowles Colliery, time and wages books, 1787–1802; and Lightwood Cottage Rentals, 1813–57. The Sutherland Collection has its own website (**www.sutherlandcollection.org.uk**) with information and articles about the family; and Staffordshire Name Indexes has a downloadable index for this collection.

The Sneyd Family Papers at Keele University comprise manorial, estate, legal and business records about the family, as well as watercolour and pencil sketches (**www.keele.ac.uk/library/specarc/**

collections/sneydfamily). The family's nineteenth-century correspondence is particularly rich and survives in greatest volume.

Other major family and estate collections covering the district (many held by the Potteries Museum & Art Gallery) are: Adams family of Hanley, Cobridge and Newcastle-under-Lyme [SD 1256]; Davenport family of Maer Hall and Westwood Hall [D3272]; Heathcote family of Longton [SD4842/11]; Broade family of Fenton Vivian [SD4842/12]; Wedgwood family of Burslem and Bignall End [SD4842/13-16]; Wood family of Burslem [SD4842/16]; and the Swinnerton family of Butterton Hall [SD4842/17]. All contain items such as deeds, rentals, mortgages, leases and agreements, sales particulars, estate correspondence, plans and accounts. These and other collections are summarized in the *Guide to Staffordshire Family Collections*, published by the SSA.

Solicitors' records are much under-rated but can contain a wealth of information, not just on large estates but also on town properties and tenants. Two important examples are the firms of Rigby, Rowley & Cooper [D3272] and Knight & Sons [D4452], both of Newcastle-under-Lyme. Mortgages, conveyances, wills, deeds, tenancies and leases, marriage settlements: all of these can end up in solicitors' records. However, as the family may have used a solicitor some distance away (or firms may have moved), a broad search may need to be made. Auctioneers' catalogues and sale notices in newspapers can provide a snapshot of an estate, or part of an estate, at the point when it was sold. Sometimes deeds can be found within the Quarter Sessions records under *Enrolments (Deeds, Wills and Papists' Estates)* [Q/RD].

Those in the upper echelons of society will have been listed in the many directories of the peerage, baronetage and landed gentry published from the eighteenth century onwards by publishers such as Burke and Debrett; copies are available via the Internet Archive and other digitization initiatives.

Staffordshire Name Indexes has a database of *Copyhold Tenants of the Manor of Newcastle-under-Lyme, 1700–1832* based on Roden (2008). Those with copyhold tenure over property had to record ownership through registering in the court roll. The property concerned was concentrated in the townships of Penkhull and Boothen, Clayton and Seabridge, Hanford, Hanley, Shelton and Wolstanton.

Other Rural Records

Mills were a key part of many rural communities. The Mills Archive holds a wealth of information about people connected with mills and milling, together with a separate database of mills across the country (**www.millsarchivetrust.org**). It includes extracts from the *Staffordshire Advertiser* for the 1830s and 1840s regarding mills for sale and to let, notices of bankruptcy and insolvency, and miscellaneous references to mills and millers.

Under Acts of 1710, 1784 and 1785 those shooting or caring for game had to have a licence. The SRO has a long series of registers for gamekeepers from 1784 to 1934 under *Game Preservation and Taxation* [Q/RTg].

FURTHER INFORMATION

Cooper, Gary, *Farmers and Potters: A History of Pre-Industrial Stoke on Trent* (Churnet Valley Books, 2002)

Durie, Bruce, *Understanding Documents for Genealogy and Local History* (History Press, 2013)

Roden, Peter, *Copyhold Potworks and Housing of the Staffordshire Potteries, 1700–1832* (Wood Broughton Publications, 2008)

Walton, Cathryn and Lindsey Porter, *Lost Houses of North Staffordshire* (Landmark Publishing Ltd, 2006)

Westcott, Brooke, *Making Sense of Latin Documents for Local and Family Historians* (Family History Partnership, 2014)

Chapter 9

IN UNIFORM

LOCAL REGIMENTS

Since the modern army began to take shape in the mid-eighteenth century, Staffordshire has been closely associated with the two regiments that bore its name. In particular, the historic North Staffordshire Regiment (Prince of Wales's) recruited extensively from the local area during the First World War and was involved in many high-profile campaigns.

The North Staffordshire Regiment

The North Staffordshire Regiment was formed in 1881 through the merger of the 64th (2nd Staffordshire) Regiment of Foot and 98th (Prince of Wales's) Regiment of Foot, both of which had affiliations to the county. These two regular regiments became the new unit's 1st and 2nd Battalions, respectively. The Militia and Rifle Volunteers forces of North Staffordshire were also incorporated into this new regiment (see below, p. 185). A permanent depot was established at Whittington Barracks, Lichfield, which also housed the newly formed South Staffordshire Regiment.

The 64th Regiment of Foot was originally raised in 1756 as the 2nd Battalion of the 11th (Devonshire) Foot, and was renumbered the 64th in 1758. It served in the West Indies during the Seven Years War, America during the American War of Independence, and South America, the West Indies and Canada during the Napoleonic Wars. Subsequent long periods were spent in Ireland and the West Indies before action was seen in India during the Indian Mutiny. The 98th Regiment of Foot, raised in 1824 in Chichester, had a much shorter history, but like the 64th had spent the majority of its time overseas. It served for a long

Officers of the 1st Battalion, North Staffordshire Regiment, shortly before embarking for France in Cambridge, August 1914. Of those who sailed, only five were still with the battalion in January 1915, most of the remainder having been killed or wounded. (Wikimedia, Creative Commons)

period in South Africa before seeing action in China in the First Anglo-Chinese (or Opium) War and India on the North West Frontier.

The North Staffordshire Regiment was heavily committed to the fighting during the First World War. In addition to the two regular battalions several territorial and service battalions were deployed. The battalions that served in France took part in many of the major actions of the war including the 1915 Battle of Neuve Chapelle, the 1915 Battle of Loos, the Battle of the Somme in 1916, the Third Battle of Ypres (generally known as the Battle of Passchendaele) in 1917, and the Battle of Amiens in 1918.

After the Armistice, the 1st Battalion was posted to Curragh, Ireland, becoming involved in the Irish War of Independence until 1922, when it moved to Gibraltar. In 1923 it was posted to India and remained in the Far East until 1948. The 2nd Battalion was initially stationed in India after the war, and later spent time in Gibraltar (1930–2) and Palestine (1936–7). In 1921, the regimental title was changed to The North Staffordshire Regiment (The Prince of Wales's).

Throughout the Second World War the 1st Battalion served in India and Burma, while the 2nd Battalion remained in Italy and North Africa. The North Staffordshire Regiment was awarded twenty-two battle honours during the conflict.

It continued to perform in peace-keeping roles up to its amalgamation with the South Staffordshire Regiment in 1959.

The South Staffordshire Regiment

The South Staffordshire Regiment was formed in 1881 through the merger of the 38th Regiment of Foot and the 80th Regiment of Foot, which also had Staffordshire affiliations. The 38th Foot, the new unit's 1st Battalion, served in Malta and Sudan, while the 80th Foot, the new 2nd Battalion, spent time in Egypt and India. After deployment to South Africa during and after the Boer War, both battalions served in France for most of the First World War. The regiment also raised eleven Territorial and New Army battalions during the conflict.

During the Second World War the 1st Battalion saw action in Palestine and Burma, while the 2nd Battalion fought in Tunisia, Sicily, Italy and at Arnhem. After the war it was granted an arm badge showing a glider in recognition of its service in an air-landing role.

Following a defence review, in 1959 the North Staffordshire Regiment (The Prince of Wales's) and the South Staffordshire Regiment were merged to form The Staffordshire Regiment (The Prince of Wales's). Under subsequent reorganizations, this became the 3rd Battalion, The Mercian Regiment (Staffords). The regimental museum is at Whittington Barracks, Lichfield (**www.staffordshireregiment museum.com**).

A list of regimental histories for Staffordshire, including yeomanry and militia units, was published in the June 2000 edition of the *Midland Ancestor* (Midland Ancestors). GENUKI's Staffordshire pages have an extensive military bibliography (**www.genuki.org.uk/big/eng/STS**).

Militia and Territorials

English militia were part-time military units established at county level for home defence. After a dormant period following the Civil War, they were reinstated by the 1757 Militia Act. The men would receive basic training at annual camps and be available to be called up in times of national emergency. When volunteers proved insufficient, a parish selected men by ballot. These men then either served or found a substitute to take their place.

In Staffordshire the militia is known to have existed since at least the seventeenth century. It was embodied as required and had units known by various names and titles. In 1797 the Staffordshire Militia was inspected by George III. He was so impressed with the regiment's smart appearance that he ordered it to Windsor Castle to take up royal duties. It was stationed there again in 1799, 1800 and 1801, when it was disembodied. The king expressed great regret at its departure; however, when hostilities with France were renewed in 1803, the regiment was reformed and ordered back to Windsor. It was welcomed by the king in person, who led it to the barracks. In 1805, George III granted the regiment the additional honour of 'The King's Own' in its title. As a royal regiment the facing colour of the uniform was then changed from yellow to royal blue. The regiment left Windsor in 1812, and was again stood down in 1814. It was re-embodied for a matter of some months in the following year, after Napoleon's escape from Elba.

At the time of the formation of the North Staffordshire Regiment in 1881 four militia and volunteer units were taken into the new regiment, each forming a separate battalion. These were: the King's Own (2nd Staffordshire) Light Infantry Militia (which became the 3rd (Militia) Battalion, based in Stafford); the King's Own (3rd Staffordshire) Rifles Militia (4th (Militia) Battalion, based in Newcastle-under-Lyme); 2nd Staffordshire (Staffordshire Rangers) Rifle Volunteer Corps (1st Volunteer Battalion, based in Stoke-on-Trent); and 5th Staffordshire Rifle Volunteer Corps (2nd Volunteer Battalion) based in Lichfield but later moved to Burton-on-Trent.

Together with the Volunteer battalions of the South Staffordshire Regiment, the new 1st and 2nd Volunteer battalions formed the Staffordshire Volunteer Infantry Brigade in 1888. This brigade was intended to assemble at Wolverhampton in time of war, while in peacetime it acted as a focus for collective training of the Volunteers.

The formation of the Territorial Force in 1908 regularized links between the old county militias and volunteers and their regular army counterparts. At that time the South and North Staffords each had six battalions: two Regular, two Militia and two Territorial. The North Staffordshire Regiment's two Volunteer battalions were renumbered as the 5th and 6th battalions, forming part of the Staffordshire Brigade in the North Midland Division.

Staffordshire Record Office has militia lists for various dates and locations, including Staffordshire Yeomanry, 1804–1946 with gaps [D1300]; North Staffordshire Local Militia returns, 1810–19 [D1788]; Trentham Loyal Volunteers, 1803 [D1554/161]; and Newcastle Volunteers Armed Association, 1819 [D1460]. TNA has a long run of Staffordshire militia lists from across the county, 1781–1876 [in class WO 13]; Gibson & Medlycott (2013) has further details or consult the TNA Discovery catalogue. The militia list for the 1st Staffordshire, 1781–2 has been published in *County Militia Regimental Returns* (**www.fhindexes.co.uk**); a transcript is available on the STCA Search Room computers. Anderton (2016) lists the names of men who joined home defence units in North Staffordshire at the height of the Napoleonic Wars. Midlands Historical Data has histories for some of these militia and early territorial units (**www.midlandshistoricaldata.org**).

FIRST WORLD WAR
Answering the Call

When the First World War broke out in August 1914 the Potteries, like many towns and cities, answered Lord Kitchener's call for volunteers to enlist. Across the country, over 100,000 rushed to sign up within the first two weeks. Within the Six Towns men gathered at recruiting stations to join up: the main station was at Stoke Town Hall. The North Staffordshire Regiment's official history recounts that: 'The streets round it were crowded with men, and inside the buildings were masses of men struggling to be accepted and passed by the doctors. It was an unforgettable sight.'

North Staffordshire Regiment cap badge. (Wikimedia, Creative Commons)

The ranks of the 5th North Staffords, the original territorial unit, were soon swelled, as the depot at Shelton was overrun by new recruits, all desperate to serve king and country. 'They were of all classes and occupations, and were the pick of the youth from the neighbourhood. A large contingent consisted of men who had been educated at the Newcastle High School.'

Leaving their new recruits behind, on 11 August 1914 the 5th North Staffords marched from Hanley to Burton, passing through Stoke, Meir, Blythe Bridge, Tean and Checkley. As they rested in a field near Checkley, their commander-in-chief, Lieutenant Colonel John Hall Knight, read a telegram asking them to volunteer for foreign service. The men unanimously agreed (as if they had a choice!) and Knight sent a telegram back to the War Office offering the battalion's services abroad.

The 1st/5th North Staffords was one of six Territorial Force battalions added to the North Staffordshire Regiment during the First World War, and the one most closely associated with the Potteries. In addition, eight Service and Reserve battalions were raised. Together with two regular and two pre-existing Reserve battalions, this swelled the number of North Staffordshire battalions to eighteen.

The 1/5th and 1/6th Battalions were among the first Territorial Force units to go to France, arriving in February and March 1915. They fought in the Battle of Loos in 1915, as well as at Gommecourt on the northern flank of the Battle of the Somme. The 1/5th was disbanded in January 1918 and the men dispersed to other units. Part of the 1/6th Battalion was involved in the celebrated action to seize the Riqueval Bridge over the St Quentin Canal in September 1918. Their commanding officer, acting Captain A.H. Charlton, was decorated with the Distinguished Service Order. Altogether, the regiment was awarded fifty-two battle honours during the First World War.

Staffordshire Name Indexes has a database of over 13,000 photographs of soldiers published in the *Staffordshire Weekly Sentinel* newspaper (**www.staffsnameindexes.org.uk**). These are typically head and shoulder shots in pictures about the size of a cigarette card. The photographs would have been provided by the soldier's family on a voluntary basis and would generally have been accompanied by a news item. Their publication may relate to the fact that the man in question was missing, wounded, taken prisoner, in hospital, or been recognized for gallantry and was not necessarily a fatality. The STCA has the original newspapers on microfilm (see Chapter 1).

The capture of Riqueval Bridge, 1918 where the 1/6th Battalion North Staffords saw action. (Wikimedia, Creative Commons)

Major Edward Blizzard, managing director of a brick and tile manufacturer in Hanley, became North Staffordshire's principal recruiting officer during the conflict. The SRO has his scrapbooks, which include the story of Lance Corporal William Coltman, VC, the most highly decorated NCO of the First World War [SRO: D797/2/2].

Capper (2014) is an authoritative history of the regular 1st and 2nd Battalions of the North Staffordshire Regiment during the First World War. Sheldon (2004) describes the experiences of men from Leek who fought and died in the conflict. Jeffrey Elson's two books document personnel from both Staffordshire regiments who have been decorated since 1914 (Elson, 2004 and 2014). STCA has records from the North Staffordshire Regiment Reunion Association, 1926–76 which includes membership books [SA/NSRA]. Commercial websites have extensive series relating to military personnel including service records, pension records, medal cards, gallantry citations and mentions in dispatches, and soldiers' wills.

Life at Home

As soldiers risked their lives on the front line, for their families and friends left at home life too was hard. This was the first time that civilians were a crucial part of a new kind of warfare. Even though men, women and children in Staffordshire were far from the guns, the authorities recognized that forming a resilient home front could make the difference between winning and losing the war.

With food in short supply, lengthy queues formed at shops. Drawn by the rumour of supplies, women and children gathered early in the morning to queue for scarce goods like sugar, margarine and tea. The government feared food shortages could spark riots. Zeppelins were seen over Staffordshire and conscientious objectors, such as Edwin Wheeldon of Burton, faced gaol for their beliefs.

Hunt (2017) describes life on the home front in Staffordshire during the First World War. The book is based, in part, on papers from the Mid-Staffordshire Appeals Tribunal, a body that heard appeals against military conscription [SRO: C/C/M/2/1-35]. The records of Military Appeals Tribunals were ordered to be destroyed after the war and the survival of those for Staffordshire is believed to be unique. Military tribunals were also reported in the *Staffordshire Advertiser*, which gives details of the cases being heard but does not give the names or addresses of those involved.

The Great War Staffordshire website served as a portal for the 1914–18 Centenary celebrations in the county and is likely to remain active for the foreseeable future (**www.staffordshiregreatwar.com**). It includes details of the Staffordshire Great War Trail which was created to connect the county's principal landmarks related to the First World War. These include the National Memorial Arboretum at Alrewas; Cannock Chase Commonwealth War Cemetery; and the Staffordshire Regimental Museum, where there is a replica First World War trench.

SECOND WORLD WAR
Air Raids and Evacuation
When the twentieth century's second great conflict came, the Potteries found itself in the front line. Not being a centre for armaments manufacture or other heavy production, the district avoided the blanket bombing suffered by some other areas. But German planes could often be seen over North Staffordshire en route to Manchester, Liverpool, Crewe and other prime targets.

There were around twenty recorded bombings across Stoke-on-Trent and North Staffordshire itself. The main targets were the Michelin and Dunlop tyre factories, the railway goods yard, the British Aluminium Works at Milton and the munitions factory at Radway Green. In January 1941 bombs fell in Old Stoke Road during a raid targeted at the Michelin works. Dorothy Hordell, who worked at Dunlops in Etruria, recalled bombing raids over Hanley for the BBC's People's War Archive (**www.bbc.co.uk/history/ww2peopleswar/categories/c1152/**):

> I used to sit and watch the German planes go over. They were after the aluminium works down Birches Head Lane and the steelworks at Etruria. They used to follow the canal that low you could see the markings on them. They came over one night and dropped a basket of incendiary bombs on Birches Head Lane. It seemed the world was on fire and everybody was running for

Air raid damage at Chesterton, 14 December 1940. (Staffordshire Past Track)

cover. I can't remember the fire brigade coming out. Our planes chased off the Germans. One German plane dropped one bomb that went through an air raid shelter up Campbell Terrace in Birches Head. Nobody was killed. They had a lucky escape they did.

One of the worst attacks was on Saturday, 14 December 1940 when a lone German raider attacked Chesterton, Newcastle-under-Lyme. Sixteen people are thought to have been killed, including several family members and evacuees from London. The Salvation Army Hall, which was fortunately unoccupied at the time, took a direct hit. On another occasion a bomb was dropped on Leek, apparently by accident.

Evacuation was introduced in order to protect children. Staffordshire was initially viewed as a 'neutral' location, meaning it was neither likely to receive evacuees nor send children out of the county. Later it was redefined as a reception area.

Evacuation to Staffordshire occurred in two waves. During the early stages of the war, under Operation Pied Piper, over 8,000 unaccompanied children were evacuated to the county from nearby cities such as Birmingham, Manchester and Liverpool. Most of these soon returned home when the anticipated bombing of cities did not materialize. A second wave of evacuation was initiated in 1940 and increased after the start of the Blitz. This time evacuees came to the county from all over Britain. Often they were evacuated with their school and accompanied by teachers. There were also children who were evacuated privately by their families to live with local relatives or friends. Many of these evacuees experienced a different way of life in Staffordshire's towns and rural communities to the one they were used to.

The Staffordshire Past Track portal has photographs of bomb damage and other aspects of life in Staffordshire during the Second World War (**https://tinyurl.com/ya88fgzc**). The Children on the Move website and associated book document the experiences of evacuees and host families in Staffordshire and provide extensive learning resources for schools (**www.childrenonthemove.org.uk**).

The Home Guard

In May 1940 the government broadcast a request for Local Defence Volunteers, the intention being to create a part-time civilian army to defend against any invasion. Within a few days several thousand men had volunteered in North Staffordshire. They were organized into six Home Guard Battalions covering all parts of the district. The 1st Staffordshire Battalion covered Stoke; 2nd Staffordshire covered Burslem; 3rd Staffordshire covered Longton and Meir; and 4th Staffordshire covered Hanley. These four Battalions formed No. 1 Group of No. 3 Zone of the West Lancashire Area. Further afield were the 5th Battalion in Leek and the 6th Battalion in Cheadle.

Although held together initially by little more than their own enthusiasm, organization was quickly tightened up and the Home Guard began to establish itself. The 2nd Staffordshire Battalion, for example, was commanded by Lieutenant Colonel Reg Brown, a Captain Mainwaring-type character who had served in submarines from 1916–19 and then, with his brother, had set up Browns Motor Company in Tunstall.

Towards the end of 1941 many factories began to form units drawn from their personnel, initially for the purpose of protecting their own premises. One such was the Royal Ordnance Factory at Swynnerton (see below).

The Staffs Home Guard site describes the British Home Guard and specific Home Guard units across the country and is particularly detailed for Staffordshire (**www.staffshomeguard.co.uk**). The STCA has a reprint of the *Home Guard List 1941* for Western Command, a rare document that lists all serving Home Guard officers (Savannah Publications, 2005). The Staffordshire Past Track portal has pictures related to the local Home Guard and the Air Raid Precautions. The BBC's People's War Archive for Stoke and Staffordshire has recollections of local Home Guard activities (web address as above). Staffordshire University has the Iris Strange Collection, comprising personal and official letters and documents relating to the position of Second World War widows.

The War Effort in the Potteries

The Luftwaffe's failure to knock out the Royal Air Force in the Battle of Britain owed much to the ground-breaking design of the Spitfire aircraft, designed by Potteries-born R.J. Mitchell (see box below). The Spitfire played a decisive role in defending the country and at one point more than 500 aircraft per month were being produced.

As noted above, other locations central to the war effort were the Michelin and Dunlop tyre factories, the Shelton steelworks and various ordnance and munitions factories. One of these was at Mill Meece, Swynnerton, between Newcastle-under-Lyme and Stafford. Construction work started in 1939, with production beginning the following year. Large numbers of people were employed, peaking at 18,000 in 1942. The factory's function was mainly the filling of ammunition cases with explosive. Such was its size and importance that a dedicated branch railway line was built to serve it. The City Surveyor's Collection at the STCA has maps of bomb damage and Air Raid Precautions from the period (see Chapter 1).

Planes at Meir Aerodrome. (Public domain)

In 1934 Stoke-on-Trent City Aerodrome had opened at Meir. It was the first of three municipal airports constructed in Staffordshire during that period, the others being at Walsall and Wolverhampton in the south of the county. From 1939 Meir became an RAF station where novice pilots were trained. Beaufighters and Blenheim bombers assembled at the nearby Rootes factory at Blythe Bridge were also flown from Meir. As the number of air bases across Staffordshire proliferated, American GIs and pilots became a common sight in the Potteries.

After the war, activities at Meir were largely confined to glider training for Air Training Corps cadets, although Staffordshire Potteries flew aircraft in the 1950s and the Staffs Light Plane Group continued until the 1970s. However, Meir was doomed from the start by its location close to a densely populated area, the sloping ground and an industrial haze which created visibility problems. The last plane took off in 1973 and the site was subsequently developed for housing. Brew (1997) has a more detailed history.

Many of the country's most important institutions and cultural assets were moved out of London during the war to escape air raids on the

194

REGINALD J. MITCHELL: FATHER OF THE SPITFIRE

Reginald J. Mitchell was one of the great designers and engineers of the twentieth century.

He was born in Butt Lane, near Stoke-on-Trent in 1895. He trained as an engineer and then joined the Vickers Armstrong Supermarine Co. in 1916, rapidly becoming chief designer. During the 1920s and early 1930s he designed sea-planes, creating revolutionary designs, such as the Supermarine S6, which set speed records and won the Schiedner trophy in 1931. From these beautiful seaplanes, the Spitfire was born.

Reginald Mitchell, designer of the Spitfire. (Wikimedia, Creative Commons)

Among his many accolades, Mitchell was awarded the Silver Medal of the Royal Aeronautical Society and made an Associate Member of the Institute of Civil Engineers in 1929, the same year that he was awarded the CBE. Unfortunately, he did not live to see the success of his Spitfire in combat in the Second World War, nor even to see it fly in anger. He died of cancer in 1937, aged only 42.

R.J. Mitchell is commemorated at several locations. There is a plaque on the house where he was born at 115 Congleton Road, Butt Lane. The Mitchell Memorial Theatre (now the Mitchell Arts Centre) in Broad Street, Hanley was named after him in 1957. Most prominent is a statue that stands outside the Potteries Museum & Art Gallery in Hanley, while the museum's Spitfire Gallery showcases the man and his aeronautical achievements.

capital. Almost as soon as war broke out the Bank of England relocated to Trentham Gardens, the former home of the Duke of Sutherland. All the major clearing banks had staff there, each bank occupying its own section in the ballroom and the foreign section on the stage. A lot of the staff were moved up from London and billeted in the local area. Many experienced profound cultural shock, being used to the big city. They tended to keep to themselves and took to calling themselves 'the Outcasts'.

The STCA has a register of Polish personnel working at W.H. Grindley & Co. in Tunstall, 1947–53, many of whom are likely to have arrived during the Second World War [SD 1332].

WAR MEMORIALS AND ROLLS OF HONOUR

Men and women who fell in various conflicts are commemorated in memorials and rolls of honour across North Staffordshire. Each of the Six Towns has at least one war memorial, generally positioned outside the town hall or in a civic square. There are many more in churches, schools, businesses and public buildings, and in outlying towns and villages. These memorials and rolls cover several centuries in some cases, though concentrate mostly on the First World War and Second World War.

Researching Staffordshire's Great War Memorials, published by SSA (2014), lists all of the county's local war memorials and provides a guide to how to research them (available as a free download from **www. staffordshiregreatwar.com**). The STCA has the *Roll of Honour Land Force, World War 2* (Vol. 5) which includes casualties from the North Staffordshire Regiment (Savannah Publications, 2002).

The Roll of Honour website has transcripts from memorials and rolls of honour across the country, including Staffordshire (**www.roll-of-honour.com***).* As well as later conflicts, it includes information about the Fenton and Hanley Boer War memorials. Civilian cemeteries in the UK containing war graves and memorials (although not individual names) are listed at the WW1 Cemeteries site (**www.ww1 cemeteries.com**). The National Railway Museum website has the roll of honour of railway employees from the conflict (www.nrm.org.uk). For those buried abroad see other sites, such as that of the Commonwealth War Graves Commission (www.cwgc.org).

Midlands Historical Data publishes many military books on CD, including rolls of honour and regimental histories (Militia and Territorials as well as Regular units).

The Military Collection at Aldershot Public Library is a useful resource for those researching military ancestors. It comprises nearly 20,000 books, most available for loan, together with many specialist databases. The library staff will undertake searches for a nominal fee (**http://tinyurl.com/nau9c24**).

THE POLICE SERVICE

Before the early nineteenth century policing in England had relied on parish constables, members of the community who were elected by their fellow parishioners and took on a variety of local duties. In 1829 Sir Robert Peel formed the Metropolitan Police in London as the first paid professional police force. This professional model began to be adopted elsewhere. In North Staffordshire the first town to do so was Newcastle-under-Lyme which set up a borough police force in 1834. The following year, the Municipal Corporation Act of 1835 compelled all boroughs to establish a watch committee, and appoint head constables and other constables.

Newcastle Police, 1890s. (Public domain)

The Six Towns were exempt from these requirements, as none had yet been granted borough status (and would not be until Hanley incorporated in 1857). In the absence of the Towns' own arrangements, it fell to the new Staffordshire County Constabulary to provide policing. A few officers and men (exact numbers are unknown) were stationed in Hanley from 1843, as part of the new Pottery Division. It was not until September 1870, thirteen years after becoming a borough, that Hanley set up its own watch committee and police force. At that time the new Hanley Borough Police had thirty-one men. Stanford Alexander, the Chief Constable of Newcastle-under-Lyme, was appointed to lead the force. He also took charge of the Police Fire Brigade: this was formed in 1871, reorganized in 1901 and survived until 1910 when the new County Borough took over responsibility for fire-fighting.

After federation in 1910, the force became known as Borough of Stoke-on-Trent Police and was renamed Stoke-on-Trent City Police in 1925. Women were first admitted in 1921 but numbers were capped at two policewomen for the next twenty years. Only in 1941, when police forces were ordered to relieve male officers for war duties, did numbers increase. Eventually, in 1968, Stoke-on-Trent City Police amalgamated with Staffordshire County Police to form a single county-wide force.

Tunstall & Cowdell (2002) describes the history of policing in the Potteries from the formation of borough police forces through to the 1968 merger. Many names are mentioned and its annex lists all of those serving on amalgamation.

Police Records

Staffordshire Record Office has a complete series of County Police Force Registers, covering the period 1842–1977 [C/PC/1/6/1-2 and C/PC/12/1/29/3]. These contain the main personnel record for every officer who served in Staffordshire Police, giving information about the officer's age and place of origin, appearance, career progression and reason for leaving the service. There is an online index to these holdings on Staffordshire Name Indexes. The SRO also holds police personnel records from 1920 to 1977, which may be consulted by special arrangement. Other police records at the SRO include registers of appointments and promotions, and superannuation registers which record the pensions paid to men who had left the service or gratuities paid to dependants.

The Staffordshire Constabulary Defaulters Register contains information about disciplinary offences committed by members of Staffordshire Constabulary, covering the period 1857 to 1886 and 1904 to 1923 [SRO: C/PC/15/1/1 and C/PC/29]. Many of the offences recorded relate to police officers' over familiarity with undesirable elements of society, such as prostitutes, or to the abuse of alcohol. Again, Staffordshire Name Indexes offers an online index to these records.

Neither of the personnel records above cover borough police forces, such as operated in the Potteries. Hence, officers who served in Hanley from 1870 and in the rest of the Potteries between 1910 and 1968 are unlikely to be included, unless they also served with the county force. The records of Stoke-on-Trent Borough (and later City) Police, 1885–1968 appear in the SSA catalogue under various headings: C/PC/6/1; C/PC/14; SD 1651; SD 1669, all of which are held at the STCA. These series include a register of applicants, 1909–26 [C/PC/14/22/2]; and a register of men from Staffordshire Police absorbed into Stoke-on-Trent Borough Police on its formation, 1910–19 [C/PC/14/22/4].

During the First World War many men signed up for roles in the Second Police Reserve, a body of volunteer police constables and the forerunner of the Special Police Reserve. This reserve helped to compensate for the loss of officers who enlisted to fight. The STCA has a register of those who signed up for the Stoke-on-Trent area [C/PC/14/22/5]. The register contains details such as previous service in the armed forces, address, year of birth, physical description and other notes, such as current employer and whether the men were willing to work unpaid or not. Many of those who joined the Second Police Reserve later left in order to enlist in the regular armed forces.

Another useful source is the Third County Force Register, 1894–1935 [SRO: C/PC/12/1/29/3], which relates to officers who joined the police reserve. A name index is also available [SRO: C/PC/12/1/29/4].

The former Staffordshire Police Museum at Baswich House closed in 2006 and its collections were transferred to the SSA [C/PC/12/19]. The Staffordshire Past Track portal has photographs relating to policing and firefighting in days gone by under the Law, Order & Emergency Services theme.

FURTHER INFORMATION

Anderton, Paul, *Called to Arms 1803–12 in the Staffordshire-Cheshire Border Region: Volunteer Infantry Corps for Home Defence under Threat of a Napoleonic Invasion* (Audley & District FHS, 2016)

Brew, Alec, *Staffordshire and Black Country Airfields* (History Press, 1997)

Capper, John, *History of the 1st and 2nd Battalions, The North Staffordshire Regiment (The Prince of Wales's), 1914–1923* (Churnet Valley Books, 2014)

Cooke, William, *Wings Over Meir: The Story of the Potteries Aerodrome* (Amberley Publishing, 2010)

Elson, Jeffrey C.J., *Honours and Awards for the North and South Staffordshire Regiments 1914–1919* (Token Publishing, 2004)

Elson, Jeffrey C.J., *Honours and Awards: The Staffordshire Regiments (Prince of Wales's) 1919–2007* (Token Publishing, 2014)

Gibson, Jeremy and Meryn Medlycott, *Militia Lists and Musters, 1757–1876* (5th edn, Family History Partnership, 2013)

Hunt, Karen, *Staffordshire's War* (Amberley Press, 2017)

Sheldon, C.W., *Roll of Honour: The Story of The Hundreds of Leek Men who Fell in the First World War* (Three Counties Publishing, 2004)

Tunstall, Alf and Jeff Cowdell, *Policing the Potteries* (Three Counties Publishing, 2002)

Appendix 1

TIMELINE OF POTTERIES HISTORY AND GENEALOGY

c. 1670	Introduction of saggars in pottery production
c. 1693	Elers brothers pioneer developments in salt glazing, sprigging and casting
1701	The Stoke-upon-Trent parish listing compiled
1730	Josiah Wedgwood born in Burslem
1738	John Wesley first preaches in Newcastle-under-Lyme
1762	First turnpike road in the Potteries
1762	Josiah Wedgwood introduces Queensware, a cream-coloured earthenware
1764	First Methodist Chapel in the Potteries built at Hill Top, Burslem
1766	Brindley begins the Grand Trunk Canal (Trent & Mersey)
1768	Wedgwood opens his new factory at Etruria
1776	Josiah Spode II starts to introduce bone china
1777	Trent & Mersey Canal opens
1793	Minton Company founded by Thomas Minton
1804	The 'House of Recovery', the Potteries first hospital, opens at Etruria
1805	Staffordshire Militia granted the title of 'King's Own' by George III
1807	Primitive Methodism formed and open air meetings begin at Mow Cop
1825	First official strike in the Potteries
1830	Consecration of the new Church of St Peter ad Vincula, Stoke

1833	Expansion of the Trentham estate and rebuilding of Trentham Hall
1834	Poor Law Amendment Act creates Poor Law unions. New workhouses are built throughout the Potteries
1837	Introduction of civil registration in England and Wales
1838	Hanley & Shelton Political Union formed
1839	A Stipendiary Magistrate appointed for the Potteries
1840	Samuel Scriven starts his inquiry into child labour in the Potteries
1841	First modern census listing the whole of the population by name
1842	Chartist riots in Hanley
1845	The Potters' Joint Stock Emigration Society advocates emigration for pottery workers
1848	North Staffordshire Railway, 'The Knotty', opens
1850	Shelton Bar Iron Company formed by Lord Granville
1852	Royal Pottery Theatre, later the Theatre Royal, opens in Pall Mall, Hanley
1854	The *Sentinel* newspaper first published as the *Staffordshire Sentinel & Commercial & General Advertiser*
1857	Hanley is the first of the Six Towns to become a borough
1858	Reorganization of the probate system to establish civil probate registries
1860	Hanley Cemetery, the first municipal cemetery in the Potteries, opens
1867	Arnold Bennett born in Hanley
1869	North Staffordshire Infirmary opens at Hartshill
1870	Hanley Borough Police formed
1873	Hanley Jewish Congregation establishes a synagogue in Hanover Street
1878	Stoke Football Club formed from other pre-existing clubs
1881	North Staffordshire Regiment formed from the 64th and 98th Regiments of Foot
1895	Diglake Colliery Disaster, Audley; seventy-seven lives lost
1895	Reginald Mitchell born in Butt Lane
1897	North Staffordshire Asylum opens at Cheddleton

1903	Charles Shaw publishes his autobiography, *When I Was A Child*
1910	Demolition of Trentham Hall
1910	Federation: the Six Towns join together as the County Borough of Stoke-on-Trent with a population of 240,000
1914	North Staffordshire Regiment raises a total of eighteen battalions to serve in the First World War
1921	Pottery unions merge to form the National Society of Pottery Workers
1922	Boundaries of Stoke-on-Trent extended to take in areas to the south and east
1923	North Staffordshire Railway taken over by the London, Midland and Scottish Railway
1925	Stoke-on-Trent is granted city status
1932	The three strands of Methodism merge to form the Methodist Church of Great Britain
1934	Stoke-on-Trent City Aerodrome opened at Meir
1938	Half of the workforce of Stoke-on-Trent is employed in the pottery industry; 2,000 bottle ovens in use
1940	Staffordshire Battalion, Home Guard formed
1940	Wedgwood Group moves from Etruria to Barlaston
1968	Stoke-on-Trent City Police amalgamated with Staffordshire County Police
1986	The National Garden Festival was held, reclaiming 180 acres of derelict industrial land at Shelton
1997	City of Stoke-on-Trent became a unitary authority, reclaiming local government services from Staffordshire
1998	Silverdale Colliery, the last deep mine in North Staffordshire, closes
2000	Shelton steel plant closes
2005	St Peter ad Vincula granted status of a Minster
2008	Spode factory closes and business bought by Portmeiron Group
2015	The City of Stoke-on-Trent acquires the Minton Archive

Appendix 2

DIRECTORY OF ARCHIVES AND RESOURCES

ARCHIVES AND RECORD OFFICES
Staffordshire and Stoke-on-Trent Archives
Staffordshire Record Office, Eastgate Street, Stafford, ST16 2LZ; tel: 01785 278379 (archive enquiries) and 01785 278373 (appointments); email: staffordshire.record.office@staffordshire.gov.uk; www. staffordshire. gov.uk/ archives

Stoke-on-Trent City Archives, City Central Library, Bethesda Street, Hanley, Stoke-on-Trent, ST1 3RS; tel: 01782 238420; email: stoke. archives@stoke.gov.uk; www.staffordshire.gov.uk/archives

Gateway to the Past (online catalogue): www.archives.staffordshire. gov.uk

As the county archive service for Staffordshire, the SSA collects and preserves archives relating to Staffordshire and Stoke-on-Trent. The service operates the Staffordshire Record Office (SRO) at Stafford and the Stoke-on-Trent City Archives (STCA) at Hanley Library, Stoke-on-Trent. In addition, it manages the William Salt Library (WSL) in Stafford, an outstanding local history library with many sources of use to the family historian among its holdings (www.staffordshire.gov.uk/salt).

Lichfield Record Office (LRO), which served as the diocesan record office for the Diocese of Lichfield and Coventry, was also part of the county archive service. It closed at the end of 2017 and its records have been transferred to the SRO in Stafford. The move was the first stage of a centralization and modernization programme that aims to bring the

SRO, LRO and WSL collections together under one roof at a new site to be called the Staffordshire History Centre. Building work is expected to begin in 2019.

Stoke-on-Trent City Archives holds many, though not all, archive collections and series relating specifically to North Staffordshire. These include parish registers, poll books and electoral registers, Poor Law records, newspapers and trade directories, and the records of local government, health and education. Its collections relating to the pottery industry are of national and international significance, and include the archives of industry pioneers and major businesses such as Wedgwood, Minton and Spode. STCA's archive on the role of Methodism in the Potteries is also of note.

Appointments are necessary at all of the SSA's sites. The Service operates an independent reader registration system and County Archive Research Network (CARN) tickets are not accepted, although they may be used as proof of identity and address. A chargeable research service is available – see the website for fees.

A family history club meets on the fourth Monday of each month at the SRO; see website for details.

Birmingham Archdiocesan Archives
Cathedral House, St Chad's Queensway, Birmingham, B4 6EU; tel: 01212 306252; archives@rc-birmingham.org; www.birminghamarch diocesanarchives.org.uk

Holds the episcopal and administrative archives of the Catholic Archdiocese of Birmingham and its predecessors, which includes Staffordshire. Also houses the records of a number of Catholic charities, societies and organisations.

Cheshire Record Office
Duke Street, Chester, Cheshire, CH1 1RL; tel: 01244 972574; http://archives.cheshire.gov.uk

Contains some records relating to estates and land holdings in North Staffordshire.

The National Archives
Kew, Richmond, Surrey, TW9 4DU; tel: 02088 763444; http://discovery.
nationalarchives.gov.uk

Discovery is the online search engine of The National Archives. Allows searches within many Midlands archives, as well as the TNA's own holdings. See the Introduction for advice on using Discovery to access the SSA catalogue.

University of Warwick, Modern Records Centre
University Library, University of Warwick, Coventry, CV4 7AL; tel: 02476 524219; archives@warwick.ac.uk; www.warwick.ac.uk /services/library/mrc/

The Centre focuses on modern British social, political and economic history, in particular industrial relations and labour history. For family history purposes, the main collections of interest are those relating to UK trades unions, employers' and trade association archives. Also records of the motor industry; radical British political groups; and pressure groups and other organizations. A series of research guides is available online, including sources by occupation. Appointments not necessary but advised; no reader's ticket required.

LIBRARIES AND LOCAL STUDY CENTRES
City Central Library
Bethesda Street, Hanley, Stoke-on-Trent, ST1 3RS; tel: 01782 238455; central.library@stoke.gov.uk

The City Central Library, Hanley is Stoke-on-Trent's largest library. As well as housing the Stoke-on-Trent City Archives (see above), it holds the city's local history collection – known as the Six Towns Collection – as well as a range of general resources. There is free access to genealogy resources such as Ancestry.co.uk and Findmypast.co.uk.

Family History Centres
Brampton Family History Centre
PO Box 457, The Brampton, Newcastle-under-Lyme, Staffordshire, ST5 0TD; tel: 01782 630178

Access to a wide range of family history resources from the Family History Library of the Church of Jesus Christ of Latter-Day Saints (better known as the Mormons). Brampton Family History Centre is the local centre for North Staffordshire. Other centres throughout the UK and overseas, for addresses see: www.familysearch.org/locations.

Keele University, Specialist Collections
Library, Keele University, Keele, Newcastle-under-Lyme, Staffordshire, ST5 5BG; tel: 01782 734159; email: library.help@keele.ac.uk; www.keele.ac.uk/library/specarc/collections/

The University holds a number of specialist collections relating to individuals, families and organizations associated with North Staffordshire. Among these, the Local Collection comprises around 5,000 books, plus pamphlets, newspapers, periodicals and directories. Features worth noting include a complete run of the *Staffordshire Advertiser* on microfilm (1795–1973), the *North Staffordshire Journal of Field Studies*, the *Collections for a History of Staffordshire*, the *Pottery Gazette* and the transcriptions of parish registers published by the Staffordshire Parish Registers Society.

Methodist Archives and Research Centre
John Rylands University Library of Manchester, Oxford Road, Manchester, M13 9PP; tel: 01612 753764; www.library.manchester.ac.uk/searchresources/guidetospecialcollections/methodist/

The Methodist Archives and Research Centre was established by the Methodist Church of Great Britain in 1961 to house the connexional records of the church. It holds the world's largest collection of manuscripts relating to the founders of Methodism, as well as Methodist institutions and organizations.

Midland Ancestors Reference Library
Birmingham & Midland Institute, Margaret Street, Birmingham, B3 3BS. www.midland-ancestors.uk

Specialist library in central Birmingham operated by Midland Ancestors (formerly the Birmingham & Midland Society for Genealogy and Heraldry – see main entry below). Has all Midland Ancestors publications as well as other material for the area covered by the Society. The library catalogue can be downloaded at the website or contact: referencelibrarian@midanc.org.

Newcastle Library
Castle House, Barracks Road, Newcastle-Under-Lyme, Staffordshire, ST5 1BL; tel: 03001 118000; email: newcastle.library@staffordshire. gov.uk; www.staffordshire.gov.uk/libraries

Now relocated within the new Castle House Civic Hub, the library holds genealogical resources and a local history collection relating to the historic borough of Newcastle-under-Lyme.

Society of Genealogists
14 Charterhouse Buildings, Goswell Road, London, EC1M 7BA; tel: 02072 518799; genealogy@sog.org.uk; www.sog.org.uk

The Society's genealogical library and education centre in Clerkenwell holds substantial material on Staffordshire. See online catalogue for details.

University of Staffordshire, Special Collections
Thompson Library, Staffordshire University, College Road, Stoke, ST4 2DE; tel: 01782 295770; email: libraryhelpdesk@staffs.ac.uk; www. staffs.ac.uk/support_depts/library/collections/special/index.jsp

Located within the Thompson Library, Special Collections houses rare books, archive materials and extensive photographic collections. The Department is open to members of the public by prior appointment. Collections of potential interest to the family historian include: a mixed collection of materials relating to the ceramics industry, including a number of illustrated catalogues; the papers of Dorothy Thompson, an eminent historian of Chartism; and the archive of the Stoke-on-Trent (South) Constituency Labour Party, 1949–79.

Wesley Historical Society Library
Oxford Centre for Methodism and Church History, Oxford Brookes University, Harcourt Hill, Oxford, OX2 9AT; tel: 01865 488319 or 01865 488455; email: wco.archives@brookes.ac.uk; www.wesleyhistorical society.org.uk/library.html

The Library has the second largest collection of Methodist books and related literature in Europe and the second largest collection of British Methodist books in the world.

MUSEUMS AND HERITAGE CENTRES
Gladstone Pottery Museum
Uttoxeter Road, Longton, Stoke-on-Trent, ST3 1PQ; tel: 01782 237777; email: gladstone@stoke.gov.uk; www.stokemuseums.org.uk/gpm/

The former Gladstone China Works is now preserved as the last complete Victorian pottery factory in the country. Typical of hundreds of similar factories in the area, it has been restored as a working potbank where visitors are able to see a range of traditional pottery making skills in action, including throwing, casting, hand decorating and bone-china flower making.

Potteries Museum & Art Gallery
Bethesda Street, Stoke-on-Trent, ST1 3DW; tel: 01782 232323; www.stokemuseums.org.uk/pmag/

Part of Stoke-on-Trent Museums Service, the museum's collection of Staffordshire pottery is widely acknowledged as the finest in the world and other collections of fine and decorative arts, natural history, social history and archaeology have local, regional and national significance. The museum is fully accredited and all the collections, totalling more than 650,000 individual objects, are designated collections. The museum is also now home to a number of artefacts from the Staffordshire Hoard, which PMAG bought along with Birmingham Museums in 2010.

In addition, the following industrial museums and heritage centres are operated by charities or private companies:

- Dudson Museum: www.dudson.com
- Chatterley Whitfield Colliery:
  http://chatterleywhitfieldfriends.org.uk
- Etruria Industrial Museum and Heritage Centre:
  www.etruriamuseum.org.uk
- Middleport Pottery: www.middleportpottery.co.uk
- Moorcroft Heritage Visitor Centre: www.moorcroft.com
- Spode Heritage Centre: www.spodeworks.org
- Wedgwood Museum: www.wedgwoodmuseum.org.uk

FAMILY HISTORY SOCIETIES
Alsager Group of FHS of Cheshire
www.fhsc.org.uk/about-the-group-alsager

A group within the Family History Society of Cheshire focusing on the area around Alsager, which borders North Staffordshire.

Audley & District Family History Society
St James's Church Hall, Audley, Staffordshire, ST7 8HL; email: famhist147@hotmail.co.uk; www.audleyfhs.co.uk

A specialist society working to make available records for Audley and its adjoining parishes. Its coverage focuses on the ancient ecclesiastical parish of Audley, which comprised Audley Township, Bignall End, Halmer End, Knowle End, Park End, Eardley End and Talke.

Biddulph & District Genealogy & Historical Society
Biddulph Library, Tunstall Road, Stoke-on-Trent, Staffordshire, ST8 6HH; email: djouthwaite@hotmail.com; www.bdghs.org.uk

The society aims to promote genealogy and local history particularly pertaining to the Biddulph area.

Midland Ancestors (formerly Birmingham & Midland Society for Genealogy and Heraldry)

Jackie Cotterill, General Secretary, 5 Sanderling Court, Spennels, Kidderminster, Worcestershire, DY10 4TS; email: gensec@midanc.uk; http://midland-ancestors.uk and http://midland-ancestors.shop/

Formed in 1963, the society now known as Midland Ancestors covers the historic counties of Staffordshire, Warwickshire and Worcestershire.

The Society holds regular meetings in Birmingham and in branches across the Midlands and in London, several of which have their own websites. There is also a Heraldry Group and a DNA Special Interest Group. The Society organizes courses and coach trips to London archives. A Reference Library is located at the Birmingham & Midland Institute in central Birmingham (see above).

North Staffordshire Family History Group, based in Stoke-on-Trent, is one of several branches affiliated to the Society. The branch holds monthly meetings in the St John's Centre, Newcastle Road, Trent Vale. There is also a branch library with local resources. Group members have transcribed many local records and are currently working to transcribe the Staffordshire Registrars' indexes for births, marriages and deaths which are being made available via the Staffordshire BMD website (www.staffordshirebmd.org.uk).

The Society has compiled and operates a series of indexes, which are available for searches for members and non-members. Costs and access conditions vary: for details see https://midland-ancestors. uk/resources/search-services/ or contact gensec@midanc.uk. Some datasets are available as downloads or on CD-ROM through the Midland Ancestors shop, which operates from a separate website (http://midland-ancestors.shop/ or via email: bookshop@midanc.uk).

Midland Catholic History Society

Vincent Burke, Secretary, 16 Brandhall Court, Wolverhampton Road, Oldbury, B68 8DE; tel: 01214 221573; www.midlandcatholichistory. org.uk

Promotes the study of Catholic history within the counties of Herefordshire, Shropshire, Staffordshire, Warwickshire and Worcestershire. Publishes a regular journal, *Midland Catholic History*.

PUBLISHERS
Amberley Publishing
The Hill, Stroud, Gloucestershire, GL5 4EP; tel: 01453 847800; www.amberleybooks.com

General histories, transport history, and the '...*Through Time*' and '... *From Old Photographs*' series on Midlands subjects and places.

Archive CD Books
Family History Research Ltd, Suite 14 Old Anglo House, Mitton Street, Stourport-on-Severn, DY13 9AQ; tel: 01299 828374; www.family historyresearch.org

Offers a range of genealogical and historical data on CD-ROM: trade directories, parish registers, census records, heralds visitations, with many Midlands titles.

Family History Indexes
14 Copper Leaf Close, Moulton, Northampton, NN3 7HS; tel: 01604 495106; email: info@fhindexes.co.uk; www.fhindexes.co.uk

Offers a range of genealogical data on CD-ROM, notably the Criminal Registers and Criminal Lunatics Registers held at TNA, and militia musters and other military records.

The History Press
The Mill, Brimscombe Port, Stroud, Gloucestershire, GL5 2QG; tel: 01453 883300; email: web@thehistorypress.co.uk; www.thehistory press. co.uk

Staffordshire-related publications are a mixture of thematic titles (e.g. crime, sports, canals) and histories of particular towns and localities.

Keele University, Centre for Local History
Room CM0.25, Claus Moser Research Centre, Keele University, Keele, Staffordshire, ST5 5BG; www.keele.ac.uk/history/centreforlocalhistory

The Centre is a long-established research and teaching department specializing in the history of Staffordshire. It offers a University Certificate in Local History and hosts the Victoria History of Staffordshire project. Its journal *Staffordshire Studies* is published annually covering all aspects of the history of the historic county of Staffordshire.

Midlands Historical Data
email: enquiries@midlandshistoricaldata.org; www.midlandshistorical data.org

Digitized resources for local and family historians relating to Shropshire, Staffordshire, Warwickshire (including Birmingham) and Worcestershire. Includes directories, local history books, electoral rolls, regimental histories and indexes.

Staffordshire Parish Registers Society
Ian Wallbank, Secretary, 82 Hillport Avenue, Newcastle-under-Lyme, Staffordshire, ST5 8QT; email: sec@sprs.org.uk; www.sprs.org.uk

Formed in 1901, the Society publishes parish registers for the historic county of Staffordshire.

Staffordshire Record Society
The Hon. Secretary, c/o The William Salt Library, Eastgate Street, Stafford, ST16 2LZ; email: matthew.blake@btinternet.com; www.s-h-c.org.uk

The Staffordshire Record Society originated in 1879 as the William Salt Archaeological Society. It publishes books and transcriptions of records on the history of the county under the title *Collections for a History of Staffordshire* (list on its website).

True North Books
Holmfield Mills, Holdsworth Road, Halifax, West Yorkshire, HX3 6SN; tel: 01422 244555; email: sales@truenorthbooks.com; http://truenorth books.com

Publishes photobooks and nostalgia books on cities and towns in the north of England, with several titles covering Stoke-on-Trent.

WEB RESOURCES

Only gateway resources, i.e. those mentioned multiple times in the main text, are listed here.

Ancestry, www.ancestry.co.uk

A broad collection of family history records, including all the UK censuses, an extensive military collection, passenger lists and emigration records, and the National Probate Calendar (Index of Wills and Administrations), 1858–1966. Specific Staffordshire material is limited, primarily extracts from parish registers. Latest additions and updates to the collections are accessible via the relevant county pages: http://search.ancestry.co.uk/Places/UK/England/Staffordshire/Default.aspx.

FamilySearch, www.familysearch.org

The massive family history website maintained by the Church of Jesus Christ of Latter-Day Saints (Mormons). A key resource for parish register and census data.

The FamilySearch Wiki, http://familysearch.org/learn/wiki/en/England, has articles on genealogical research within English counties written and maintained by volunteers.

Findmypast, www.findmypast.co.uk

Commercial website owned by DC Thomson Family History. A broad collection of family history records, including all UK censuses, the 1939 Register, military records, occupational records, newspapers and trade directories. There are major location-specific collections for Staffordshire (see separate entry below) and some other counties, and strong Midlands coverage within the National Burial Index.

FreeBMD, www.freebmd.org.uk

Non-commercial site that aims to transcribe the civil registration indexes of births, marriages and deaths for England and Wales, and provide free online access to the transcribed records.

GENUKI, www.genuki.org.uk/big/eng/STS/

Non-commercial directory of genealogical resources across the UK and Ireland. Many useful links available via the Staffordshire county pages.

Potteries.org, www.thepotteries.org
Local history website maintained by amateur historian Steve Birks. A key resource on the history of the pottery industry and the Potteries in general.

Staffordshire BMD, www.staffordshirebmd.org.uk
A collaboration between Staffordshire's register offices and family history societies to transcribe the original, locally held indexes of births, marriages and deaths back to the start of civil registration in 1837. The indexes are not yet complete for all years and districts. However, coverage pages for each index type show what is included and coverage for North Staffordshire is generally good.

Staffordshire Collection (on Findmypast), www.findmypast.co.uk
Online collection of Staffordshire records under licence from SSA. Contains parish registers for approximately 200 Staffordshire parishes, including all those within North Staffordshire. Coverage comprises entries for baptisms, marriages and burials from the beginning of the registers through to 1900, and includes digitized images of the original registers. In addition, the Staffordshire Collection covers probate records and marriage allegations and bonds (both with digitized images) issued through the Consistory Court of Lichfield, previously held at LRO.

Staffordshire Name Indexes, www.staffsnameindexes.org.uk
A series of online indexes taken from the records held by the SSA. Subjects include: apprentices, canal boats, jurors, police officers, prisoners, workhouses and wills.

Staffordshire Place Guide,
www.staffordshire.gov.uk/leisure/archives/history/placeguide
A finding aid for information on Staffordshire parishes, maintained by the SSA. Information is summarized under various headings, with direct links to the online catalogue, Gateway to the Past. As yet, not all parishes are covered.

Staffordshire Past Track, www.staffspasttrack.org.uk
Also maintained by Staffordshire and Stoke-on-Trent Archives, this website showcases photographs, images, maps and documents relating to Staffordshire's history, using a range of easy to use search tools.

MISCELLANEOUS
Carmountside Cemetery and Crematorium
Leek Road, Milton, Stoke-on-Trent, ST2 7AB; tel: 01782 235050
Enquiries and search requests relating to burials within municipal cemeteries managed by the City of Stoke-on-Trent.

HM Coroner for Stoke-on-Trent and North Staffordshire
Coroner's Chambers, 547 Hartshill Road, Hartshill, Stoke-on-Trent, ST4 6HF; email: coroners.office@stoke.gov.uk

Enquiries re inquests subject to the seventy-five-year closure restriction.

Newcastle-under-Lyme Register Office
20 Sidmouth Avenue, The Brampton, Newcastle-Under-Lyme, Staffordshire, ST5 0QN; tel: 03001 118001; email: registrarsenquiries @staffordshire.gov.uk; www.staffordshire.gov.uk/community/lifeevents/ homepage.aspx

Holds civil birth, marriage and death registers for historical registration districts within the Newcastle-under-Lyme registration area.

Stoke-on-Trent Probate Sub-Registry
Combined Court Centre, Bethesda Street, Hanley, Stoke-on-Trent, ST1 3BP; tel: 03001 231072

A sub-office of Birmingham District Probate Registry and has limited opening hours. It may be able to help with enquiries regarding historical probates.

Stoke-on-Trent Register Office, City of
Hanley Town Hall, Albion Street, Hanley, Stoke-on-Trent, ST1 1QQ; tel: 01782 235260; email: register.office@stoke.gov.uk; www.stoke. gov.uk/info/20011/births_marriages_and_deaths

Holds civil birth, marriage and death registers for historical registration districts within the City of Stoke-on-Trent. Facilities for ordering searches and certificates online.

For other Staffordshire register offices search by postcode at the staffordshire.gov.uk address given for Newcastle above. All offices offer facilities for ordering searches and certificates online.

LOCAL HISTORY GROUPS AND SOCIETIES

The following is a list of local history societies, groups and general websites for North Staffordshire. Staffordshire Heritage Group is an umbrella organization for all local history, genealogy, archive and archaeology groups and societies within the county (https://staffordshireheritage.weebly.com).

Blo(o)r(e) Society (an association focusing on the name Bloore and derivatives which has a high concentration in the North Staffordshire area): http://bloor.org

Burslem History Club:
www.burslemhistoryclub.btck.co.uk

Congleton History Society:
www.bmsgh.org/BorderHistory/conghs/ congleton.htm
Eccleshall Historical Society:
http://staffordshireheritage.weebly.com /eccleshall.html

Leek & District Historical Society:
www.bednallarchive.info/misc/l&mhistsoc/leek_hist_soc.htm

Potteries Heritage Society:
www.potteries.org.uk

Stafford and Mid-Staffs Archaeological Society:
http://samsas.co

Stafford Historical & Civic Society:
http://staffordshireheritage.weebly.com/stafford-historical-society.html

Staffordshire Archaeological & Historical Society:
www.sahs.uk.net

Staffordshire History Group:
ma.george@btconnect.com

Staffordshire Industrial Archaeology Society:
www.staffsia.org.uk

Stoke-on-Trent Museum Archaeological Society:
www.stokearchaeologysociety.org.uk

Tean & Checkley Historical Society:
www.checkleystaffs.co.uk/historical

The Old Nortonian Society (Norton in the Moors):
www.northstaffsresearch.co.uk/Oldnortoniansociety

INDEX